DAVID STEALTH

ARCHWAY
PUBLISHING

Archway Publishing books may be ordered through booksellers or by contacting:

Archway Publishing
1663 Liberty Drive
Bloomington, IN 47403
www.archwaypublishing.com
1 (888) 242-5904

Because of the dynamic nature of the Internet, any web addresses or links contained in this book may have changed since publication and may no longer be valid. The views expressed in this work are solely those of the author and do not necessarily reflect the views of the publisher, and the publisher hereby disclaims any responsibility for them.

Any people depicted in stock imagery provided by Thinkstock are models, and such images are being used for illustrative purposes only. Certain stock imagery © Thinkstock.

ISBN: 978-1-4808-3606-8 (sc)
ISBN: 978-1-4808-3605-1 (hc)
ISBN: 978-1-4808-3604-4 (e)

Library of Congress Control Number: 2016915409

Print information available on the last page.

Archway Publishing rev. date: 9/28/2016

CONTENTS

INTRODUCTION

This book is dedicated to the men and women of the Detroit Police Department who have given the ultimate sacrifice, as well as those who have severed and continue to serve proudly with integrity, while wearing the badge of honor.

These proud officers are from various backgrounds and cultures, all of whom took an oath to protect and serve, while upholding blind justice for every resident of this city.

Unfortunately, many citizens of Detroit stood unaware that they were being protected by two separate factions within their police department. There's a White and Black faction, who often operates in unity, but occasionally performs intentionally separate. Yes, the ugly force of racism is alive and well in the Detroit Police Department, and it exists on both sides!

This is one man's view of a-City that has been served by a Force Divided, counterpoised with the dreams of another who desired for men to be judged by the content of their character not the color of their skin, a dream that sadly in many cases has yet to be fulfilled.

Even though this account begins some 40 plus years ago and brings us to date, the readers will be eerily aware that the same ugly force of racism that existed half a century ago remains with us today. It may not be as blatant, however, I assure you it exists within many ethnicities. Although some would suggest the roles have reversed and many of the self-proclaimed victims have now become the bigots. Racism is not unique to the City of Detroit. It unfortunately exists throughout our great nation!

While this entire book is based on first hand observations and recollections, it's an uncensored account of racism within the world of law enforcement. Readers will be taken into an unambiguous realm which at times can be crude and brutally honest. Many of the names, locations and situations have been altered to protect the privacy of those involved.

Furthermore, readers should be acutely aware that the author is in no fashion attempting to intentionally disparage any individual, race, culture or organization.

A SPECIAL SALUTE TO

Officer Bob "Bubba" Field, one no nonsense cop, who is perceived by many to be one of the finest police officers who ever donned a badge in the City of Detroit. He also has the dubious distinction of being one of the many casualties' that the city intentionally sacrificed to remain politically correct.

ABOUT THE AUTHOR

The Author, a retired Detroit Police Officer, worked the streets of Detroit for his entire career in various capacities. These assignments included uniform patrol, felony plainclothes car, as well as 16 years as an undercover narcotics officer.

During his tenure in Narcotics, Dave worked many high profile cases while serving with a number of federal task forces, including the Drug Enforcement Administration (DEA), Federal Bureau of Investigation (FBI), and Alcohol Tobacco and Firearms (ATF).

As an undercover officer, the author has a very unique perspective of the law as well as lawbreakers. His unusual ability to blend in with the criminal element allowed him to infiltrate and descend to depths that most criminals never reach, much less law enforcement officers. He believes you must understand and think as your enemy before you can pursue them.

In addition to his law enforcement career, Dave is a United States Army veteran, who served on the Korean DMZ with the 2nd Infantry Division as well as a tour with the 101st Airborne Division in Iraq as a Law Enforcement Professional (LEP) during the "Surge" of 2007-2008.

THE YEAR OF AWAKENING

AS I GAZED AT THE CLOCK, I thought. Why did I even set the alarm? I have not slept a wink all night. How could I sleep on the eve before the day I was to become part of a great fraternity, a brotherhood with approximately five thousand members. Today was the day I would become a Detroit police officer just as my father before me, a man I admired for his ethics and the fact that he was an honest lawman who loved enforcing the law.

After a quick shower and a cup of coffee, I put on my newly purchased rookie uniform, which fit like a glove, if I must say so myself; I attributed my excellent physical condition to being a recently discharged Army veteran, standing at six feet and tilting the scale at approximately two hundred pounds. My sandy brown hair complimented the tan uniform; I certainly looked like a cop, my objective was now to become one.

I arrived at 1300 Beaubien (Detroit Police Headquarters) at 6:30 a.m., an hour- and- a- half early. I sure didn't want to be late my first morning, the day I would be sworn in as one of "Detroit's Finest."

As I stared at this large historical, gray, multi-story building, that had obviously been built at the turn of the century, given its stately architecture along with the fabulous sculpturing in the mortar. I felt as though this grand old lady was demanding respect from all who gazed upon her including the moon that shined brightly overhead.

My stomach was in knots; the dream I had held since childhood was only a short time away from becoming true. Oh God, I thought. Please don't let anything happen to prevent me from becoming commissioned. Just then the ringing of bells came from a distance. As I turned towards the sound a man exited a small greasy spoon that was located kitty-corner from Police Headquarters. Great, I thought, because I sure could use another cup of coffee.

The bell hanging on the door rang once again as I entered the little eatery causing the patrons to turn and look in my direction. Immediately, I observed a short chubby man dressed in the unmistakable tan student patrolman uniform, which all police rookies are required to wear during their 16 weeks in the Police Academy.

As our eyes met, we both smiled, realizing each was most likely a member of the new Police Academy class. I walked over and introduced myself, "Hi, my name is Dave Stealth; you look like a new guy, too," extending my hand. He said, "I'm Bill, Bill Stephan" grabbing my hand and shaking it eagerly. "Are you also being sworn in this morning?" "Yes, I guess will be classmates," I replied. Little did I know, I had just shaken the hand of one of our class's future fatalities.

At the end of the counter was a slightly older black officer in uniform. He was apparently deep in thought, which would explain why he ignored us, two of his new brothers in blue, oh well. We ordered breakfast; I don't believe my food ever touched my teeth because I nervously ate so quickly. The only thing on my mind was that in less than an hour I was going to finally be sworn in as a Detroit cop!

As Bill and I entered Police Headquarters with spirits high, we observed what seemed like hundreds of officers of all ranks, detectives in plainclothes with guns and badges attached to their belts as well as those in full uniform. Some were beginning their tour of duty while others who appeared fatigued, from working the graveyard shift were obviously going home. Strangely enough, just as the black officer in the restaurant had, these officers were ignoring us as if we were apparitions. Did we exist? I didn't expect a party; however, a simple hello or a casual nod of recognition would have been nice!

Suddenly, I realized Bill was no longer involved in our conversation or at my side. As I turned I found him silently looking at a wall that was littered with photos of Detroit officers who had given their lives in the line of duty, the Wall of Honor. There was something eerie yet holy about the shrine and I'm sure we both were sharing the same thoughts. How were they killed and would one of us experience the same fate?

It was now 7:45 a.m. as we entered the gym. Many of our fellow colleagues were now beginning to arrive, all displaying enthusiasm, and a little arrogance, on their faces. The gym quickly began filling up with tan uniforms, all awaiting our first orders or instructions. As introductions were being made between classmates, I could sense the bonding of our group taking place, even before we were officially sworn in as law enforcement officers.

At 8:00a.m., all 28 members of Class 72 L, one of the smallest classes in the last two years, were present and awaiting the arrival of our training officers, who obviously were late. As I looked around, I noticed two distinct groups forming, one black group and the other white. Thoughts of my three years in the army came to mind where racial tension was blatant and occasionally violent. Surely the police department would be different; after all we are all brothers in blue who will be depending upon each other daily in the fight against our common enemy: crime.

Just then a voice from the rear shouted "Front and center people, all you wannabe's shut up and fall into formation, now!" Our training officers, one sergeant and two patrolmen had arrived. They weren't quite what I imagined. I had thought they would be a reflection of Sergeant Johnson, my D.I. (Drill Instructor) in the army, well built with the eyes of a shark. But these guys were your everyday Joe's, with average builds and rather pleasant faces. The only thing outstanding about them was their police uniforms and pistols hanging from their sides.

"All right people. My name is Sergeant Mustaff and these are Officers German and Glowski. For the next sixteen weeks, we will have the misfortune of being your parents. It is our job to weed out the boys and those who just don't have the right stuff. God only knows we don't need any more incompetent or bad cops out there! We will teach you to respond as a team and you will learn to act as one! Now listen up for your name to be called and respond with, Here sir, student patrolmen and your last name, is that understood?" The class responded simultaneously, "Sir, yes sir!"

We had an enthusiastic class, most cadets had been recently discharged from the military service, so PT (physical training) was not considered a challenge. Those of us who were physically fit would be able to assist any classmates who were having a difficult time, because we would never leave one of our own behind, a mindset we had been taught in the military.

As the weeks passed, our class began to form a strong brotherhood. We were operating as a team where color was not an issue and all were becoming more confident with each passing day. This was just how I had imagined the brotherhood to be. As well as everything was going, what could possibly go wrong?

As with the many classes graduating before us, the future would not be kind to all. During the following four years, three of our 28 classmates would commit suicide, one would be shot and killed in a domestic dispute, half a dozen would become divorced and many of us would become alcohol abusers. It was becoming clear that the perfect matter-of-fact world I believed in had a dark and often hidden side. Suicide, divorce, alcoholism and racism are very prevalent in the field of law enforcement, which we would all learn in the very near future!

In the spring of 1972, I proudly graduated from the Detroit Police Academy and was assigned to the Seventh Precinct. The Seventh was located on the southeast side of Detroit, bordering the Detroit River. It was considered to be one of the more dangerous and active precincts in the city. Not only had my dream come true, it came with a real bonus, a precinct with a high level of crime and a lot of action.

The Seventh Precinct was divided into ten scout car (patrol) areas one through ten. Theoretically two men were assigned to each patrol car and area during each shift. However, this was not always possible due to a manpower shortage. Scout cars would be assigned an area number as their radio call signal i.e.: 7-1, 7-2, 7-3 and so on.

On day one, a classmate and I arrived at the Seventh Precinct expecting the officers to welcome us with open arms, their new brothers in blue. Wow, were we mistaken! Not one officer greeted us, as a matter of fact, most were just outright rude. We were directed to the squad room by an overweight sergeant who talked to us like we were pizza delivery boys.

As we entered the squad room, most of the officers glanced in our direction then quickly turned their backs to us, while the others looked at us like we were aliens. We quietly stood by the Coke machine appearing as if we were reading the bulletins on the wall, while awaiting the arrival of the shift supervisors to begin roll call, at which time we would receive our first assignment.

Shortly thereafter, a lieutenant along with three sergeants entered the squad room and announced, "Roll call. Fall in." The lieutenant was Bill Chimes, a large white male who stood about 6'3and weighed approximately 250 pounds, with salt and pepper hair. The Lieutenant's commanding presence left little doubt about who was in charge.

The sergeants on the other hand were far less impressive, at least in appearance and stature. They were Ken Jacobs, an older, short gray-haired man with a slight belly and a large pipe hanging from his mouth, definitely number two in charge. Then, there were sergeants Tom Stockton and Bill Anthem, both obviously recently promoted due to their young ages.

Lieutenant Chimes began calling officer's names and handing out their assignments for the afternoon. "Robbie, Perry, you've got 7-10 (referring to scout car area 7-10). Field, Bagger, 7-3. Kingston, Rogers, 7-4. Thomas, you've got the rookie Stealth on 7-2." To my surprise Thomas immediately spoke out, "Aw come on lieu, why in the hell do I always get stuck with these kids? You know damn well they can get us killed out there!" The entire formation started laughing, which made me feel even worse, if that could be possible. It was sure nice to be wanted!

Most rookies are assigned to walk a beat (foot patrol) for months before they are eligible to ride in a patrol car. I should have been flattered but instead, I felt humiliated and useless because the only reason I wasn't walking a beat with the others was due to the fact that Thomas partner called in sick at the last moment.

Lieutenant Chimes spoke up, "All right you guys knock off the bullshit, everyone gets their turn in the barrel with new officers. It wasn't too long ago you guys were the rookies." I knew this to be true because our academy instructors told us the average time on the job was 2-3 years.

The lieutenant then completed the assignments and began giving out information from the teletypes concerning wanted vehicles and criminals in our area. Suddenly, those in the front row began to giggle as they attempted unsuccessfully to conceal their laughs. The lieu then looked up from his report and said, "Nods, what in the hell do you think you're doing?" It was at this time I observed whom he was addressing; it was the officer second from the right in the front row. He was an old-timer in a sloppy uniform, with food stains on his tie and a broken down hat, which looked as though it had been through 20 bomber missions in WW II.

As this officer began to reply to the lieutenant's question, he turned slightly which allowed us in the second rank to observe what everyone was laughing about. I could not believe my eyes. Nods had his pants unzipped exposing himself to the entire shift, as he replied, "If you are going to work us like damn livestock we might as well look like them." The entire squad room, including me, roared with laughter, as the lieutenant shook his head from side to side stating, "Nobs, you are one crazy asshole. Sergeants, you got anything?" asked the lieutenant, to which they responded negatively. "All right guys, get out there, back each other up and watch your asses!"

These supervisors seemed to accept, if not condone this type of behavior. Now, I must tell you I had experienced a lot of strange behavior in my three years in the Army, but young kids forced to grow up overnight performed most of those acts. I just didn't expect this type of behavior from adults who in my mind should be setting an example, not to mention we're supposed to be the professionals that hold the city together, the only force stopping complete chaos. I was totally confused; as humorous as this was, it is not the way I envisioned the police department. Although, I would soon learn that laughter and a sense of humor is a defense mechanism that allows officers to vent as well as mask their innermost feelings.

I was beginning to understand why the black officer in the restaurant and all the others ignored us. Just because you wear this uniform doesn't make you a "brother." There is a definite rite to passage in the Detroit Police Department (DPD) and it's mandatory for all rookies. You must prove yourself as a cop prior to being accepted as a trusted partner or brother.

After roll call, I nervously walked up to Officer Thomas, who was at his locker, and extended my hand saying, "Hi! Officer Thomas, my name is Dave" and he reluctantly shook my hand, "How ya doing! I'm Jerry." I then asked if I should sign out a prep radio (which is a hand held radio that attaches to ones belt) and a shotgun. Thomas snapped back "Look kid, let's get something straight, you can get a radio but you won't need a shotgun, not unless you plan on going squirrel hunting." I could see it was going to be a trying eight hours.

As I was walking in the parking lot, I observed one of the black crews loading their scout car with a shotgun, M-1 carbine rifle and other miscellaneous police equipment. They obviously felt that there might come an occasion when a weapon more powerful than the 38-caliber revolver we all are issued by the department would be advantageous. Now, I'm not a hotdog or some kid that is infatuated with guns. However, I have been engaged in combat and I surely wouldn't mind having a shotgun or rifle if the crap hit the fan. Why couldn't this jerk I'm working with recognize the importance of firepower just as the black crew did?

I understood I was the new guy on the block, but it didn't take a detective to realize that a definite segregation existed, the black officers stood on one side of the squad room and the white officers on the other. Furthermore, there were no integrated scout cars. Maybe this was just a fluke and their assigned partner was off that day. Was there something going on here I wasn't aware of, or was I just really naïve?

As Thomas and I pulled out of the Seventh precinct parking lot, we received our first radio run from dispatch. "7-2, East Grand Blvd. and Jefferson they hear a women screaming," to which I responded, "7-2 on the way radio." Thomas murmured "Just wonderful, first I get stuck with a rookie and now I can't even stop for a coffee."

Upon our arrival, we found a large black woman who was obviously intoxicated standing in the street screaming as she wiped blood from her nose, "Get that son of a bitch in the house officer." Just then the screen door opened and a black male rushed out screaming, "That's right, I beat that bitch's ass and I will beat her ass again if she opens that damn mouth." Officer Thomas grabbed the irate male by the arm and I restrained the woman who was attempting to attack the man. I was right in the middle of my first of many domestic disputes.

We separated the fighting couple and calmed them down. I then advised the lady that I was going to arrest her boyfriend for cursing in public, an old law that had never been removed from the books. Officer Thomas abruptly turned towards me with a look of disbelief and said, "What in the hell did you say rookie? You aren't arresting anyone unless I say they're going to jail." He then demanded the couple stop drinking and make amends, while informing them if we were called back, both of them were going to jail!

Once back in the car, Jerry gave me my first lesson in in the racial divide that existed in Detroit's inner city "Look kid, you'd better wake up and wake up quick, people like this act like animals and we are the zoo keepers. Quit thinking of them as civilized citizens, these folks just get high, make babies and kill one another." Wow, my first day on the job and I get stuck with "Bobby Bigot!"

We weren't even a half a block away when a gunshot rang out from the direction of the couple we had just investigated. "That's it damn it, I've had it!" It was apparent Jerry was hot and one if not both of these folks were going to jail. "Kid, tell radio we're going back and shots have been fired," as he made a sharp U-turn heading back to their house.

As we approached the location, I observed the boyfriend lying in the street face down in a pool of blood. The girlfriend was standing on the front porch with a silver pistol in her right hand screaming, "I had to shoot the son of a bitch officer, he started beating my ass as soon as you left."

Jerry and I approached the frantic lady with guns drawn, advising her to lay the weapon on the porch and come down immediately. She looked at us in a distraught fashion and for a moment, just a moment, I was sure she was considering taking a shot at us. Suddenly, the lady complied, laying the gun on the porch. She then fell to her knees burying her face in her cupped hands crying out loud, "Oh my Lord, I have killed the man I love."

I retrieved the nickel-plated revolver from the porch, carefully placing it in my pocket, so that I didn't contaminate any fingerprints, which would be needed to confirm the identity of the shooter should this case go to trial. Officer

was involved in a combat situation and failed to assist that person, they would be court-martialed and tried for cowardliness, that's if they made it back to base camp alive. I never experienced this type of behavior while serving in foreign countries, yet now that I've returned to the world (stateside), I find that I must unfortunately watch my back because I'm unsure if all of my brothers-in-blue would be there to support me when needed.

By time we completed our statements and paperwork at the Homicide Division it was 12:30 pm. As we were getting on the elevator, Jerry who was lighting his pipe, said, "See kid that is why you don't get a lot done on this job. An arrest that takes moments generates hours of paperwork. It's just not worth it." Even though I nodded in agreement, I was thinking to myself, I'm not going to let bureaucracy or paperwork prevent me from doing my job. I joined this Department to lock up bad guys and by-God I'm going to do just that.

Jerry immediately drove to a small restaurant on East Jefferson and told me to advise dispatch that we were clear from Homicide and now request a code 9330 (lunch). Two of our scout cars were already at the restaurant. Once inside we joined our comrades in a booth for lunch and again, I was ignored as if I was the saltshaker. At that moment in the booth, I made a silent pledge, that when I became a senior officer I was going to make some serious changes. Rookies might not be accepted initially, however, they would certainly be treated civilly.

The final three hours of my shift consisted of an auto accident report and two alarm runs. I thought it was an awesome shift but I'm sure Jerry would say it was just another day at the office; nothing seemed to excite this guy. As we pulled in the precinct parking lot and began to unload the scout car, one of the senior patrolman walked by jokingly saying "Long day Jerry?" I could not believe Jerry's response. "Aw, the kid seems alright, I've had worse." For Jerry, that was like him offering me the honor of being the Godfather to his child!

I couldn't drive home fast enough to share the day's events with my wife and two- year- old son, a day filled with disappointment, excitement and inner satisfaction all in one. I dominated the conversation throughout dinner and the entire evening, giving my point of view on what was wrong with the department and how some day as a senior officer I intended to change things for the better.

This evening no doubt would be a sleepless one, as I was sure I would lie in bed with anticipations of what tomorrow would bring. I could not believe how exciting my first day was, the first day of twenty-five years on a job that has already become the love of my life. The alarm went off awakening me from a healthy two-hour sleep. After a shower, cup of coffee and a slice of toast, I was out the door.

That day and for months to follow, I would be assigned to walk a beat (foot patrol) with another rookie. This actually was not a bad detail because it allowed us to meet the people in the community, as well as making our own decisions regarding investigations and arrests. It was nice not having some judgmental old timer watching your every move, while making condescending wise crack remarks. Don't get me wrong, constructive criticism is an excellent learning tool; however, certain officers would correct you just to belittle you, or provide a good laugh for other senior officers.

Walking a beat in uniform gives one a whole new perspective of those who live in the neighborhoods of our cities. You meet all varieties of people, prostitutes, pimps, winos, vagrants, hardworking decent citizens who love their city, as well as those who are just stuck there because they're old, poor or just a product of their environment. Some are fine people with great ethics and others are purely opportunists who are too lazy or unwilling to get a job and provide for themselves. Subsequently, they tend to blame society for their predicament conveniently turning to crime or entitlements, which they consider the easy way out.

I, myself, was raised on the Westside of Detroit in a racially mixed neighborhood, so I was somewhat familiar with the ways of the street and people from various backgrounds. This was unlike a few of the rookies who moved to Detroit from the suburbs to experience the action a big city police department provides. My father had also enlightened me regarding the streets from a police officer's perspective and I would find the combination invaluable throughout my career.

During the first year I, as every other rookie would be used in whatever capacity is needed. Many found this indefinite schedule discomforting, whereas I considered it an opportunity to learn the infrastructure of our Department. Each day brought new challenges, and with each test we became better officers.

Tomorrow would be a big day, my six-month anniversary as a police officer, which meant I was only six months away from completing my first year. This is very important because it means my probationary period will have been successfully completed. I will then become a member of the Detroit Police Officers Association Union (DPOA) more importantly; those officers with a year or more on the job were no longer looked upon as rookies. My God, it will be great to be treated like a man instead of something lower than a sea urchin.

The clock in the squad room read 3:35 p.m. As usual, I stood silently by the Coke machine reading the same bulletins and wanted posters I have read over and over waiting for roll call to start. Suddenly, the doors opened and in came Lieutenant Chimes and the sergeants. My assignment for this day was Beat 7-22, Chene Street between Mack Avenue and the I-94 Interstate freeway. My assigned partner for today was Officer Jay Johnson or J.J., a tall thin black male who appeared to be very pleasant, sporting a smile which I interpreted as a sign; we will be just fine as partners.

As I have indicated, a rookie's assignment varies daily, since they are pretty much used as fill-ins for those on leave or who call in sick. If no one calls in ill, your assignments could include walking a beat, precinct security or working inside behind the desk as an extra clerk, which is not very appealing to a rookie. We wanted to experience action. Although it is understood as a rookie, you are understandably just an extra body at the bottom of the food chain.

J.J. and I were dropped off at the corner of Mack and Chene by Scout 7-3, Field & Bagger, who advised us "Watch your asses when you're walking by the pool hall at Illinois & Chene because there's a lot of dope in that place. Just make sure they hear you approaching. You don't want to surprise anyone." I felt as though they were advising us to turn our heads by letting the criminals know we were coming. However, I would later learn that this location was notorious for dope and shootings, Field and Bagger were genuinely concerned for our wellbeing.

The fact of the matter was that we might not respond promptly to a narcotic situation taking place. As rookies, we weren't familiar with the area or key players (violators) and if we walked up unwittingly into a narcotic transaction, we could very well become injured or worse. As with most rookies, we would soon discover ignorance can be very costly.

As we began walking North on Chene Street, we could observe a crowd of black folks several blocks away standing in front of an old white building, a building I would soon discover was the Chene & Illinois Pool Hall about which 7-3 had warned us. It was still early and there was plenty of daylight remaining, which allowed the crowd to see us as well. The closer we got, the more people slipped inside the pool hall.

"Hi officer, how you doing?" asked one of the black males that remained in front of the pool hall as we passed. "Fine sir, what's going on with you folks?" "Aw, nothing much, just hanging out, sir." Another man looked at my partner saying, "What's up my brother?" J.J. nodded and continued to walk along my side. Once we were several houses away from the pool hall, I asked J.J. if he observed the brothers inside the pool hall peeking out from behind the curtains. "Yea, I seen them, they probably have outstanding warrants." Once we passed, the crowd reappeared and cars once again began pulling up and taking part in what I'm sure were narcotic transactions. Damn, if we only had a scout car, we could make a narcotic arrest.

Upon reaching the intersection of Chene and Warren Avenue, we observed a black male with crutches in hand lying on the ground in front of a bakery. He obviously had fallen and would need assistance to get back on his feet. As we approached the incapacitated individual we detected a strong and disgusting stench of alcohol and body-odor. He was murmuring something that sounded like "Bitch, bitch, stay away from me, bitch." I leaned over this unfortunate crippled individual and placed my hand on his shoulder stating "Sir, can we give you a hand?" Suddenly, this poor handicapped man grabbed me with such force that it felt like a bear trap had closed on my arm. This drunk pulled me to the ground with little effort, and began striking me with one of his crutches. He had a strong grasp on one arm and I was blocking his blows with my other arm, leaving me virtually defenseless. I recall saying, "You crazy idiot, I'm trying to help you."

J.J. immediately came to my aid, grabbing him around his neck. At this point, "Sampson" dropped the crutch and flung J.J. against the wall like a human dart. Just my luck, the first fight I get into is with a drunken cripple with the strength of ten men. I finally got the crutch that he was striking me with away and kicked the second into the street. I now found myself rolling around on the sidewalk exchanging blows with this nut. J.J. returned and between the two of us, we were finally able to break his grip from my arm, allowing me to crawl out of his reach.

Now that we were out of harm's way, J.J. and I looked at each other, slightly smiling, reminding me of two professional wrestlers who had just won a major tag team title. We had faced a situation that required teamwork and unfaltering commitment, which we both successfully displayed. This was significant in my mind because it reinforced my belief that black and white officers could work together as brothers with the same common goal.

A scout car was requested to assist us in transporting our prisoner. I could not believe what had just happened, our first arrest without the presence of a senior officer was an insane disabled drunk who just kicked our asses and had yet to be handcuffed - how embarrassing!

Of all people to respond, was Sergeant Ken Jacobs. As he pulled up, I could see him shaking his head in disbelief. There we stood, J.J. with the knees of his pants torn out and me with my ripped blood-covered shirt, blood which was mostly mine. He leaned out the window with his pipe clinched in his teeth. "What the hell are you kids doing with him?" "This man assaulted us Sir," I replied. "No shit, that's quite obvious, look at you guys, you're a mess, if he's under arrest, why isn't he cuffed?" "Boss, we tried. This guy is strong as a bull!" Sergeant Jacobs, with his eyes closing just shook his head side-to-side in disbelief.

Just then, 7-4, who had received the radio run pulled up. As Rodgers and Kingston got out of their car, they, too, began shaking their heads while laughing. "I see you guys have met Jonathan, nice guy isn't he?" Rodgers leaned over our prisoner and said, "Jonathan, its Rodge, are you OK?" I thought, is he OK? We're the ones who just got our butts kicked by this crazy. "Hey Rodge, I'm alright. I was just playing with the rookies and shit got a little out of hand." Rodgers had our subject crawl into the rear seat of his scout car, where the handcuffs were placed on him with no resistance whatsoever. Unbelievable!

We would later learn that the handicap gentleman we encountered was known as Jonathan, who frequently got drunk and loved to fight, especially with police rookies. Everyone at the precinct knew and welcomed him as if he was one of the family. He was placed in the lockup (jail cell) to sleep it off and upon sobering, he would be released. So much for our first big arrest; he goes free and we are left with torn uniforms, aching bodies and bruised egos.

Sergeant Jacobs advised us to write a quick Preliminary Compliant Report (PCR) on the incident, change our uniforms, lick our wounds and get back on the street for the remaining five hours of the shift. As he walked away with his back to us he shouted, "And try not to get into any more trouble, damn it." J.J. and I looked at each other in disbelief. Our attempt to assist a fallen handicapped citizen had turned into a fiasco where we not only got our clocks cleaned; we now appeared like mischievous kids or bumbling idiots. What's wrong with this picture?

Once we were driven back to our beat, we walked toward the northern end of the precinct in search of a place to take a code 9330 (lunch). The north end of the Seventh Precinct was a racially diverse area. There were black and white, Polish, as well as those of Arabic descent, residing in an area that covered approximately four square miles. This area was referred to as the United Nations because of the many cultures represented. And, surprisingly, the crime rate was lower than many of the other scout car areas within the precinct.

As we crossed Milwaukee Street, the bright neon sign that read "Famous "Restaurant" lit up the sidewalk, welcoming customers. It was an older restaurant with pre-World War II décor, which consisted of a long counter with wooden stools, small wooden tables covered with red and white checkered table cloths, along with a number of wood booths against the wall. We sat at the counter and began viewing today's specials, which were displayed on a large black chalkboard hanging on the wall.

Just then the door opened and two older officers walked in. I nodded and said, Hi, guys, how's it going? They replied with a courteous nod prior to seating themselves in the furthest booth away from us. "J.J. I'm getting so tired of this bullshit. Who in the hell do these guys think they are?" His response was not quite what I expected, "Don't take it personal, Dave, it's me. They don't like a brother in their white restaurant." "No way, J.J., it's because we are rookies, I replied. "Dave, you're a nice guy but you have a lot to learn about this race thing." As I looked around the restaurant, it was apparent my partner was the only black patron. Surely, this wasn't the case. He's not some suspicious street thug, he's a police officer in full uniform.

Later, at off duty roll call, everything returned to business as usual. J.J. went and stood with the black officers and I stood on the white officers' side of the squad room. Even after all we went through during the last eight hours; it all came back to the reality of the ugly truth, racism. Maybe J.J. was right, I'm living in a dream world. Racism not only exists, it's a cancer that refuses to die, spreading throughout society and now residing within the Detroit Police Department.

For the next few weeks, J.J. and I walked beat 7-22 (Chene Street) together, during which time we got to know each other quite well. J.J. came from a large family, four brothers and three sisters that had moved north from Alabama during the 1950's. He, too, was recently discharged from the Army after returning from Vietnam.

I found we had much in common until it regarded race, then we took on two totally different views. J.J. believed many black criminals are victims of society, or are a trapped people, forced to remain a product of their environment. On the other hand, I was far less forgiving. I believe that each and every one of us is free and quite capable of making our own decisions, as well as facing the consequences of those choices. In my opinion, many blacks declare racism when caught in an illegal act, which provides a smoke screen for the crime they have committed. Sometimes, ignorance is convenient, and it's easier to blame the world for your misfortunes rather than attempting to make a positive change.

Fortunately, J.J. and I were able to separate our ethnic and political views from our patrol duties. We had both proven our loyalty to each other, fighting side by side without mistreating any suspects. This was a concern of mine because of the stories I had heard about old-timers beating suspects half to death because they were black. Thank God I had not witnessed anything like that! I surely would like to believe it's an exaggeration, although J.J. assured me not only did it exist, it's very prevalent.

I also expressed my concern that there appeared to be a racial divide within the Seventh Precinct and I prayed this was not the case department-wide. Once again, J.J. reminded me that I was either blind or awfully naïve, that racism is not only prevalent in the Seventh Precinct, it's everywhere and it's about time I wake up and see the light. I totally disagreed, saying that we may not be able to change the world but we can certainly make some changes within our precinct.

Let me make something very clear: I'm not a bleeding heart liberal, or an activist in the civil rights movement. To the contrary, I come from a southern background where traditionally, integration was considered totally unacceptable and, unfortunately, racism was widespread.

My roots are in a small town in western Kentucky, a town by the name of Russellville. I recall as a young boy, my grandfather, whom we respectfully referred to as "Daddy Claude," would take me into town where he would trade pocket knives in the square with other old timers.

On one occasion, he took me to a little hole-in-the-wall restaurant. While ordering a soda, I observed a sign on the back door that read "Colored Eating Area." I walked to the screen door and gazed outside where I observed several wood picnic tables occupied by black folks who were eating. When I asked why they were not allowed to come inside and eat with the whites, my grandfather stated, "That's just the way it is, son whites don't eat with colored folks." This was an answer that I did not understand or find appropriate at the time, but it would become very clear during the next decade, a time in history that was to become known as the Era of the Civil Rights Movement.

Now, my forefathers were anything but rich, actually they were poor white sharecroppers going back several generations. I recall my great grandpa Billy, who lived to the ripe old age of 105, relating a story from his childhood. He said he and his siblings would join the black farm hands in the barn to worship, singing gospel songs. What was so unique about his account was the manner in which he said they worshipped, actually placing wooden water buckets over their heads while singing. They did so in an effort to muffle the sound so they would not disturb the rich landowner up in the big house. How pathetic!

I would be less than truthful if I implied there were no prejudices within me because I was exposed to certain beliefs in childhood, ugly teachings that I have since abandoned or fully intend to conceal, protecting my son and daughter from these ugly traditions. I pray this cycle stops with me.

I'm a man who believes that change can be very constructive and should be implemented by those with true conviction. No man, no creature should be treated with less dignity than God intended and to declare oneself superior over another, actually reveals how inferior you really are. I fought side by side with people of color in the Army and now with fellow black police officers. It's just beyond me how we could bleed and die for one another; yet still eat in separate restaurants. My God, this was not 1910!

J.J. and I did compromise and agreed to eat at locations in which we felt comfortable and considered race-friendly. One of these locations was Donnie's Pizzeria, located on our beat. Donnie treated us well and always had hot pizza ready for policemen in the back room, which was great because it kept us away from those customers who always had a ton of what would be perceived as ridiculous questions. This is not the way one wants to spend their lunch hour.

My partner and I were beginning to get this police thing down; almost to the point it appeared that we knew what we were doing. We lead the shift in misdemeanor arrests for the month and wrote two books of tickets each, mostly parking tickets. Now, while I did not enjoy writing tickets, as rookies on probation it was necessary to display your aggressiveness in all areas until we reached our first year anniversary. During the probationary period rookies have absolutely no representation nor protection from the Detroit Police Officers Association. This meant in effect, we could be terminated at will for essentially any reason.

July was now upon us and criminal activity was beginning to soar. It was not out of the ordinary to get 12-15 police runs a night. Hot summer nights just seem to bring out the worst in people. I'm not sure if it's because the homes are far too hot due to the lack of air conditioners, which eventually drives everyone out into the streets. Drinking also becomes a huge factor influencing one's behavior, especially when among large crowds. Then, you have those individuals who are just plain evil and find pleasure in causing trouble.

It was a Friday night and the temperature was holding in the upper 80s with little if any wind. The streets were crowded and tempers were rising, all the ingredients for trouble. Our radios were transmitting non-stop and they were all serious calls. We had just left the lot when information came over the radio that a S.T.R.E.S.S. crew had been ambushed during an investigation, followed by a description of three suspects. I wanted to throw up; with these four it made six officers shot in my first seven months on the job.

Later that evening, we were advised that all four members of the S.T.R.E.S.S. crew were shot by three black male subjects, who were eventually identified as Boyd, Bethune and Brown, men who would later be described as "Mad dog killers" by Police Commissioner John Nichols, a statement that would return to haunt him during the upcoming Mayoral election.

To say that S.T.R.E.S.S. was a controversial unit within the Detroit Police Department would be a great understatement. S.T.R.E.S.S., which was the acronym for "Stop The Robberies Enjoy Safe Streets" was the child of then Police Commissioner Nichols and one of his deputy chiefs. Nichols was also a controversial figure in his own right, respected by most of the white population and detested by many within the black community.

In the near future, Nichols would be running for mayor of the City of Detroit. His opponent, a black candidate by the name of Coleman A. Young has been involved in the political game for years. Young was well known for his rude and outspoken mannerisms as well as being recognized as a black activist for the civil rights movement. This campaign set the forum for one of the most heated mayoral debates in the history of Detroit. The majority of the issues would be race-related with the dismantlement of the S.T.R.E.S.S. unit in the forefront.

S.T.R.E.S.S. was created as a decoy type unit and recruited the best of the best throughout the police department. The officers, both black and white, were placed in covert operations in high crime areas citywide, usually portraying themselves as helpless or unaware citizens, who are typically the prime targets for the criminal element, especially holdup men. Since the unit's inception, there have been a number of officers involved in fatal shootings where the suspects were either killed or wounded during the commission of a felony or the actual arrest.

The unit was loved by conservatives, who believed that hardened criminals were being taken off the streets. Whereas, much of the black community and liberals truly believed that S.T.R.E.S.S. was a gang of white cops declaring open season on the city's black citizens. Many accused the white establishment of enticing blacks into committing felonies by posing as easy targets. Again, it was not about right or wrong, it was about black and white!

My partner on this particular evening was Officer Arne Greyson, a stocky red headed fellow who was very opinionated on any topic that might arise. He displayed a very bitter attitude toward blacks in general, blaming them for just about every problem that existed in society. I must admit that I, too, had a bitter taste toward the black criminal element but did not consider the entire black population a product of evil.

"These black bastards continue to shoot us and the courts just keep letting them go free (A statement directed toward the shooting of the four S.T.R.E.S.S Officers). You know why? I'll tell you why. Because they're black and in today's society that gives them a free ticket!" "Arnie, you can't blame the entire black race for the shit a few maggots do." "Bullshit, they all hate us and it's quite obvious."

There was no talking to this guy: he was one of those that loved to hate. I too get infuriated at the black idiots that just live to stir up trouble, causing this country to constantly be on the brink of internal war. However, I know lining up blacks and executing them as if they are all criminals is not an option. That's been tried in Germany and it didn't work, not to mention its outright evil. No, there is enough responsibility to go around for both races.

Suddenly, the radio sounded off, "7-6 East Grand Blvd and Farnsworth, there's a black male in a red shirt threatening people with a large stick." "On the way, radio 7-6," I relayed. As we approached Farnsworth, some kids advised us that the suspect had just gone into the alley that runs adjacent to the street.

Upon entering the alley, we observed the suspect stagger-ing and carrying a baseball bat as reported, which he pointed at our scout car while advising us how he was going to kick our asses. Arnie and I approached the drunk from different di-rections and attempted to convince him to drop the bat which he now had over head in a threating fashion, our request were met with insulting racial remarks, indicating rational compliance was not an option. While I was negotiating with the suspect, Arnie came from behind, grabbing him in a bear hug, which gave me the opportunity to take away the bat.

What followed next was shocking to say the least: Arnie threw the suspect to the ground and went crazy on the old guy. I don't know what got into him. He began kicking and hitting the suspect while screaming racial slurs. This guy was no longer resisting, he was just attempting to block the blows. "Come on, Arnie, he's had enough. You're going to kill him." "Fuck him, I'll teach him how to respect the law." I thought to myself that the only thing you are teaching him is to hate cops!

Finally, I was able to get my cuffs on the old timer who was a mess. He was then transported to Detroit Receiving Hospital where he was registered as a police prisoner and ironically charged with Assault &Battery of a Police Officer and Resisting Arrest. I found this strange due to the fact that Arnie and I had only obtained minor wounds, as where the defendant was the one that would require minor medical attention. I must tell you I do believe this prisoner was dealt with appropriately up to the point he stopped battling and no longer presented a threat.

That night after the shift, I drove around for quite a while just thinking about the episode with the old man. Eventually, I stopped over my parents' home and had a long discussion with my mom, a lovely old southern gal who had a heart the size of Texas and was always willing to share her wisdom. I expressed how disappointed I was in myself for not stopping the beating of the old man. "Momma, it just wasn't right, the old guy got a beating far more than he deserved and I stood by idly and let it happen. This makes me as guilty as my partner."

Her statement was simple but profound. She said, "Son, you can't change another man's heart, but you must answer for yours. You cannot turn the hands of time back so what happened today will always remain, but you can make sure it never happens again." Her advice became the foundation of how I would carry myself throughout the rest of my career. If I made a mistake or a fool out of myself, it would be because of my actions, not because I was going along to get along.

The following day I was assigned to Scout 7-7 with Ed Harrison, an average- sized, well-groomed, professional black gentleman. Once we got out in the parking lot, Officer Harrison tossed me the car keys, saying, "You drive officer, I will jump." This meant he would ride in the passenger seat and be responsible for jumping out and chasing suspects if necessary.

This kind gesture was highly unusual, because few senior officers allowed rookies to drive. The reason for this was two-fold; first being your driving was not trusted and the second was you were unfamiliar with the precinct. It is essential you know your location at all times, in case you need to call for assistance or must get somewhere in a hurry, there is no time to look at a map!

"Hi Ed, my name is Dave." "Yea, I've heard all about you, kid. JJ says you're cool." "I don't know how cool I am, but I assure you I can be trusted," I offered with a slight smile, which received a slight grunt that I interpreted as OK, we will see about that.

Ed directed me to a small restaurant located on the south end of the precinct off Jefferson Avenue. This was a location frequented by a predominantly black clientele, a preferred stop for black officers for their morning coffee. As I put the car in park, Ed glanced in my direction saying you can wait in the car if you're more comfortable. "Why, are you ashamed to be seen with a white boy?" "Not at all, just giving you a choice," said with a half grin.

Once inside, we joined two of our fellow officers, Spacy and Kenwall who were already seated. I must admit, I felt very uncomfortable because I could feel the tension throughout the restaurant and certainly at our table. Shortly after we were seated, an attractive black waitress began to take our order. "What can I get you, sir?" she asked kindly. "Just a coffee ma'am please." An innocent reply that erupted a firestorm of angry questions from Kenwall; "You afraid to eat our food? Not good enough for you, or do you think you might turn black?" "Aw come on man, cut the kid some slack," intervened Ed. "You think he will cut us slack Ed when he's with his own?" The hate Kenwall displayed for whites was so transparent.

I wasn't ready for this drama so early in the day so I decided to remove myself from this ugly situation before it escalated.

"Look guy's, I think I'll go out to the car and start the daily log." As I got up and walked out I could feel eyes burning a hole in my back. I was never so relieved to get out of a place in all my life. I now had an understanding of how J.J. felt at the Famous Restaurant, where he was the only black patron.

Shortly after I started our log, the passenger door opened, "Sorry about that, Dave, said Ed as he seated himself in the passenger seat. "You know, Ed, that guy has some real issues. How in the hell can he be fair to people with an attitude like that, he's a cop, not a Black Panther!" "Look Dave, I don't agree with what he said in there. However, he is justified in feeling that way in many respects. You're new, kid, and you have not experienced the ugly things that we have on this department.

Do you realize just a few years ago it was not uncommon to hear cops on the radio stating, "Kill that Nigger or Kick that Nigger's ass." And that's no shit. I've worked with old white guys who would tell me to stay in the car while they went into a restaurant and had lunch with all their white counterparts. You just don't have any idea of the hurt we have felt." "So, that gives him the right to treat me like some substandard animal? I don't think so, Ed that was not me or the entire white race on that damn radio making the racial slurs!"

7-7, East Grand Blvd. and Lafayette, "In the alley, a man stabbed, description of suspect as follows: A black male, 5'10", 175 lbs. wearing an army field jacket and a red ball cap, armed with a large butcher knife, last seen walking west on Lafayette from East Grand Blvd."

Upon our arrival, we found a black male approximately 70 years of age sitting on the ground with his back against a garage, bleeding profusely from his right shoulder and left hand. The hand wound was apparently sustained from grabbing the knife as the assailant was stabbing him. He had lost a lot of blood and was beginning to slip into shock. Fortunately, the hospital wagon arrived and the old-timer was transferred to Detroit General Hospital for treatment.

Ed and I gathered what evidence we could and advised dispatch that we would be busy, in route to Detroit General Hospital. As we pulled out of the alley west on Lafayette, Ed observed a guy matching the description of the stabbing suspect walking south on Field from Lafayette. I made a U-turn and began to slowly approach the individual from behind. Suddenly, he turned and observed us. "Oh shit, he's going to bolt Dave; I can see it in his eyes." Just then, he took off west between the houses. "Let me out here, Dave, you see if you can go around and cut him off."

"Radio 7-7", "go ahead 7-7", "My partner is chasing a suspect believed to be involved in our stabbing, west between the houses from Field south of Lafayette. He's described as a black male 5'10" an army field jacket and a red ball cap." "All cars in number seven, 7-7 is on foot in the area of Lafayette and Field chasing a suspect wanted for Felonious Assault with a knife. The suspect is described as a black male, 5'10" wearing an army field jacket and a red ball cap."

I drove two blocks over in anticipation of surprising the

suspect as he came from between the houses. I couldn't believe my eyes. The suspect was jumping fences and was going to eventually be running right into my arms. I hid out of sight until he reached the house in which I was situated. My heart was pounding so fast and loud, I thought for sure it would give my location away. I could hear his shoes hitting the ground, any second now, I thought. Just then, there he was, I tackled this dirt bag who went down for the count. The cuffs barely fit around his wrists, an obvious heroin junkie with hands that were swollen like footballs from shooting up. The suspects coat was soaked with the old-timers blood and contained several dollars and a butcher knife.

"Hey, Ed, I'm over here, I got the idiot in custody." "Good job Dave, does he have the knife?" "Yea, he had it in his jacket along with four dollars." "7-7 calling radio," "Go ahead 7-7." "We have our Felonious Assault suspect in custody." "All cars in number seven, go easy, 7-7 has the suspect in custody, good job 7-7."

I placed my hand on Ed's back, while he was leaning over with attempts to catch his breath. "You Ok, Ed?" "Hell no I'm not Ok, I'm too damn old to be chasing these stinking knuckleheads around." After catching his breath, Ed took on this somewhat puzzling look, which was followed by a curious question. "Let me ask you something kid. Why didn't you get your licks on this asshole, there were no witnesses?" "Why should I kick his ass? He didn't resist." "Boy, you can tell the old white guys haven't got to you yet, you'll change." "Bullshit, Ed, if this idiot would have resisted at all, I wouldn't have hesitated to split his damn head open. However, I have not, nor will I ever beat a man like a help-less dog to impress anyone, black or white." With a look of skepticism, Ed said "I sure hope you keep that outlook, kid."

Scout 7-8 arrived on the scene and advised us they would convey our prisoner into the station, "Did you guys get the weapon?" "Yea, we got the knife and money he took from the victim. He got a little bruised up when Dave tackled his ass. Just let the desk sergeant know we'll be in to do the pa-perwork as soon as we interview the complainant down at the hospital." Little did we know the old-timer had expired shortly after he arrived at Detroit General Hospital, he just lost too much blood. The idiot stabbed him in a main artery, all over a few stinking ass dollars!

At off duty roll call, I observed Ed standing near the locker room talking to all the brothers, who would occasionally look in my direction, then quickly turn away to avoid being too conspicuous. It was obvious I was the topic of conversation. Oh, to be that fly on the wall.

CHAPTER "IT'S TIME FOR CHANGES" 2

"FIELD, RONOWSKI, 7-3. LAST BUT NOT least, Stealth, you got Angle on 7-5. Got anything for the troops, sergeants?" asked Lieutenant Chimes, to which they indicated in the negative, with facial and head gestures. "OK guys, get out there, keep your eyes open and watch your asses."

God, I can't believe 14 months have gone by. I now have my own scout car and I'm considered a senior officer. In most suburban cities you would still be considered a rookie. But 14 months on the streets of Detroit is considered equivalent to serving five years elsewhere. I like using the analogy, serving in Detroit is like serving in Vietnam or Iraq; you learn quickly or you die, as opposed to working in most suburban police departments which could be compared with doing a tour in Europe.

This is not to insinuate their job in the suburban areas is any less hazardous than big city cops, because this is simply not the case, whenever you pin on a badge, you become a target and believe me criminals are not concerned with geography's.

"Hi! Sir, I'm Jim Angle," as he extended his hand. I replied, "How you doing Jim? Forget the sir stuff buddy; we are both patrolmen, the names Dave. Why don't you go get us a prep radio and a shotgun, Jim?" "Sure thing, Dave," followed by a large smile. The kid felt welcome and was obviously hyped and raring to get out there and do his job.

"How about we start with a coffee Jim? I'll introduce you to some of the gang." "Yes sir, I mean that sounds great Dave." Jim was fairly short in stature, I would say approximately 5'8" and about 170 pounds, but very muscular. I thought I looked young, but this kid looked like a high school senior quarterback. He carried himself very well and came across as a very intelligent young man.

"*So* do you have a family, Dave?" "Yea, I'm married and we have a two-year old son." "That's cool, I have a fiancée and we're going to get married next year, now that I have graduated from the academy. I'll be moving her here as soon as I get settled in and get an apartment." "Where are you living now Jim?" "Oh, I'm staying with two of my academy classmates on the Westside. I want to move to the eastside now that I've been assigned to the Seventh." "Where's home Jim?" "I'm from Midland, a small community in central Michigan." "I'm very familiar with that part of the country; I have hunted in Harrison County for years, actually. So, what makes a farm boy like you come to this hellhole?" "Well, the way I figure, the only way I'm going to learn how to be a good cop is by experience and what better place to gain experience than Detroit, the murder capital of the world?" "You've got a point," I responded.

"Turn right and then left into the parking lot, Jim." The Click Restaurant already had several scout cars in the lot, each team attempting to get a morning coffee prior to the radio going crazy with runs. The criminal element is primarily active at night and sleeps at least until 10 or 11:00 a.m., then their law breaking cycle begins all over again.

As we were parking the car, we received our first run "7-5 Milwaukee and Chene, the NBW bank, a holdup alarm." "On the way, radio, 7-5." While in route I advised Jim, "We have been getting a lot of false alarms at this bank, nevertheless, we always treat them as if they're the real thing as it's better to be safe than sorry." "Got it Dave," Jim nervously acknowledged.

I pulled up just short of the bank to prevent from being in the line of fire should this be a legitimate call. We got out of our vehicle and approached the bank on foot. As we cautiously peered through the bank window everything appeared to be business as usual with tellers waiting on customers. Once inside, the bank manager confirmed it was indeed, a false alarm inadvertently set off by one of his employees. "Radio 7-5, Milwaukee and Chene NBW is a false alarm. Please advise any cars responding to cancel and we're back in service." "Ten-four, 7-5, you're back in service."

Jim had a look of disappointment on his face as we drove away. He obviously wanted this to be an actual bank robbery, which is not uncommon for working cops. Bank robbers are typically the worst of the worst, the type of criminal you really want to put behind bars. They walk into the crime with gun in hand and all too often are willing to shoot those who interfere or fail to comply with their demands.

It was quiet for the next couple hours and it seemed as though the bank robbery run would be the highlight of the day. We had investigated several vehicles and a number of gang bangers, who on this day were clean and in possession of nothing but a bad attitude.

"7-5, we're getting multiple reports at Milwaukee & Chene, of a man shot in front of the bank." "On the way 7-5." Again, we were only several blocks away. Could this be an omen, I thought as we approached. Two runs to the same locality within hours? Upon arriving at the location, it was clear this was not another erroneous police run. There was a white male lying on the sidewalk, face up. As we exited our vehicle, I could see the man was indeed, shot and bleeding profusely. "Jim, let radio," Jim interrupted, "I'm already on it, Dave, a wagon is on the way." This kid has initiative; he's going to be a good cop!

The victim was still conscious but in bad shape. He took a round to the chest, almost center mass. "You're going to be ok, partner, we'll get you to the hospital right away." His eyes opened, acknowledging my words with a yes head gesture followed by an expression of shock. "Dave? It's me Jeff, Ken's brother in-law." I then recognized the gentleman. We had both been groomsmen for my cousin Ken's wedding two weeks earlier, oh my God! "Jeff, the wagon is almost here, you hang in there, we will get you to the hospital right away."

As they placed Jeff in the back of the wagon, I advised him I would notify the family, who would be joining him at the hospital. He appeared to be falling into shock due to the excessive loss of blood, taking on the chalky look that can be found in ICU wards, not looking good!

Prior to the victim being transported, he informed us that he was just leaving the bank after cashing his check when he was approached by a black male, 5'10, 160lbs wearing dark clothing and a black gangster hat who demanded his money, saying "Turn it over cracker." Jeff without hesitation complied; nervously handing over his money envelope, at which time the piece of garbage smiled and shot him, anyway.

We were obviously dealing with a cold-blooded killer and the only people in this area who wore the dark clothing and gangster hats were members of the infamous Chene Gang, a ring of black teens that had claimed control of the north end of the precinct with graffiti that warned all this was Chene Gang territory!

The Chene Gang was responsible for various crimes in the area including multiple robberies. Their preferred targets were small businesses, the elderly and whites who were typically oblivious to their surroundings, such as their latest target, Jeff.

Once at the precinct, I contacted my cousin, Ken, advising him of his brother in-law's despicable incident. I informed

Ken that Jeff was conveyed to Detroit Receiving Hospital and suggest he and the wife get down there ASAP because he took one to the chest.

Prior to completing my report, I called the hospital for a condition update on the victim, to which I was advised he expired on the operating table about 20 minutes ago. Just great, Ken and his wife will be arriving to greet a corpse. She won't even be able to tell her brother goodbye. This parasite finds it easier to kill a man over $500 rather than working for a living, simply because robbing the innocent requires far less effort.

I would wager that the suspect never once took into consideration the residual effect this horrific act would have. In this case, the victim was survived by a wife and two small children, all of whom are now left alone to fend for themselves. The only thing this vicious thug could see was a white man with cash, money he deserved but was deprived of because he was one of the "have-nots."

For the next week, Jim and I gave the north end of the precinct a lot of special attention in attempts to get information leading to the arrest of Jeff's murderer. We questioned numerous Chene Gang members, all of whom had convenient amnesia. Not that I expected them to turn in one of their gangbanger cohorts, but sometime when a question is repeatedly asked, one can slip up and provide information that even they are unaware they're giving.

Our efforts had thus far brought little results, which concerned me because if this thug was not captured soon, he would very likely, through arrogance, commit additional rob-beries that could escalate to murder once again!

Several days later Jim was on leave, which meant I would either be given a rookie or be reassigned to another car. As luck would have it, I was assigned to 7-3 with Officer Bob Field, which was just fine with me. We had developed quite a relationship and both of us were very enthusiastic concerning crime and arresting those who would harm our people, the people of the Seventh Precinct. It was never about race but it was good and evil in our eyes!

"Bob, if you don't mind, can we cruise up to the north end and see what we can dig up concerning that shooting in front of the NBW bank?" "No problem, Dave, let's grab a quick coffee and then we'll take a look." "Thanks, Bob, I just want to get that piece of garbage off the street."

After a quick stop at the Click Restaurant, we went di-rectly to the south end. "Ok Dave, what are your thoughts?" I found it very flattering that this senior cop was asking for my advice. I must be doing something right. "I would suggest we start in the Milwaukee and Chene area Bob, if that's OK?

We were north on St Aubin approaching Milwaukee when we observed one of the Chene Gang, a member with whom I was very familiar, Ed Henry aka "Muff Dog." As we ap-proached, I observed the right side of his jacket was bulging. "Bob, watch his hands! He has something in his jacket, Bob replied, "Yea I got it." Henry turned and stopped, looking at us as if to say "ÓK, let's get this shit over with." Upon patting him down, we found an open bottle of Vodka in his right pocket, which we confiscated, advising him he was going to receive a Minor in Possession of Alcohol (MIP) violation citation.

Once we checked Henry for outstanding warrants, I asked if he had heard about the man killed in front of the bank, to which he replied sporting a smile, "Yea, the honkey got his due and screw you and your fucking ticket. I don't have to answer anything," as he turned taunting us while back-stepping. Bob grabbed his arm and the fight was on.

One would think two healthy cops, both exceeding 200 pounds, would be able to subdue a wiry kid with no problem, but Henry was putting up one hell of a fight and things were about to get worse. Bob was holding him down while I attempted to put on the handcuffs. "Dave, hurry up! I can't hold him much longer." "I'm trying Bob!" I got one cuff on, one more second."

As if things weren't complicated enough, an unexpected scream came from a house across street, "Hey what in the hell you doing with him? They are beating up on Ed, Y'all " Suddenly, the house emptied and we had Ed's entire family running toward us. Seconds later, we had approximately 15 males and females attacking us. Bob was able to break loose and radio for assistance. "Radio 7-3, Milwaukee and St Aubin, officer needs assistance." "Ten four, 7-5 and all cars in seven, 7-3 needs assistance, Milwaukee and St Aubin.

The family was on us like flies, attempting to forcibly

take our prisoner while throwing punches and kicks from all different directions. I could hear sirens off in the distance and my only thought was if they don't get here soon, we are going to be short one prisoner, not to mention our clocks were being cleaned.

What the average citizen fails to realize is that when a police officer gets into this type of situation, he has several concerns, such as his partner's safety, his gun being snatched from his holster and pure survival. Whereas, the angry mob has no concerns, they attack like a pack of wolves with an unquenchable thirst for violence and blood.

As I looked up for the arriving good guys, I observed a young black male off to my right swinging a red brick down on my head as he screamed, "I'll kill your ass, you white motherfucker!" Within seconds, my vision was obstructed by the warm red blood flowing down my face. That was it, I released one of the two assailants I was holding and pulled my gun, at which time I heard the screeching of tires. Thank God, the Calvary has arrived!

As I got to my feet, the same thug that split my head open with a brick was charging at me to finish the job, screaming the same old racial slurs as he swung the brick. However, this time, I was not attempting to restrain two men. I grabbed the arm with the brick in hand, twisting it behind his back, at which time I could hear it snap like a twig, causing him to drop the brick and scream like a little girl. He wasn't so tough now that I wasn't on the bottom of the pile.

We arrested the entire family for Assault and Battery of a Police Officer, conveying all to the precinct except the punk with the broken arm, who went to the hospital. Once at the station, all of the suspects were separated in hopes of minimizing the screaming and threats, a technique that I must admit failed. I have never been called a white motherfucker, cracker, and honky so many times in one day.

On a positive note, our efforts paid off, one of the suspects arrested gave us information that led to the arrest of the gang member who murdered Jeff in front of the bank. It made us getting our clocks cleaned almost worthwhile, I said almost.

Needless to say, this ended our day, our uniforms torn and covered in blood. By the time the doctor at the hospital emergency room stitched me up, our shift was over. Bob and I were just beginning to come down from our adrenalin rush. Both of us realized things could have really gone south out there if that mob had been able to overpower us and get one of our guns. There is nothing more sorrowful than a cop being shot with his own service weapon.

The next day, Jim returned and immediately expressed his disappointment for missing the action and he was noticeably upset. "Jim, if it makes you feel any better, I wish it had been you on the bottom of the pile having your head split wide open with that brick instead of me," as I chuckled. Jim smiled, "I would gladly take one for you Dave." "I know you would, partner, I'm just joking and I respect you for that."

Radio to 7-5, "Go ahead radio" 7-5 we are getting a

boyfriend causing a disturbance at 5367 Grandy. "On the way, radio 7-5." Once at the house, we spoke with the boyfriend, who had been drinking and was attempting to resolve a problem between him and his lady. We arrested the boyfriend, not for the domestic dispute, but rather for outstanding traffic warrants he had failed to pay. No assault had taken place, and the gentleman was actually a nice guy who was having relationship problems, to which we as cops could certainly relate with.

As we placed the handcuffs on Mr. Robinson, I advised him they were necessary for his safety, not to mention policy. "They will only be on you for a bit partner; the station is just a few blocks away." I failed to mention a lot can happen in just a few blocks! "So listen, buddy, do us a favor, when you make bond on these tickets, please go home and get some rest and talk to your girlfriend tomorrow, ok?" "Yes sir, I don't need any more problems. The bitch has been sleeping around on me anyway. She can go to hell, I'm done."

"Dave, something is going on up there with those folks on the right." "Yea, I see it Jim." A crowd was gathered in front of a house screaming at some people entering a blue Mustang. "Sir, you might want to lie down on the seat until we find on what's actually going on here." Now I have seen men move fast in my time, but I must tell you, our arrestee was on the floorboard buried between the seats before I finished my warning.

As we approached the scene, we could see a black male

lying on the front lawn with a blood stained shirt. A heavyset lady began screaming, "Officer, officer they shot this man," as she pointed to the Mustang. "Jim, watch your ass and stay to the rear of car." I grabbed the shotgun and we began to approach the vehicle, which appeared to have multiple passengers, yet we were unable to determine who and how many were in the car due to the dark tinted windows. I announced, "Police, everyone exit the vehicle now!" Suddenly, a shot rang out from the car and the Mustang began to pull away at a high rate of speed. As Jim and I took cover behind some parked vehicles, I fired at the two driver's side tires with my shotgun.

"Radio, 7-5 priority!" "Go ahead 7-5." "Radio, we have shots fired west of Mt Elliot on Pierce and we have a citizen shot. Suspects fled in light blue Mustang, license number LLT-325, south on Elmwood from Pierce." "7-5, EMS is ordered and any and all units available to assist 7-5 proceed to Pierce west of Mt. Elliot."

"Jim, are you ok?" "Yea, I don't think they were shooting at us." "How's our prisoner doing?" "Oh shit Dave, I forgot about him." Upon opening the rear door of the scout car, we found our man hidden between the seats. "Sir, are you ok?" "Hell no, I'm not ok! I could have been killed over all this bullshit. Carry me to jail where at least I'll be safe." The gentleman had a point, having a couple delinquent tickets certainly doesn't warrant a situation like this, if it was up to me it would be time served and released. Oh well, some things just can't be avoided.

Fortunately, we had not entered in the period of our society's lawsuit frenzy where monetary claims are filed at any given opportunity, especially with municipalities where the big bucks are available. I would suggest in the not too distant future this fellow would have shysters fighting over his case. It would be considered a no brainer and very lucrative. However, this young man just wanted to get behind bars and away from the crazy streets.

Scout 7-7 found the blue Mustang about a quarter mile from the scene, abandoned with the rear driver's side tire blown-out. At least one of my shots had a positive effect. The screwdriver sticking out of the ignition was a pretty good indication it was stolen. The vehicle was towed to the Seventh Precinct garage and held for fingerprints. However, in all reality, unless the victim dies, there will not be a lot of effort trying to solve this case, especially considering the victim was shot in the arm.

While filing our report at the precinct, Scout 7-9, manned by Anders and Simpson, also members of the "Protectors," came in with the arrest of a white businessman for traffic warrants. Now, I could care less what race a violator is, right is right and wrong is wrong, but these guys flaunted the fact that they had a white professional arrest, which was rare to find due to the fact that the population of the precinct is primarily black and lower to middle class working folks.

"Almost shot another brother, huh Guys?" "Give it a rest Anders the only thing black I shot was a tire. I see you got another hardened white criminal, though." Said with sarcasm I must admit. "Hey Dave, if you're wrong, you're wrong. Just because he is white doesn't mean he's right!" "I agree, Anders, and I could care less about the guy. However, if you are only stopping him because he's white and the fact you can, what does that make it?"

This conversation was not going anywhere. I was dealing with a man who claimed he was an activist fighting for a cause, when in reality he was acting out of revenge, seeking out the opposite race to make a statement. Now tell me who the racist is? How ironic.

After processing our arrest, Jim and I decided to stop by the Goodyear bar for a bowl of Art's famous chili and a meatloaf sandwich. The Goodyear Bar was located in the north end of the precinct, and was considered to be one of the toughest bars in the area. What was unique about Art's bar was the fact that not only was it a preferred place for cops to hang out; it was also a bar where some real shady characters frequented.

"Hey Art, how you doing, buddy?" "Come on in guys I just put on a fresh pot of chili." Art, the owner, was a small red-headed fellow who loved cops, at least the fair and honest ones. The bar itself was not a place you would ever want your mom to see. It was furnished with small wooden tables with four chairs, none of which matched, a long wooden bar with a tarnished brass foot rail and stools that were worn and held together with duct tape. Behind the bar were wooden coolers dating back to the 1920s, a long mirror which had numerous cracks from flying beer bottles and a long shelf that contained the finest cheap whisky one could buy. The floor was made of old hardwood boards that were coated with years of spilled beer and whisky, which made walking without sticking almost impossible. The entertainment consisted of a pool table, long shuffleboard table with an old jukebox that contained nothing but honky-tonk, Elvis music and a few Christmas songs, which remained all year round.

A good night at the Goodyear bar for most patrons, consisted in, getting drunk out of your mind, a little bit of dancing, a fight with your girlfriend and smashing a beer bottle over the head of the guy who was flirting with her, who in many cases would be a friend or family. On some nights, there were more teeth on the floor than in the mouths of the patrons. Not quite the place you would want to have a wedding reception.

You may ask yourself why cops hang out in such places: bars where the very elements we arrest daily patronize. My answer would be twofold. One is that these establishments are located within their precinct, purely geography. Two, is that the customers in these bars could care less when the cops "let their hair down" and start telling war stories, getting loud or bitching about their organization. This actually supplies the customers with some form of entertainment, as well as a look into the world of law enforcement. A world where the only contact they have had most likely occurred at the end of a nightstick while being arrested, not to mention it is the closest they will ever come to knowing someone in city government.

"Art, let us try some of that fresh chili and we'll split a meatloaf sandwich. So everything's been quiet, Art?" "Yea, pretty much. You heard about the

black vice crew that came in Friday?" "No, what happened?" "I knew something was up because of this and that." "this and that" was a term that Art used to a point of being annoying. "First, this light skinned black guy came in and ordered a beer and asked me if I had change for a hundred, and I said no." I then asked for his ID because he appeared so young and this and that. He indicated he left his wallet at home and would return with it shortly, as he turned and walked out.

"A short time later, five black vice cops came in and identified themselves as vice officers and asked to see my license, which was right there on the wall, as he pointed to the license. They checked my license out and this and that, then they ran all my patrons on the radio for warrants. After searching the entire bar they walked out without saying a word. I am sure that young guy was a set up to see if I would serve a minor."

"Oh well, looks like you slipped by again Art." "Bullshit, Dave, you know damn well those niggers were only in here because I am a white bar owner. I'm just another honky to them and this and that. Why don't they pick on their own people, they're the ones selling dope and running whores out of their bars and this and that." "You need to calm down,

Art, you're going to have a heart attack or upset that sleeping ulcer."

Art was absolutely right. It was common knowledge that numerous liquor establishments were targeted because of race, especially with crews that were entirely of the same race. The white crews would target many black establishments because they were so plentiful and the black crews, in turn, would seek out white violators to make a statement. A statement that says, "We are not going to just lay down any longer, you come after ours and we'll come after yours." This was a cry heard around the country within the civil rights movement, now it's in the ranks of the police departments.

There is a faction black folks that not only excuse petty crimes that take place in their neighborhood, they condone them, believing they are justified due to years of oppression by the white society that continues to hold them down. In their eyes, it is simply a way to acquire things they believe they deserve but cannot afford. It is all about the haves and the have not's! Many of the crimes that were condoned or ignored were typically non-violent crimes or wrongdoings where the likelihood of anyone being harmed was minimal, misconducts such as receiving and concealing stolen property, breaking and entering (B&E), fraudulent checks, grand theft auto, playing the numbers (gambling) and prostitution, to mention a few.

"Art, my Mother always says there are good and evil in all races." "I know that, Dave, you have black people and then you have niggers." A statement used by many whites, who in their minds excuses their bigotry, however, I assure you blacks find this much less than amusing. I guess you could say its right up there with: "Some of my best friends are black." "Just stay straight, Art, and they can't touch you. The best defense is an honest one," generating an expression from Art that said, "yea, right Dave," "Thanks for the great food my old friend and we will talk to you later; it's time to go lock up some bad guys. Here Jim, you drive, I've got some paperwork to catch up on."

"Radio 7-5 back in service," "Ten Four 7-5 we have you back in service." "Ok kid, what is on your mind?" I always knew when Jim was pondering on something, since he took on this somewhat puzzled expression with a slight smirk. "I'm just thinking Art has a point. Those vice cops only came in there because they know it's a white bar and white cops hang out there. It's merely a form of harassment." "Jim, I know why they went in there as well as you do, but white crews do the same thing and have for years. So, the way I see it is we can both continue hating each other and divide our resources or we can start working together as professionals, at least for eight hours." "You're dreaming, Dave, they don't want to work together. They want us to turn this entire city over to them on a platter. You may feel you owe them, but I don't owe them a damn thing. I did not enslave their people and I didn't kill Martin Luther King."

Boy, I sure got him riled up. What happened to that young meek rookie I was breaking in just a few weeks ago. "Look

Jim, you can loosen your jawbones now. All I am saying is it's time for a change on both sides. I'm not the Messiah here to release them from bondage and I certainly don't have all the answers. But what we have been doing for years is broken and needs fixing. It needs to start somewhere, why not with us? I, too, hate some of those self-serving racist bastards, but this is my city, too, and I refuse to turn it over to them or to anyone else."

Jim was by no means a Klan supporter. To the contrary, he was a very fair man as well as intelligent, who in this case just got his feathers ruffled by the transparent acts of some cops who were attempting to make a statement. It is so easy to justify detestation in those who are different or perceived to be different. Jim, along with many others in both races, was struggling daily with these emotions. It is difficult to be fair to those who are treating you unfairly.

I was so tired of going home at night and turning on the tube, only to watch these cop shows that portrayed our lives as being so glamorous, while insinuating we all got along so well, on and off duty. Nothing could be further from the truth, there existed an enormous amount of dissention and resentment at all levels, from the chief down. Yet, the perception of the vast majority of the public was that we were one big happy family who had overcome society's ugly gift of racial discrimination. At most, I would say we had a tolerance for one another. This is not to say there weren't those black and white professionals who were dedicated and advocated positive change. But their presence was dwarfed by the huge numbers that were quite content with the status quo.

The shift was at an end and the question was not if we were stopping for a drink, but where? Once again, the day's events including the shooting would be rehashed repeatedly with our peers. On this occasion, we ended up at one of the local Brewers, which allowed officers to drink free beer directly from the kegs, their way of saying thank you.

As usual, the absence of black officers was quite obvious. This was a traditional white stop. To invite black officers in would be an unpopular gesture, to say the least, just as it would be looked upon unfavorably to invite a white officer into a black establishment.

One of these stops that comes to mind was a BBQ restaurant, a well-known black establishment located in the heart of the Seventh Precinct. I recall one evening a few of us white officers went there to eat after a night out on the town and other than some disparaging looks from a few customers, we were treated just fine. The ribs were excellent and were covered with a secret BBQ sauce that was "to die for." The owner was a typical businessman, never discriminating against patrons with cash money no matter what color.

The aged white clock on the wall was now showing half past 4a.m., and we all looked like Garfield the Cat clones, with our eyes half closed from a long day and quite a few cold ones. "Well, I'm out of here, guys. I have to be in court by nine and the wife has a laundry list of things for me to do during the next two days while I'm on leave." Rodger spoke up, "Yea, I'll walk out with you, Dave. I told the wife I was just stopping for one." I sure wouldn't want to be Rodger walking through that door knowing his 200 lbs. plus red headed wife has been waiting for him for over three hours – no thanks!

CHAPTER 3

"MALCOLM-X WANNABE"

FINALLY, MY TWO DAYS OFF WERE nearing an end. I was ready to get back to work and there was no better day to return than a hot Friday night, which, unquestionably, would be chock-full of new challenges. After a year, the novelty of the job had not worn off. To the contrary, I was just as excited about going to work today as I had been a year ago. How many are fortunate enough to love their career as much? I attribute this excitement to the uncertainty or anticipation of the job; what will the next police call bring, what is around the corner or what's behind that door? It is just something about the unknown that we find extremely intriguing. I'm being paid to do what all boys do as children, playing "Cops and Robbers." However, unlike the childhood game, those who are shot usually do not get up and walk away!

Jim was off today, and I had no idea what my assignment would be. Ordinarily, I would remain with my regular car and would have an officer temporary assigned with me for the evening. As I entered the precinct garage, I was met with laughter from a group of guys from my shift. "Hey, Stealth, good luck tonight. You are working with Malcolm X," a nick-name given to Jerome Patterson, one of the black officers on the shift who had quite a radical outlook on life and the civil rights movement. He made it quite clear he was not too fond of whites. "Don't worry Dave; we will back you up on your runs." "Thanks Bob, I can use all the backup I can get." With guys like Field backing you up, it relieves some of the pressure when working with a man who will be scrutinizing my every move.

"Stealth, Paterson, 7-7." With this final assignment the lieutenants stated: "Keep your heads down. It is a hot summer night and the natives are restless." Lieutenant Chimes was quoting a line from an old Tarzan movie, but I'm sure it was interpreted as a racist remark by a few black officers as well as white. Knowing Chimes, it was an innocent quote used to express safety; he was just way too fair of a man to make a racist remark. When it came to his shift, they were all his men regardless of color.

Paterson had been on the job for three years, which made him the senior officer and, as such, he would ordinarily call the shots. "Paterson, you want me to get the radio?" "No, I'll get the radio." "Ok, I'll get a shotgun." "You don't need a shotgun. We ain't shooting anybody tonight." Oh shit, I can see now this is going to be a long eight hours! Just what I need is some radical asshole just waiting for me to screw up or make a wrong move. God forbid I have to get physical with anyone, much less use my gun. This character will see things through the blurred vision of hate.

Officer Paterson certainly was not the most professional looking officer. His appearance left a lot to be desired, sporting a wrinkled uniform with his sweat stained shirt half tucked in and shoes that were old and badly in need of polish. To make things worse, he had a sparsely tangled beard, which is totally against regulations. However, Paterson had provided a written excuse from a doctor which indicated shaving caused his face to break out in bumps. In essence, I was working with a cop who resembled a homeless person.

"How about getting a coffee, Jerome, before the rush starts?" "It's your world officer, I don't drink the stuff." Oh God, I'm not sure I can make it through the entire shift. I am running out of things to talk about. "So, why didn't you want me to get a shotgun, Jerome?" "I'll tell you why, because it is just another weapon used to kill folks out here." "Yea, but only when it is necessary, and it's a nice weapon to have when you need it." "Yea, I hear you are pretty familiar with it." His remarks, no doubt, were referring to my recent incident, where I shot the tires of the fleeing shooter's vehicle. Obviously, the brothers have been holding court on my incident.

"All I'm saying, Jerome, is that the shotgun is better then using our side arms if we find ourselves in the middle of a gun battle." After a few seconds of dead silence, Paterson spoke up and said in a very condescending manner, "Officer

Stealth, if I had my way, I would not carry a weapon at all. I know I can handle any situation out here without a weapon. These people are not animals in a circus that you need a chair and a pistol to control. Cops in this city are way too quick to shoot a brother and you know that is a fact." My reply was immediate and sincere. I had never seen a brother or anyone else shot just for the hell of it. I could not nor would I tolerate such behavior. "Stealth, you are either blind or have not been around long enough to see that there is indeed an open season on blacks." "Jerome, I can see we are only going to agree to disagree, so I suggest we drop it." Well, that only leaves 7 hours and 47 minutes to go before the shift is over, just fricking dandy!

How lucky can I get? The first night back and I got stuck with a Malcolm-X wannabe who believed he could patrol one of the toughest cities in America without a gun. Even Black Activist groups were wise enough to carry guns in these neighborhoods. I sure would have liked to see Anderson attempt to sweet talk a gun out of a murder or holdup man's hands. I think his philosophy would have changed awfully fast and, if not, I would be using two guns, his and mine. They did not pay me enough to die just to prove to a racist that I'm not one!

"Sure is a hot one, uh Jerome?" "Yea, its summer time, it gets that way." His insulting reply was the final straw. I thought to myself this is going to be a long night anyway, so I might as well lay my cards on the table. "Look Jerome, I don't know why you have a hard-on for whites and frankly I don't give a damn because it has nothing to do with me. So, if you don't mind, deal with me as an individual, if I should disappoint you, then categorize me as one of them you hate." "Yea, I heard you were straight, but that is easy to do when it is just me and you. I'm sure it would be different if your boys were around." "Jerome, look, you are not going to convince me to become black and I damn sure am not going to convince you to become white, so let's just deal with to-night and do our job, ok?" "I hear that," which was the same as saying I had a point. At least it was a start.

"7-7, Disturbance at Chene and I-94, Buddy's Timeout Lounge, there's a man stating he was robbed during a card game." "On the way, radio 7-5." Well, this should be inter-esting. We were headed to a bar that had a racially mixed clientele and I wondered how my partner would handle the situation. We very well could be dealing with a circumstance that involved both races.

As we pulled up, I could see a white male standing outside the bar, clad in blue jeans, a knock-off T-shirt and white tennis shoes. I must admit he was in dire need of a bath and carried an odor only matched by that of an outhouse. He was also ob-viously drunk beyond the point of walking, much less driving.

"Officer, those motherfuckers ripped me off. They took my whole weeks check." "Slow down, big fellow (He was actually slight in size, but flattery often made the individual easier to handle,) tell us what happened." "I came into the bar for a couple drinks and they talked me into playing cards. Before I knew it, they had taken all my money, $190" "Ok, did you lose your money playing cards or did someone actually take it?" "Both, I lost some and they ripped the rest off when I wasn't looking." "Can you describe the guys who took your money?" "Damn right I can! It was Freddy, the bartender, and that black bastard, Clarence. Oh, sorry officer (as he noticed Paterson). I didn't mean any offense." Jerome snapped back immediately, You're not sorry and it don't mean nothing anyway."

As we opened the doors of the bar, we could observe several women who were definitely working ladies (prostitutes). They were either taking a break for a drink or searching for prospects in Buddy's place, most likely some poor factory worker who had worked his ass off all week for $200 or less. Farther down the bar past the drunks was a group of men playing cards.

To say Freddy the bartender was a large man would be an understatement. He was huge, about 6'7" and had to weigh about 380 lbs. But as with most large men, he was quite docile and thank God it took a lot to rile him. "Hello gentlemen, how are we doing tonight?" The four men closed their fanned hand of cards and laid them face-down on the bar. "We're doing fine, officer, just having a friendly game of cards. What can we do for you?" "Well, this gentleman says he was playing cards with you guys and he was ripped off for $190. You guys know it is illegal to play for money, right?" "Yes sir, we just play for fun, no money involved." which we all knew was the politically correct answer, but we also knew it was an outright lie.

"Look, Freddy, even if this guy didn't lose his check playing cards with you folks, you know he was served too much alcohol and we both know that is against the law, right?" "Yea, Dave, he may have had a lot to drink but it was before he arrived here." "Freddy, I am not going to split hairs with you. He's drunk and you're the bartender, so how are we going to solve this problem?" Freddy knew I was attempting to give him a way out of this uneasy situation. There was no doubt in our minds that someone took advantage of this guy's drunken state and ripped him off, at least part of his money. "What do you suggest, Officer Stealth?" "Well, I'm sure if this gentleman received at least a part of his money back, he would be content and we could drive him home, which would make the whole problem disappear. What do you think?" Freddy thought about it for a second or two and then reluctantly reached into his pocket and pulled out a wad of money large enough to choke a horse, he then ripped off a one hundred dollar bill and handed it to the complainant, who accepted it with a smile.

We then escorted our intoxicated accuser out of the bar and home, where I'm sure he still had a lot of explaining to a wife who will have to work with half a check for another week. This was not a situation in which any man wants to find himself.

Paterson hardly said two words through the entire ordeal, he just sat back and let me handle it. Now, ordinarily the jump man (passenger) does ask the questions because he will be doing the paperwork if needed. However, in this case, I think it was because it was a white on white crime and it gave him an opportunity to size me up.

Two hours had passed since our last run at Buddy's Bar and I must say the night was going by excruciatingly slow, with little if any conversation other than an occasional word or two. I sure would have liked something to happen to make the time go by. At this point, I would even settle for an auto accident, which in most cases are tedious and time consuming. That is, unless you are required to be a referee for the two or three parties involved. Then, it can get pretty hairy with tempers flaring and unfriendly verbal exchanges.

The radio suddenly blared interrupting the awkward silence, "7-7, Gratiot and Mc Dougall in the parking lot of Kingston Restaurant, man with a gun. Suspect is described as a black male, heavy-set, wearing a black tank top, white baseball cap and is sitting on the hood of a red car." "On the way radio, 7-7."

Great, I got my wish! Now, how was I going to handle this situation? This was not only a serious run, it was also a hot location, known for idiots carrying guns as well as selling dope in the parking lot. I could only imagine how my liberal partner was going to handle it. I knew one thing for sure. I was not going to be shot trying to prove to this clown that I was not a bigot. My gun would be un-holstered and I would react accordingly.

Typically, respectable hard working cops want a radio run such as this to have some validity. It not only allows us to arrest a drug dealing parasite, it also gives us an opportunity to take a gun off the street, a gun that could possibly be used to either kill an innocent citizen or even one of us. Yet, I found myself hoping this was a bogus run because of my lack of trust in my so-called partner.

As we pulled into the parking lot which was full of loiterers, I observed a man fitting the suspect's description standing next to a red car with several other individuals. I certainly hope we get some backup. "Jerome, can you see him, between the cars?" "Yea, I got this one." What the hell does that mean, "I got this one?" So much for the partnership, maybe he is going to convert the brother and recruit him to become a Detroit Police Officer.

Once the suspect looked in our direction, he leaned down between the cars for a brief second, making a swinging motion with his right arm. This surely appeared like he was discarding something. He then stood up and began to walk away from the red vehicle along with three other black males. "Hold on fellows." "I said I got this one Dave. Gentlemen, please come over to the vehicle." They began to reluctantly comply, when suddenly the man fitting our suspect's description stopped and began waving his arms screaming, "Hell no, this is bullshit! Y'all just wanna fuck with some brothers." I thought to myself, here we go, this guy is going to get stupid, and he'll probably attempt to rile the crowd to cause a diversion.

I have found this tactic is used quite often by the black criminal element when they fear they are going to be arrested or have something to hide. They start screaming unfair discrimination which diverts the attention from them and places it on the officers. This offensive distraction usually ignites the crowd into a rage, which quickly draws more hostile people. If this volatile situation is not put under control immediately, you will have a large unruly mob on your hands, a mob which is quite capable of almost anything. It's something about people in a mass; it's as if they believe they are invincible and unaccountable for their acts under the cloak of the chaos.

Jerome walked toward the man with his gun holstered saying, "No one wants to fuck with you, my brother. We just need to ask you some questions. Someone reported there was a man out here with a gun. So, let us straighten this shit out and you and your brothers can be on your way."

By the time we had these clowns up to our vehicle; two other scout cars arrived to assist us, thank God. I walked over to the red vehicle where the men had been standing. I immediately observed a blue steel .38-caliber revolver along with several packs of suspected heroin in brown coin envelopes under the car. This was in the very spot where the suspect had made the overt motion as we arrived.

While walking back, I could see the crowd was getting

larger and much more boisterous. The other officers and I knew it was imperative we do what needed to be done quickly and get out of there. "Jerome, here's the gun and heroin he tossed under the car as we pulled in the lot." "Alright my brother, let's go to the station and straighten this out. You have the right to remain silent, anything you say can and..." All of a sudden, I could see the suspect's facial expression change as he began to scream in a final attempt to get out of this mess. "Hey, ya'll, they trying to put some bullshit on me. Don't let these pig motherfuckers put this case on me." Jerome and I quickly began placing the handcuffed suspect in the rear seat of our car as he yelled, "Help me, they're beating me. These motherfuckers are going to kill me."

Finally, the suspect was subdued and secured in our car and not a moment too soon. A whisky bottle which was hurled from the rear of the crowd exploded on the hood of our car. The crowd was now more disorderly than ever, escalating from screaming to physical violence. It was definitely time to get the hell out of Dodge, which we all did, ducking bottles and rocks in our escape.

On the way to the station, I asked the suspect for his identification, to which he indicated he left it at home. He was then asked for his name and date of birth (D.O.B.), which would probably be bogus. But his fingerprints will most likely give us a positive identification. I can't imagine this character not having a criminal history record. His temperament suddenly became docile and much more reverent without the backing of the hostile crowd. How typical, this raging idiot has now turned into a calm and accommodating citizen. His change of attitude was not out of respect, but rather out of fear of an old time ass beating which was not going to happen, unlike him we had to follow the law.

As we pulled into the station parking lot, I could see our prisoner was sweating like hell, with an expression on his face that one might have found on a passenger of the Titanic as she sank, stark fear and anticipation. "You know mister, you could have gotten us killed back there by pulling that stunt." "I'm sorry, officer. I never meant for anything to happen, but I swear on my momma that .38 and the three packs of dope are not mine. That belonged to the other brother. Y'all got the wrong man." "That's interesting, my man, because I never showed you the gun or dope, yet you know that it is a .38-caliber three packs of dope. You are either a psychic or our man!"

Jerome remained silent and expressionless during our brief conversation, leaving me with the impression that he either didn't give a damn or was unhappy about the arrest. I must believe it is just his way of protesting another brother's arrest, which I must say amazes me because "his brothers" were throwing bottles at him as well as at me!

Once the suspect was placed in the lockup (Jail cell), Jerome and I advised the sergeant on the desk of our arrest for Carrying a Concealed Weapon on Person (CCWP) and Violation of Controlled Substance Act (VCSA) for the possession of the heroin.

Due to the fact that I was jumping, it was my responsibility to write the report of our arrest. "So, Jerome, you want to be the complainant or should I?" "It's your arrest. I didn't see the brother with a gun and I'm damn sure not going to say I seen something I didn't just to lock a brother up. I will write my report the way I seen it go down and you can give your version." "Look, Jerome, I really don't care what you put in your report. This piece of trash had a gun and heroin and I am not letting him go free because you are trying to make a statement to the world!" God is this guy annoying!

My report indicated precisely the way I witnessed the incident take place, which was observing the suspect making an overt action under the vehicle and my retrieving the gun and narcotics from exactly the same area. It would now be up to the courts to determine his innocence or guilt. And, believe you me, with the state of judicial system, the odds were definitely in his favor.

However, my partner Jerome's report indicated he observed the man kneel down between the cars and then stand back up, never seeing a weapon or narcotics at any time. I guess it is all in one's perspective or attitude. I still felt Jerome believed that the only reason my report wasn't more creative was due to his presence. Trust me, nothing could be further from the truth, but I would not dignify this jerk with an explanation.

I realized early on, that there is no need to manufacture the facts to arrest the criminal element. They would eventually be their own demise, even after our liberal courts released them time and time again. My only concern was and still is how many victims must pay the price, some even with their lives, prior to the thug's overdue incarceration? I did my job and if the court found this character innocent and turned him loose, oh well! I'll get him next time. I would only suggest if it looks like a Duck...!

"You ready, Jerome? I could sure use something to eat. How about we pick up something and bring it back to the station?" "Yea, that's cool, you like fish?" I could tell by his facial expression, he expected me to reject his suggestion. Little did he know, I love fish. "Sure, that sounds great."

A short trip down Gratiot Avenue brought us to the Fish Shack, a business I was familiar with from my days walking a beat. It was a small eatery that was commonly frequented by a black clientele. As we entered the restaurant, I observed several patrons enjoying a large shrimp basket with fries, and a basket full of loaf bread, which they were dipping in an oversized cup of tartar sauce. Sure looked greasy, but good.

I was the only white face in the establishment and received my share of looks from those present. Jerome was recognized and welcomed by the employees. This was not surprising because it is a well-known hangout for black officers who, no doubt, receive a discount on their purchase, a practice extended by many businesses. It is just a way to thank officers for serving their community, not to mention it certainly doesn't hurt to have a reputation for having uniform officers frequent your business.

Jerome ordered the shrimp basket and I had the fried catfish dinner, a meal reminiscent of many I had back home in Kentucky, with cornbread, fried potatoes and greens. The kitchen was not the cleanest I had ever seen. There were dishes piled in the sink, flour and cornmeal residue on the floor and the grill area was caked with dark grease from all the frying. But, like many other greasy spoon eateries the food was home-style cooked and has a taste that would haunt you, not to mention take five years off your life. I must admit I watched the girl prepare our dinners, not because she was black, but because there have been cases in many restaurants where employees would spit in officers' food or worse. It is their manner of getting back at "the man" for some run-in or ticket they may have received in the past.

Once back at the station, Jerome and I ate our lunch in the squad room, which was sparsely furnished with the exception of a podium, coke machine, Ping-Pong table and a table with a few chairs. Hardly a word was spoken during lunch. But afterwards, Jerome leaned back in his chair, loosened his pants and just stared at me. He had a half-eaten toothpick hanging from his mouth, which he pulled from his Afro upon completing dinner.

After a few seconds of silence, Jerome spoke first: "So what's your story, Dave? You seem like a pretty straight guy unlike most white cops, so why did you come on the job?" "What's that supposed to mean; are you insinuating one must be evil to become a cop?" "No man, but most of the white boys come on this job because they hate niggers and what other job pays you to shoot and beat brothers?" "That's one hell of a profound statement, Jerome, one that is full of hate and certainly not true of the majority. You know it is people like you that thrive off the dissension between the two races. I really think you have a need to keep things stirred up just to rationalize your mean and hateful agenda."

I continued, "There are a ton of white cops out there that are really trying to make a difference and believe in what they are doing, many of whom have given the ultimate sacrifice." "Are you telling me you have not seen some white cops beat the shit out of a brother for some petty bullshit?" "Damn right I have seen cops kick the shit out of some poor bastard, who in my book did little to warrant it. But that doesn't mean I condoned it and there are many others out there that feel the same way." "So, let me get this straight, Dave," I could see Jerome was getting hot as well; the veins on the side of his face were pulsating profusely. "You and these other wonder cops have witnessed men being beat which you indicate you did not condone, so why in the hell didn't you stop it? Far as I'm concerned you are as guilty as those kicking the brother when he was down. You are sworn to protect not punish, as a man you must take a stand!"

This radical ass was really beginning to get to me. "Look, you pompous militant, this shit didn't get this way overnight and it is not going to be a quick fix. You're damn right I could and should have stopped the beatings and that is something

I will have to live with. However, you certainly don't help matters any by walking around hating us just because we're white."

After a breath I continued: "Jerome you know damn well we are both in a work environment that has historically been run with an old-boy network attitude. Do I believe it can be changed? Absolutely it can, but not from one tyranny to another. We need to start looking for a solution and quit placing the responsibility on each other's race. Believe me, there is enough blame to go around."

I might as well have been speaking to the wall. It was obvious Jerome was not buying anything I had said. This guy was like many other self-proclaimed civil rights activists. They realize if a solution to racism is discovered, they would be out of a job and God forbid they don't have anyone to hate or blame for their misfortunes in life.

All the way home, the words of Jerome kept erupting in my head concerning my lack of response to the brutality by officers. As much as I dislike the man, I must admit he had a point. If I didn't agree with what was going on, I should have attempted to stop it, even knowing it would cause me to be immediately blackballed by the old cops and declared a "bleeding heart liberal who loves blacks." Yet, I knew my silence was interpreted as acceptance. I had sworn approximately a year-and- half ago that I would not be as close-minded as some of my mentors and would initiate a change for the better.

Nevertheless, here I was, still lacking in my progress. How strange fate is. I had been enlightened by a black racist and made to realize I could make a difference, even at my patrolman level. Being silent was not an option. Spectators who stand by and watch a mob of vigilantes hang a person are just as guilty as those who place the rope around his neck.

Fortunately, the majority of officers I have come in contact with knew how to harness their prejudice while working and would never beat a man just for the sake of beating him. They were willing to put their lives on the line daily for the public, black and white. Yet, as always the rogue few are viewed as the majority by the faction with an agenda.

The following is a good example of a case in point which takes place several weeks later. A scout car from the Eleventh Precinct broadcasted that they were in pursuit of a vehicle that was wanted for suspected murder. We would eventually learn that the scout car crew had observed the occupants of the car being chased, placing bodies in the trunk of their vehicle.

The chase was now entering the Seventh Precinct, north on St Aubin at Milwaukee, where the suspects blew right through a red light almost striking cross traffic. Keep in mind, car pursuits are very dangerous and scare the hell out of cops because of the high possibility of collateral damage to citizens, property and to the officers themselves. Criminals will blow right through a light at 100 miles an hour without a second thought, whereas officers who have their sirens blaring and adrenaline flowing, slow down, if not briefly stop, at red lights out of fear of colliding with oncoming traffic or another scout car approaching to assist with their siren blaring as well. While we attempt to be as cautious as we can, the bad guys drive their three thousand pound bullets through lights and stop signs with no regard at all for human life.

We joined the pursuit at St Aubin and Warren, still going north approaching Mack Avenue, which was showing a red light that this asshole no doubt would ignore. As expected, he went right through the light only to come to an abrupt stop after T-boning a car occupied by an innocent family coming home from church services.

As we pulled up, we observed the two occupants, one of whom had got out and attempted to escape, were now in custody and handcuffed. The suspects' vehicle trunk had flown open from the enormous impact exposing the lifeless bodies of two black males whose hands were tied behind their backs with their severed heads lying next to them, a calling card of one of the city's most notorious heroin dealers. This was a fate that was experienced by anyone who double-crossed him or "snitched" to the cops.

We directed our attention to the innocent family, whose vehicle had been propelled back about ten feet from the impact location and was leaking gas. The car was a bloody mess, with cries for help coming from the interior. We immediately began extracting the passengers out of fear of an explosion from the leaking gas. I reached in the back seat where a lady was screaming "My baby, my baby!" We entered the vehicle and pulled the little girl out at which time we observed she was totally non-responsive and not breathing at all. I immediately began CPR along with mouth-to-mouth, while advising my partner it was imperative we get her to the hospital immediately!

Once in our vehicle, dispatch was notified that we were rushing this child to Detroit Receiving Hospital and requested the trauma team be notified and standing by for our arrival, as well as requesting that all intersections be blocked as time was definitely a major factor. I was delighted to see every intersection to the hospital had scout cars blocking traffic, which allowed us a straight non-stop shot. What a great feeling to see all these officers come together to save this innocent little two-year-old girl!

Upon arriving at the hospital, I observed the little lady was beginning to take shallow breaths, thank God! I handed the child off to the trauma team, who went to work on her immediately.

At the end of our shift, I called the hospital to get a condition on the little angel. To my deep regret, I was advised she had expired about an hour ago. Her frail little body just couldn't handle the trauma of such an impact. Yet both of these heinous criminals walked away with minor injuries.

You know, not once during this emergency transportation did I hear any of the officers racing to the intersections to clear a path for us, ask the race of the little girl! How odd? Just for the record, she and her family were black and so very innocent. Where's the justice?

CHAPTER 4
"GROWING PAINS"

THE SQUAD ROOM WAS RATHER QUIET, no laughter, horseplay or war stories. The somber atmosphere was a direct result to us doubling back from the afternoon shift to days leaving us with just a few hours between shifts. We were some tired cowboys. But, all would be well after a coffee or two.

My partners were on leave, so I was assigned a rooky by the name of Ed Lapeer, good looking smaller-framed man who I had the pleasure of working with on several occasions. "Dave do you want me to get the radio?" "Yea sounds good Ed, I'll grab a shotgun and meet you on the ramp."

"What do ya say we stop for a quick cup of coffee before we get going Ed?" "That sounds great Dave." I like this kid a lot. He has a ton of heart and loves to hit the street running, a real go-getter.

There was about seven scout cars in the Click parking lot, you can tell we all have jet lag from the quick turnaround. "Do you know everyone on the shift yet Ed?" "Not everybody, I've been walking allot of beats lately."

"Hey guy's you know Ed don't ya?" Ed was welcomed aboard by all. "Who'd you piss off to get sent here?" asked, Rodgers our eternal optimist. Now most policemen are cynical but Rogers takes cynicism to a whole new level. If this guy found a brick of gold he would complain it was too heavy to carry to the bank. Rodgers was the type of guy who flaunted his authority to impress rookies and citizens, by playing the tough cop. However, many times this ploy only caused friction, which often led to confrontation or at least made the situation uncomfortable. On this job, you need to know when to be that tough guy and when to be diplomatic.

"Rodge back off the kid; it's difficult enough being a new guy without you contributing to his anxiety." "Just trying to educate the kid Dave, he needs to know how things are." "Educating him is fine Rodge, however, filling his head with bullshit is something entirely different." My words fell on deaf ears, he continued to address Ed, "You see kid; they don't like it when I tell it like it is. This job sucks, you've got bosses trying to write you up for every little fucking thing you do and liberal judges letting these fucking thugs out on technicalities or because their fucking black." "Rodge that's enough, let us have our coffee, it's too damn early to listen to your one-sided bigoted hate philosophy's." "Bullshit Dave, you know I'm right, these fucking liberals and niggers are ruining our society." I could see Rodge was working himself into a frenzy again and when he gets in this hate state the best thing you can do is let him rattle on until he calms down. Thank God he wasn't drinking.

"7-5 Kirby and Chene, the Chene Party Store, we're getting a report of a holdup alarm" "On the way radio 7-5, let's go Ed." The kid was so excited he tipped his coffee over as he stood up. "Slow down buddy, it's probably a false alarm and even if it's not we can't help anyone if we get in an accident."

Once in route, Ed became noticeably quiet. "Listen Ed, majority of the time these holdup alarms are set off by accident or there is some sort of glitch in the system. Yet, you must treat each and every one of them as if they're the real thing. It's your ass if you get careless or complacent. Unlike most professions Ed, our mistakes cost lives." "Got it Dave thanks!"

The Chene Party Store was located just moments away, which certainly increases the odds of an encounter if it proves to, indeed, be a valid robbery. Now there's times on this job you just have that gut feeling that this one is the real Mc Coy and this happened to be one of those occasions. "Hey kid stay on your toes, I don't have a good feeling about this one."

The green Chrysler running in front of the store was the first and most obvious indication that this could be a legitimate call. "Stop short of the car Ed. Oh shit Ed, not next to the car!" I was looking dead in the eyes of the driver of the Chrysler, which was running. "Pull up, pull up damn it you're going to get me shot!" "Sorry Dave," as he attempted to rectify his mistake.

Suddenly two black males came running out of the party store wearing Army field jackets and ski masks one had a shotgun and the other had a blue steel revolver. Upon observing us, they both opened fire. Ed and I immediately exited the vehicle and positioned ourselves behind the scout car, seeking whatever protection we could from the gunfire. "Radio 7-5 Milwaukee and Chene at the party store, officer in trouble we're being fired on" "All cars in seven, 7-5 is calling for assistance, they have shots fired."

God, the gunfire was loud; I could hear the pellets striking the ground around us. I looked over and Ed was holding his own, he had already emptied his revolver and was in the process of reloading. I had three rounds left before I would need to reload and was waiting for a clear shot at these ass holes. Suddenly, I heard tires screeching. The holdup men threw their car in reverse, striking a blue Chevy and then did a U-turn and began driving south on Chene. Let's go Ed, if they get to the freeway they'll be a vapor. I must tell you I felt a slight moment of relief hearing them pull off, that meant we no longer were a bull's eye, at least for now.

"Radio 7-5 the suspects are escaping South on Chene in a green Chrysler, license number KEC-251." Now, for those who have never been in a shooting or in a life-threatening situation, you cannot begin to understand how one's anxiety levels can go off the charts, you are running on pure adrenaline, a state that allows you to turn raw fear into a level of courage that would astound most.

The perpetrators were now approaching the I-94 Interstate where 7-6 and 7-8 had blocked the entrance ramps to the freeway. "Ed, stay in the left lane, when they get to the service drive and realize we have them blocked in there going to attempt to come back our way, so try to pin them in and take cover. I'm sure they're going to come out firing." Just as I expected the suspects attempted to turn around when they observed the roadblock. Ed handled himself like a real vet, he rammed their car, not quite what I expected but very impressive, we can do the paper work later.

As I anticipated, both suspects exited their vehicle firing at us as well as the cars blocking the freeway ramps. Ed and I exited the vehicle taking cover while returning fire. Ed's man was struck in the shoulder and fell like a wet towel. Seconds later, the remaining suspect dropped his gun raising hands screaming "I give up, I give up officer, please don't shoot" It would not be until later we would learn the only reason this idiot surrendered was that he ran out of ammunition. That's the price of being the good guys, we must play by the rules unlike our advisories, which I'm certain would not cease firing if we were yelling "I'm out of ammo, don't shoot!"

Once the smoke cleared, I observed Ed leaning up against the car with a perplexed look on his face; his complexion had adopted a pale color, a shade only seen on a corpse lying on a slab in a morgue. I was familiar with this expression; it's often displayed by an individual following a trauma or combat type situation. You experience a dry cotton taste in your mouth as your adrenaline level drops leaving you with a sensation of exhaustion or out of body experience. You now begin to replay the events in your head at warp speed in an attempt to justify your actions or determine what other avenues if any you may have considered. Cops in these types of situations frequently second-guess themselves silently; we can be our worst critics.

"Eddie Boy, are you OK?" He continued staring out into space with this oblivious look on his face. Sirens could be heard off in the distance still headed our way even though it was announced there was enough cars at the scene and the situation was now under control. Police officers being inquisitive creatures by nature frequently continue to show up to give support to the officers involved in the shooting as well as curse the injured or killed suspects for attempting to harm one of theirs. Everyone wants to be part of the show.

"Hey, Eddie snap out of it, come on back to earth." I could see he was beginning to get his color back. Suddenly, he shook his head, "Sorry Dave, I was out of it for a moment, I can't believe how drained I feel." His blue uniform shirt was so saturated with perspiration it appeared to be jet black. "You're ok kid, your just experiencing a little post trauma symptoms, it is totally natural Ed, we have all been there. Just let it out, don't attempt to hold it in, because if you do, eventually you will explode like a balloon."

There are lawmen who attempt to disguise these symptoms from their peers and display traits of being unconcerned or unaffected by a shooting. They almost appear inhumane or invincible; some call this the John Wayne syndrome.

Unfortunately, many times their anxiety will be released later when they're alone or with family members who could not fathom in their wildest imagination what their love one has experienced.

"You did one hell of a job kid, it was a clean shooting and there is no justification for scrutiny on your part, you did what you are trained to do and I must say you did it well." "I know you're right Dave, I just have never shot anyone before, I wasn't even sure I could when it came right down to it. This guy was walking and talking five minutes ago now he's lying there shot." "Ed, listen, this piece of dirt was not only walking and talking five minutes ago; he was also shooting at us with full intent to end our lives. That could be you lying on the ground with half your head missing. Do you think he would have any remorse for your death or any concern for your loved ones that would be left behind? I don't think so, the only remorse this guy would have displayed is the fact that he was apprehended, so let it go and come to grips with the fact that the only thing you have done today is shoot a parasite that was trying to kill us. He's a cancer to society and if he lives, he's going away for a long time."

On the way downtown I made a quick stop at a local party store. Leaving Ed in the car, I picked up a pint of Crown Royal and a pack of gum, commonly referred to as a trauma kit, what a combination. "Here Kid, take a couple swigs of this," handing Ed the pint. "This will take the edge off; we have a lot of paperwork and questions to answer. I'll take the scenic route down to homicide." Ed looked at me like I was crazy. "Look Eddie its ok, the dicks (detectives) at homicide understands that this is about the only therapy you will receive from the department today." He began drinking the whisky like someone announced prohibition on alcohol was being implemented once again. "Slow down kid, I said a couple swigs, not the entire bottle. I want you to take the edge off not go over the edge."

After about six hours downtown processing paperwork and answering questions from our attorney and homicide detectives, Ed was placed on administrative leave, meaning he would be assigned to a desk job pending the review of the shooting board, which consisted of a number of high ranking officers who would determine whether his shooting was justified or not.

We headed back to the precinct to drop off our equipment and reports. This task would be followed unquestionably with a visit to "Big Z's bar where our peers were waiting. As we approached the front desk, the clerks began to clap and congratulate Ed and the sergeant stood up and put his hand out "Good job officer that could have been one of us out there". The old sergeant knew this to be true, due to the many officers he had buried during his tenure. All the hype gave Ed a since of temporary security in the fact that he had acted as a professional.

"Now, listen to me partner, these guys have been putting cocktails down for a couple hours already, and they're going to be giving you a lot of opinions, some worthy of filing away and others that should be shredded and forgotten immediately." "I hear you Dave."

As we walked through the door, our comrades in blue began to sing the police song of praise in a loud base tone voice: "Here's to Ed, raise your glass. Here's to Ed, he's a horses' ass." A song obviously not written by Neil Diamond, yet filled with admiration and approval for a job well done.

Before long, Ed was feeling no pain. "Hey buddy, you OK?" "Oh-yea, I'm good Dave." "Partner listen to me, it's easy now you have all your friends here making a lot of noise and buying you anything you want, but, later when you're alone in your little silent apartment it can get pretty bad. Promise me you will call if you need to talk, OK?" "Dave come on, I can take care of myself." "Yea I know, that's what I'm afraid of!"

"Hey, kid good job! You should have killed that fucking black bastard!" Oh, just great, Rodger's. Just what we need, our loud mouth resident racist, I thought. "It's just another piece of garbage off the street." Now, I could not disagree with that, he was a piece of garbage and if we had not run into him today, we would have had to deal with him tomorrow. "Rodge, not tonight, he's out of it right now." Fortunately, Rodge had not been drinking yet, so he complied and struck up a conversation with the other guy's. All we needed now was to turn this into some loud mouth Klan like meeting, the kid was confused enough.

"Last call guys. I don't care where you guys go but, it's time to leave." The bar was filled with the stench of smoke and stale beer, you would have thought we would have been glad to leave and go home, yet each and every one of us was willing to continue telling war stories and drinking until dawn, as we had on so many other occasions. Nevertheless, tonight Z was tired and wanted us out.

As we walked out of the bar a "blue and white" (marked police car) passed by slowly, occupied by two black officers. They nodded, with blank expressions on their faces, looks that in one sense, appeared to recognize us as their peers but, on the other hand, could be interpreted as disgust for our celebration of shooting a black man, one of their brothers. "What is their problem Dave?" "Don't worry about them Ed, those two belong to the "Protectors" and some of the Protectors believe that we have declared open season on blacks and are just looking for the opportunity to kill or mistreat them whether they're guilty or not."

"What they fail to realize Ed, it's not about celebrating the shooting of a black man, we are celebrating your survival and the fact you took a cold-blooded would be murderer off the street, who just happened to be black. He would have gladly shot a black officer as quick as he would a white one. It's all about blue, which is the only color these criminals recognize."

The Protectors is an organization created for the purpose of representing black police officers as well as protecting and preventing abuse to any black citizen by the hands of the white establishment, which in their minds had failed to represent them fairly. In theory, it would sound like their cause may have had some serious validity, but as with most organizations, black and white, you will have those with their own agenda, which in many cases is driven by pure racism.

This organization is not recognized within the Detroit Police Department or the DPOA (Detroit Police Officers Association). Yet, they caught the eye of the black community as well as the ear of the media. I must tell you I did agree with the premise in which the organization was founded, but not with many of the tactics used, which often appeared to be racist in nature to prove their point. You can't eliminate a racist by becoming one!

I followed Ed home and made sure he got to bed. His apartment was typical of a young bachelor, sparsely decorated with only the necessary furnishings. He was not feeling any pain, matter of fact he wasn't feeling anything at all. The next morning would be an entirely different story; he would awake alone and begin rehashing the shooting over and over again, asking many questions, some of which can never be answered.

I would make it a point to return first thing in the morning for coffee and to give him any support he may need. Unlike today, there was very little post- shooting support for officers by the Detroit Police Department. We found our support within the ranks, which typically consisted of a stiff drink and slaps on the back from our peers, accompanied by a whole host of advice which mostly consisted of "Fuck him" or "You had no choice, it was you or the asshole." Each piece of advice as shallow as it may have been was sincere and contained legitimacy.

Oh damn, I have had some hangovers in my time, but this one felt like my facial skin was being pulled over my head. The sensation in my mouth was dry, leaving a taste that can only be described as having a rodent stuck in your throat. As I laid there mustering up the nerve to lift my head off the pillow, the disgusting odor of stale cigarette smoke entrenched in my hair gave me symptoms only a women with morning sickness could understand.

Looking toward the window, I could see the dawn was giving birth to a new day; a day I suddenly remembered would be Ed's first day after the shooting, which gave me the burst of energy I needed to get out of bed.

After a quick shower I grabbed a cup of coffee and a cigarette as I ran out the door. I allowed myself extra time, because I suspected Ed would be moving a little slow. We had to sign the warrants on the robbery suspects and I had a separate trial, a case that likely would be dismissed on some technicality or would allow the predator to cop a plea. The Detroit Court System was quite often like a carnival or flea market where merchants made deals that were questionable to say the least. Actually, officers have given the 36th District Detroit Recorder's Court the nickname of "The Circus," a name so befitting and deserved on many occasions.

If I knocked any harder I will wake up the entire building. "Ed, wake up boy, you are going to make us late for court, come on Ed open the door damn it." The stench of the stale beer coming from his apartment was disgusting and reminded me of the smell of a homeless shelter full of winos. Suddenly the door opened and there stood one pitiful sight: Ed was clad only in his boxers and black socks, a real sex God! His face was swollen and his eyes were blood red, which indicated he was experiencing one hell of a hangover or he had been up all night crying. "You ok kid?" "Yea, but I feel like shit." Suddenly he began turning pale white and started licking his lips. "Ed get to the bathroom quick." It was too late he tossed his cookies all over the carpet. This was going to be an interesting day!

After cleaning up my newly adopted son, we were off to the good old 36th District Court to play let's make a deal. Upon checking into my assigned courtroom I was advised there would be at least a two-hour delay, which is oh so typical of the court system, a system that reflects the Army's policy of hurry up and wait. This delay allowed Ed and I time to go up to the Prosecutor's Office, where the warrants for the three holdup men would be signed.

We were advised that the suspect that Ed shot would survive and would be arraigned when his condition was upgraded. Once the warrants were signed, the other two slime balls were arraigned and ordered held with no bond, pending their preliminary examination, which was scheduled eight days from today, just one of the many stages offered to the accused in our system, a system I do not necessarily agree with, however, I do realize there are none better worldwide.

Ed seemed elated with the referee's decision concerning

the bond. "Partner don't get too excited, this is the first battle of many, and things are going to get very ugly before these pieces of dirt get put away. You need to realize many factors are going to come in to play during this judicial process." "Like what Dave, it's a slam-dunk, we have witnesses that observed them rob the store, they fled from us and subsequently got out of the car shooting at us. We got them dead to rights with the guns and money, what could possibly go wrong?" "Kid, this goes way beyond right and wrong, the sad truth is you are a white cop and the defendants are black, not to mention you shot one of their friends. The defense attorney, whom very well could be one of Detroit's high-end attorneys, due to the high visibility of the case, will do everything in his power to turn things around, making you the bad guy as well playing the race card."

It was almost a week before the Shooting Review Board declared the shooting justifiable and allowed Ed to return to full duty. Up until then, Ed was assigned to desk duty while awaiting the board's decision. He was delighted to be returning to the street, he needed it; you must get back in the saddle as soon as possible. Time off allows too much idle thinking, which can negatively influence a good street cop. It's imperative that you respond without hesitation to a situation and this is difficult to do if your head is crammed with garbage or regrets. The consequences of not reacting in a timely fashion can be extremely costly.

I warned Ed that his reception could very well be varied

on his first day back and boy was I correct. As he walked through the squad room door the white officers greeted him with smiles saying job well done, while the black officers on the other side of the room looked at him with disgust as they stared silently. I overheard one of the black officers say, "Well they have turned that one," insinuating that Ed is now one of the good old white boys who has adopted the racist ideas and beliefs of the old. Nothing could have been further from the truth. This kid had real character, integrity and a mind of his own, traits that are God-given and can't be bought.

You talk about sitting on a keg of dynamite; you could have cut the tension in that room with a knife, many of the blacks were under the impression that Ed was proud of the fact that he shot a black man and many of the whites believed he should be proud of the way he reacted to a potentially deadly situation. I, along with others was proud of the way he handled himself during the shooting, race was never a factor it was purely a survival instinct. There were cops on both sides who thrived on causing dissension between the two races and would get quite upset when we were acting civil toward one and other. On the other hand, you had those that had serious concerns of injustice.

Thank God, Lieutenant Chimes and the sergeants entered and began roll call. After the assignments were read the lieutenant addressed the ranks. "All right guys I have been around long enough to know when something is cooking. Listen up, we have enough trouble with them ass-holes on the street, we do not need and I won't tolerate any dissension on my shift. The times are coming that you all are going to have to depend on each other, black and white. So leave all your other bullshit beliefs at home. When you walk through these doors everyone is equal and will be treated with respect. Now get out there and do what you are paid to do and back each other up."

I have heard a lot of the traditional, "Go out there and win this one for the Gipper" speeches, but this one struck home with a few of us and it made me more determined than ever to change some of the old ways. I could only imagine how powerful we would be if we were united!

The lieutenant honored my request to have Ed assigned with me on his first day back, I thought it would be much easier being with the partner that he had experienced the intense incident with. Once we hit the street, I knew Ed would be ok. He was not nervous at all; to the contrary, it was almost as if he had aged five years since the shooting. He has taken on a persona of an old salty cop with an air of confidence and a slight touch of cockiness. These traits are quite acceptable and even needed, as long as they're harnessed properly and accompanied with a trace of humility.

Being arrogant in the world of law enforcement is quite common and actually necessary to a certain extent. Our profession requires us to react to life and death situations within a split second as well as determining if we should take an individual's life or freedom through incarceration. This is an awesome amount of responsibility with a ton of liability hanging over one's head. Law enforcement officials are not intended to negotiate each arrest. They are paid to take control of a situation and make an immediate decision, choices which they will be ultimately accountable for.

"VOTE ACCORDINGLY, OR WE RIOT"

SUMMER OF 1974, A VOLATILE TIME in Motown, the economy was not doing well, crime was running rampant and the upcoming November elections unquestionably promised a heated campaign. Many believed the outcome of the elections would determine whether Detroit would experience another riot or not. This option was unfavorable for the majority, with the exception of a few advocates of hate, which would love nothing more than to drive a larger wedge between the two races. Thankfully, for the most part, blacks and whites were disgusted with the last decade of violence around the country and were willing to explore different alternatives.

Each candidate brought entirely different ideas to the table, making it very obvious that there would not be any love lost between the two during or after the election. Coleman Young's camp demanded that John Nichols give up his appointed position as Police Commissioner during the campaign. Stating it was a definite conflict of interest, because it is unlawful for a city official to run for a second position while holding a current one. Eventually, John Nichols would succumb to the demands and reluctantly resigned as Police Commissioner, focusing his efforts entirely on the campaign.

The lines between the races were drawn, with Young targeting the black population, particularly, liberal Democrats, black businesses and the black clergy who are normally looked upon as the pillars of the community. One undeniable fact about the black culture is they have an unwavering belief in God, whom they give credit for delivering them from bondage and believe some day will make all men equal.

Coleman Young's promise to the citizens of Detroit was to reform the Police Department, putting an end to the police brutality and the persecution of blacks. He swore to dismantle the controversial S.T.R.E.S.S. Unit and put more cops back into the community, where they could become familiar with the people and their needs.

He would also implement the concept of the Police Mini Stations around the city. These locations would be small storefront police stations within the community, manned by two or three officers, which in theory would be more accessible for citizens to file police reports without leaving their neighborhood. Mr. Young believed by placing officers in the community, they would be compelled to interact with Detroiters which would be instrumental in changing attitudes as well as mending the relationship with the police, which at best was poor.

Nichols, on the other hand, would concentrate on the

conservative white vote. This included big money businesses, police, firefighters and the upper middle working class. His campaign pledge was also strong; he would make the streets of Detroit safe once again, by having a zero tolerance for the criminal element. In his opinion, crime was one of the main factors big businesses were reluctant to move into the city and exactly the reason many citizens were fleeing to the suburbs. He also swore that S.T.R.E.S.S. was here to stay and that rather than disbanding the unit he would increase its size by adding more officers.

The police and firefighters were clearly divided racially, with the white standing behind Nichols and the blacks supporting Young. From all poll indications, John Nichols was favored to win. This was not surprising when taking into consideration that a majority of the city's employees, who in a large part were white, supported him.

Young, was not thought of favorably by many whites, he was perceived as a loud, radical black man who sported ideas from the sixties and at times spoke like a street gangster rather than a respectable politician, many times using slang and cursing like a sailor to express himself. He allegedly had ties with the communist party and was certainly associated with the ACLU and other liberal activist groups. Surely, a man like this could not win. Or could he?

The black community however, was very excited about the election, they sincerely believed victory was possible. Detroit was finally ready for a black mayor and in their eyes there was none better qualified then Colman A. Young. Even though Young was looked on as the underdog, blacks truly believed with hard work and determination he could beat the odds, just as many other black mayors have done throughout the country. The entire country was going through a metamorphosis and Detroit wanted to be part of it.

Young and Nichols campaign stickers were materializing around the entire city as well as the suburbs. It was clear this was more than an election; this was two different factions of society making a powerful, heartfelt statement, both sincerely believing they were right and the other was wrong. One thing was apparent, a change was coming and it would be a drastic one!

An obvious change of attitude was evident in the citizens of Detroit; it reflected a sense of urgency, promise and pride. If a black mayor was elected he could lead them into the 21st Century and restructure the city government by appointing blacks to higher municipal positions, positions traditionally held by whites.

It was apparent that the whites believed in the polls and didn't think Young had a snowballs chance in hell to win the election and certainly lacked the charisma and knowledge of his predecessor, Mayor Roman Gribbs. This over confident attitude throughout history has proven to be dangerous and many times will be the precursor to defeat.

It wasn't long before a directive came down from headquarters, advising all city employees to cease placing campaign stickers on city property, which included all police cars, and refrain from discussing politics while on duty. This action was taken largely due to the fact white officers were placing "John Nichols for Mayor" bumper stickers on police and fire vehicles.

Things were really starting to get ugly with slander coming out of both camps daily, not to mention the repercussions from S.T.R.E.S.S. incidents, which seemed to take place daily. The unit was gaining a reputation of a group of rogue cops who shoot first and ask questions later. Some even accused a minute number of them with planting weapons on suspects after they were shot. An accusation that, unfortunately, appeared to have validity, at least with one of the officers when a knife allegedly possessed by a suspect he shot was found to contain cat hairs, hair that was traced back to the officer's feline.

The one incident that would not die was a shootout that occurred between S.T.R.E.S.S. cops and a group of black Wayne County Sheriffs. Apparently the sheriffs who were off-duty and involved in a card game, were suddenly raided by a S.T.R.E.S.S. crew, which initiated an immediate gun battle, a shootout that would tragically leave one Wayne County Sheriff deputy dead. This incident was a cop's worst nightmare, mistakenly shooting it out with your own, just one of many hazards working in an undercover capacity. Fortunately, if there is a fortunate side to this tragic incident, is that the S.T.R.E.S.S. crew was also black. This somewhat eased the tensions of the public as well as black officers. God only knows what would have happened if it had been a white crew involved in the shooting.

As it was, Young's colleagues were having a field day with a statement made by John Nichols several months ago following the shooting of four S.T.R.E.S.S. officers. During this news conference, Nichols referred to the suspects: Boyd, Bethune and Brown as "mad dog killers." Young charged Nichols with making an outrageous racist statement when referring to the suspects as animals, which in his mind insinuated that they were less then human because of their blackness. He further stated that every man has the right to a trial before being declared guilty. A decree he and his administration would violate some twenty odd years later when they would accuse two white officers involved in an on-duty arrest in which the suspect died, as rogue murderers, declaring them guilty less than 12 hours after the incident.

Others however, believed that referring to the suspects as "mad dog killers" was a compassionate statement, coming from a man who thought of his officers as family and felt their grief each time one would fall, black or white. Was he angry? Damn right, he was furious, how anyone could be so callous to ambush police officers and then declare themselves as victims and civil rights warriors who were fighting for the cause, a declaration which was an outright fabrication.

In reality, these men were immoral opportunist with criminal backgrounds who were wanted for holding up dope houses around the city, most of which were black operated. After shooting the S.T.R.E.S.S. officers, they conveniently cloaked themselves in the beliefs of Martin Luther King, a man who certainly did not advocate violence from either side. In other words, they were cowards who hid behind a great man and idea in order to justify their crimes, which included cold-blooded murder.

The atmosphere around the precinct was tense as hell; these elections were making an ugly situation worse. White officers would candidly speak of the upcoming mayoral race with condescending comments toward Coleman Young. Many times these remarks had racial overtones and were less than appropriate to those in earshot, often times disregarding the presence or feelings of black officers. The black officers were far more discrete, they would gather in small groups and discuss Young's progress within the black community, sometimes throwing a little humor in with a hidden meaning, with remarks that could be over-heard, such as "Things sho going to change when we get a black mayor" or "The city is going to have a new Masser real soon." These candid remarks were often met with ugly replies or nervous laughter from the white officers.

I often thought to myself, what could we expect if another riot erupted, whose side would the black officers be on? I truly believed most would perform as professional lawmen enforcing the law they swore to uphold, some would call in sick, just to avoid any chance of conflict with their people.

The radicals would, oh hell who knows what they would do, they change like the wind. However, I did know this; the black officers would not tolerate police brutality at the level that was purportedly used by some in the 1967 riots.

How frightening it would be to go to war and find out that the man you share a foxhole with is on the other side. Your brother in blue is now just a brother with an attitude. It appeared more and more to be about black and white as opposed to right or wrong. Whites continuously attempted to be politically correct, to the point it became embarrassing, bosses felt they must justify each decision and assignment to avoid a complaint, because it is common knowledge that a civil rights complaint against a white supervisor could derail a promising career in the blink of an eye, a fear that was quite evident to the black officers and, believe me, they took advantage of this mindset.

Anymore, being right is a matter of perception. If you truly believe in an idea or movement, it is difficult to consider that there could be an opposing view, we become blinded by our beliefs and inconsiderate of those who disagree.

The black community could sense the fear in white America and many of them felt it was not only justified but also long overdue. They believed whites had purposely held them back for hundreds of years by maintaining a monopoly on financial and political positions. Whereas, most whites felt they were not responsible for the evils of their forefathers, many times stating, "I never owned a slave, and my ancestors who were poor white laborers certainly never possessed slaves either, so why should I be held accountable for something I am not related to?" I thought things were volatile between the races in the Army, as high as the tensions were back in the 60s and 70s, it couldn't compare with the anxiety being felt within the walls of our police precinct.

With the upcoming elections growing closer the "Protectors," the unrecognized black union, was becoming quite outspoken toward the election and their purpose. They were being interviewed by a number of the local TV stations, announcing their support of Coleman A. Young for Mayor and advising the citizens of Detroit that their purpose as an organization was to uphold the law as well as insure that the civil rights of Detroiters were not violated. Well, needless to say, this did not set well with most white officers, for the simple reason they felt they were being indicted for the actions of a few and did not need a bunch of revolutionaries making the streets any more hazardous than they were by inciting the people.

As expected the Detroit Police Officers Association (D.P.O.A.) were pledging their support behind their previous Police Commissioner, John Nichols, a man whom they trusted understood their needs as cops. It was just another division between the races that was quite apparent to all. Both sides were using these opposing views to their advantage in the campaign, with the blacks inferring that Nichols wanted to keep business as usual within city government by keeping the whites in power and holding the black man down. The whites disputed this by saying blacks were more concerned about the criminals' rights then the safety of the good citizens in Detroit.

The apprehension in the upper echelon of the department was at an unprecedented high. The command structure was far more cognizant of expressing their opinion of either candidate, unlike the officers on the street, who were more than happy to share their opinion with anyone who was willing to listen. It was almost humorous to see command officers run for cover if someone would make a derogatory statement against Young in public. Most would do whatever they needed to do to appear neutral, in an attempt to assure a place on the new team, no matter what the outcome of the race.

It is well understood that whoever wins the election would restructure the upper ranks, placing their supporters in key positions and bury those that opposed them, by either demoting or placing them in some second-rate job that would virtually end their career. This was no longer simply a black and white issue; this was politics at its best!

The months were flying by and the elections were fast approaching, it seemed like all conversations around the water cooler involved the campaign. With each passing day, the media was allotting more time to the candidates. It didn't matter what TV station you turned to, you were sure to see one of their photos followed by a story or accusation concerning the two.

There was also a tremendous amount of rumors flying around, particularly directed toward Coleman Young, everything from being associated with the Black Panther's to being indicted on federal charges by the FBI for treason, all of which were obviously unfounded at the time. However, it was common knowledge that the feds have had a special interest in Young for a number of years due to his association with a number of political groups that were on the FBI's watch list.

Young, for the most part responded to each allegation as simply accusations coming from a racist or a Jim Crow government that would do whatever was necessary to keep a black man out of office. He did acknowledge that he was quite aware that the federal government had their sights set on him for years, attempting to associate him with questionable people or organizations. Yet, none of their claims were ever substantiated and if there was any validity to the allegations at all he would have been charged accordingly.

There was certainly no love lost between Coleman Young and the Fed's and he never attempted to conceal his resentment of them. Most politicians would avoid being so bold as to make such insulting remarks against federal law enforcement agencies, if for any other reason, out of fear of reprisals or sparking off a new investigation and in today's world an investigation alone can cost you thousands of votes. But Young had this "Bring it on" type attitude and with each public accusation from the government, he would advise them to put up or shut up, not to mention that all public confrontations added to his defense of entrapment and harassment should he ever get indicted. This wise old fox was obviously not afraid of the hounds.

One thing was for sure, if you as an officer had any type of relationship with a federal agency there was no danger of you ever being assigned to Coleman Young's security detail, should he be elected. Without question he would insulate himself with only those that he indisputably trusted and their job would consist of keeping out anyone who was not totally reliable, blind loyalty was demanded.

Jim and I were one of the first scout cars off the ramp and upon notifying radio that we were in service; we received the first run of what would turn out to be a very busy night. "7-5 Chene and Kirby, three men assaulting a man in the alley" "On the way radio 7-5" We were only about two miles from the location so if it was a good run there was a decent chance we could make it there in time to assist the victim and possibly catch the perpetrators.

As I turned in the alley I almost hit the suspects who were really putting the boots to this poor guy. If I didn't come to a squealing halt, I don't believe these characters would have even noticed us. The one facing us looked up and screamed "Cops" and took off running like a deer with Jim right on his heels. I was able to apprehend the other two before they could run off, placing both face down with their hands enter locked on top their heads until I could handcuff them. "Radio 7-5, my partner is in foot pursuit north in the alley from Kirby west of Chene. The suspect is described as black male 6' thin build, wearing blue jeans and a white T-shirt, wanted for assault. I have two in custody and request backup to assist and transport prisoners."

After securing the two suspects in cuffs, I went to give aid to the victim who was lying in a pool of blood, as I turned the victim over, I recognized him immediately. It was Buckie, one of the neighborhood winos and he was bleeding like hell from injuries to his head and face. "Radio 7-5, you better send a wagon, we have one for the hospital." "OK 7-5, Scout 7-4 is on the way and will transport your injured." 7-4 was a station wagon which was equipped with stretchers that was used to transport injured parties to the hospital when needed, often referred to by the officers as the "meat wagon." (These vehicles would eventually be replaced by the Emergency Medical Services, commonly referred to as E.M.S.)

Most winos are considered harmless with only one goal in life, that is to drink themselves to death with the cheapest wine or alcohol they can find. We estimated Buckie's age at approximately 30 years old, a guess that could never be verified because of a lack of identification along with the fact he could never remember his date of birth. The one unmistakable trait of these winos was their disgusting body odor, a scent I can only describe as a combination of sour milk and stale beer. They often would go for months without bathing and were usually infested with lice, fleas and host of other diseases. If you were unfortunate enough to transport one of these guy's you and your vehicle would more likely than not have to be deloused prior to going back into the population, a process that was time consuming as well as humiliating because you were stripped nude for sanitizing.

Buckie, was a terrific source of information because he literally lived in the streets and was thought to be a burned out drunk who was oblivious to the world around him, when in fact this ghost knew and observed a lot more than he was given credit for. On many occasions his information proved to be invaluable in solving crimes committed in the area. Finding him was less than challenging, because he frequented the north end of the precinct and would go from one doorway to the next, consuming his drink of choice, whatever was available and then sleeping off his last bottle. His face was weathered, unshaven and always a mess, not from beatings like this one, but from falling down drunk and hitting his head on the concrete.

"Hey buddy, are you ok? We are going to get you to the hospital real quick." "Hey Dave, can you spare a couple bucks for some food until I get on my feet?" He would never get on his feet and it is common knowledge you don't give wino's money, the only groceries he would buy comes in a bottle. On extreme cold nights or around the holidays we would buy hot food and coffee from some nearby restaurant and give it to them instead of cash. We also would advise them of local abandon buildings where they could get out of the subzero temperatures and bed down safely for the evening.

"What the hell happened here, why'd these clowns jump you?" "I don't know Dave, I was cutting through the alley when they came out of nowhere and started kicking my ass yelling you white mother fucker." "Did they try to take anything from you or use any weapons?" "The only weapon I seen Dave was their size twelve's coming down on my head and do I look like I have anything worth taking?" "Good point" as I chuckled, this guy just had his head kicked in and he still has a sense of humor. If he drank one bottle less a day he could meet the requirements to become a cop.

Some would classify this as a hate crime and maybe it is, but the reality of the matter is there are no weapons and no robbery, so these thugs will be charged with assault and battery, which will no doubt be reduced to simple assault at best, that is if we can find Buckie and get him to court, which is highly unlikely. Now if this were some executive whose vehicle broke down in the area, they would have hung these guys out to dry. Is it a double standard? Absolutely there is, and on both sides. Buckie is just another homeless person who has fell through the cracks, so the system will more than likely let these dirt bags go with a slap on the hand.

As I looked up I could see Jim coming back down the alley with his guy cuffed and bleeding from the nose. "Good job Jimmy boy, I thought this one would get away from you" "No chance Dave, I'm not as old and decrepit as you." Yea right, I had a whole three years on Jim. "What happened to his nose, did you have to tussle with the idiot?" "Nah, when I tackled his ass he hit his face on the cement, it's no biggie, it's just a nose bleed."

The suspect, as large as he appeared was unquestionably a juvenile, with no facial hair and a baby face. "How old are you man?" "I'm fourteen and I want to make a complaint against you mother fuckers for busting my nose, this is bull-shit." I cannot believe this punk, he and his two buddies just kicked the shit out of this helpless drunk for no other reason than he was white, down and out while walking in a city alley. Now this tough guy wants to make a complaint, un-believable! "Look big fellow you are not dealing with some destitute homeless person now, I will take those cuffs off of your young ass and see just how bad you are without your two pals. You want to make a complaint, I'll give you some-thing to complain about." "Fuck you, all you white mother fuckers will be out of a job, soon as my man Coleman Young becomes mayor. That's right, he said he's going to get rid of all you white boy's."

This statement was a good indication of how this cam-paign had come under the watchful eye of the entire city, even the lowest criminal element was aware of the battle and the high stakes. A number of recent statements by Coleman Young inferred that the days of the brutal white police offi-cers and heavy-handed tactics would no longer be tolerated, consequently delivering the respect the citizens of Detroit have been deprived of for far too long. A statement at face value could not be argued, however, there was that element of society that would take these statements and interpret them as a green light for criminal activity, a mindset this city could not afford, regardless who wins. Throughout the entire country we lead in the number of homicides and violent crimes, which had gained us the dubious distinction of "The Murder capital of the world," a less then flattering title for any city.

All the way back to the station, the two suspects I apprehended remained quiet and orderly, while Jim's suspect had diarrhea of the mouth, he just would not shut up. He continuously informed his two accomplices that they did not have to say anything because they were juveniles. "Look man why don't you shut the hell up, we don't need a statement, we witnessed you guys kicking the hell out of the victim." "Ya'll ain't got shit, that old mother fucking drunk ain't going to court and besides we're under 17 so ya'll can't do shit to us, we are juveniles. You hear me, mother-fucker, ya'll ain't got shit, not shit!" "Yea we do" "What ya'll got? Huh mother fucker, what ya'll got?" "We got shit, because we have you." This disrespectful thug suddenly got a bewildered look on his face as he attempted to understand what was said, and I wasn't about to break my statement down for this mental giant. But at least we all experienced a moment of silence while he attempted to figure out.

As I was turning my report into the sergeant at the front desk, I noticed a black lady walking out of the Juvenile Division office with our loud mouth suspect who smirked as they approached. "That's one of them right there momma" indicating me by the pointing of his finger. "That's alright baby, these mother fuckers will be hearing from our lawyer real damn soon." You know there are times a man needs to know when to keep his opinion to himself, this however was not one of those occasions, yet I knew the moment I opened my mouth I made a big mistake. "Ma'am, I'm not sure if you are aware of what took place out there today, but your son and two of his friends beat and kicked an elderly gentleman half to death in an alley, the man is currently hospitalized with head injuries." To which she so eloquently replied. "Look Mr. Po-lice-man, for your fucking information that old drunk mother fucker called the boys niggers, that's why he got his white ass kicked and if I was there I would have helped them kick his drunk white ass too."

Now, I know Buckie, and he is far too street wise to call these kids anything; he would walk around the block to avoid any potential problematic situation, he is simply a harmless drunk wandering the streets in search of his next bottle. But, attempting to talk to this poor excuse for a mother would be totally useless, not to mention it could escalate into an all-out brawl. "Come on baby, Mr. Young is going to put a stop to all this bullshit in November, these mother-fuckers will find themselves unemployed and standing in line for government cheese. Whitey has stepped on black folks long enough, now it's our turn."

It's parents like this that dwarfs their children mentally as well as socially. I can now see where the kid gets his attitude and lack of respect; he does not have a chance in hell with a support system like his mother. I will be seeing this kid again down the line; he has all the makings for a holdup man or murderer. His mother has instilled all the necessary traits, dishonesty, and disrespect for the law, property and life along with the art of blaming society for all your misfortunes because of race. The odds of him being shot and killed by a law enforcement officer or someone on the street in the future are better than not, and when it happens his mother will be screaming: "Lord why did you let them take my baby?" I would suggest the Lord or the streets did not take your baby; you yourself surrendered him to the streets!

Now this is not to insinuate that black mothers, are as careless with their children's lives as this poor excuse for a parent, because that is simply not the case. Black mothers are just as protective and concerned about their children's well-being and proper upbringing as is the millions of other mothers around the world. However, every now and then in all races you will find a dysfunctional mother like this one who should have never been blessed with the precious gift of having children.

How ironic, the defendant is walking out the door even before my supervisor has reviewed the report. This is not unusual at all when it concerns juveniles; the law is much more lenient and forgiving when it comes to adolescents, not to mention having a youth offender confined almost takes an act of Congress. In the eyes of the judicial system, these little felons should be less accountable for their crimes than the adults. I would suggest in some cases this may be true, however, majority of them conveniently veil themselves from the law with this knowledge. As my mother often said, "You can hide from man, but you can't hide from the good Lord, he knows what's in your heart." Unfortunately, God's wrath may be the only justice these young thugs will see in our forgiving society.

This mindset of "support Coleman Young and hate police" displayed by the mother and son was becoming more prevalent throughout the city and certainly appeared to be very contagious throughout the country. Blacks and liberal whites felt every decision being made by the current establishment was designed to undermine and discourage any progress in the black community. Whereas, the majority of the white population felt the blacks were just attempting to receive another free benefit through government and welfare programs, programs that are typically financed through tax heights. The amazing fact is that both sides genuinely believed in their hearts their cause was just. I find it absolutely astonishing that our society is so decisively divided by race that both sides think the other is mentally challenged because they cannot understand the others' view points and stance.

The summer was finally over and what a bloody summer it turned out to be. The wanted S.T.R.E.S.S. killers had ambushed and shot two more S.T.R.E.S.S. officers who were on surveillance. One was killed while the other was left impaired from the waist down and consequently would be confined to a wheel chair for the remainder of his life.

Boyd was subsequently shot and killed down south by a good old country boy sheriff, Bethune killed himself and Detroit officers arrested Hayward Brown during a drug raid. The odds of Brown being taken alive were less than fair in most officers' minds, not because he would be revengefully executed, but because he was part of a crew that viciously targeted and killed police officers and this made him a real and present danger, for the simple reason if you are bold enough to kill one cop or ten, you are ultimately facing life in prison, if not the death sentence.

Elections were just a week away and both candidates were still going strong, making accusations and promises most of which could hold no water. The election sites would have security at an unprecedented level, out of fears of foul play, including voter intimidation and ballet tampering. There would not only be police officers assigned to the polls there would be supervisors assigned to watch the watchers.

The polls released by the local papers indicated Nichols was leading by a comfortable margin, but as most know, polls and opinions can change with a simple statement or remark from either candidate. Young's camp was playing the race card like it had never been played before, while Nichols camp stayed the course dealing with the campaign issues and was kept busy putting out fires sparked by accusations. In the end Detroiter's would have the final word and I must say I would be glad when it was behind us, regardless of the outcome, so we as a city could move on.

There were rumors throughout the city that if Coleman Young lost the election the city of Detroit was going to burn to the ground. These threats were taken very serious by the upper echelon and preparations were being developed to handle any disturbance that might arise. The governor alerted the National Guard to be ready to move on a moment's notice and all leave days and vacations for police and firefighters were canceled during the two-day election period, with all first responders being placed on our highest alert level.

Both candidates publicly requested that civil peace prevail no matter what the outcome of the election. Our city had yet to recover from the damage of the 1967 riots. Coleman Young advised the citizens of Detroit that the battle should take place in the voting booth not in the street, advice that only cool heads would take heed to.

There were those of us who believed that the element of black citizens demanding a victory or else, was nothing more than a form of extortion and intimidation, a tactic that is becoming all too common in this country. How can a community have a fair election when you are threatened with bodily harm and property destruction if you don't vote for the candidate being endorsed by these hooligans?

I was present for the 67 riots, although only 16-years-old at the time, I can still recall the army tanks and soldiers patrolling our streets and watching the looters breaking into the stores and escaping with arms full of stolen goods laughing as they ran. These were hardly people who were trying to make a political statement, in my opinion they were common thugs who were taking advantage of a bad situation and when arrested they would put their political hat on and scream racism and police brutality.

By the third day of the riots my father put mom and us kids on a Grey hound bus headed south to Kentucky, out of harm's way. I will always be haunted by the vision I observed from the rear window of the bus as we escaped from the chaos: the city of Detroit was on fire, with hundreds of individual smoke stacks climbing into the sky, taking on an eerie lingering purple haze.

The thoughts of another riot like that in Detroit frightened most, but on the other hand, many of us young officers were intrigued by the thoughts of experiencing and reacting to a civil disturbance such as that of the 1967 riots. This is not to say we wanted to witness the deaths and destruction that would be unavoidable, but rather because of the experience one gains from a combat type situation or campaign. Our views or longing to experience a riot could not be publicly expressed for fear of being labeled warmongers or racists, but I truly believe, one becomes a better soldier with each battle. Experience is a priceless gift.

When we would hear the veterans of 1967 reminiscing and relating their intense ordeals experienced during the riots, working cops were left with a sense of envy. This is not to say we agreed with all the stories or tactics used, because in some accounts, police engaged in cruel and sometimes racist behavior. I say sometimes, because in a case where an officer reacts and kills a man who is shooting at officers or firemen from the top of a building, it has absolutely nothing to do with racism, it is simply a situation that needs to be controlled and handled immediately. However, if officers were to prevent a black man from escaping from a burning building by shooting in his direction, consequently leading to his death, now you have a case for racism, not to mention murder.

The alarm went off with a sound that for a moment mimicked sirens from a fire truck, a noise that was intensified; I'm sure, by my hangover. Once again I awoke with a splitting headache from our nightly choir practice at Zs. I laid there for a moment having a cigarette in bed as my wife got up to put the coffee on. Kristy was a lady who I met in California after returning from Korea and later married, she would eventually make me the proud father of my first child, Dave Jr.

Suddenly, through the spider webs in my head, I remembered it was Election Day; oh shit this is the day all hell could break loose. I jumped out of bed like someone called "Officer in trouble". After a quick shower and a brief conversation with my wife as I ran out the door with a cup of coffee, a cup that I would find out is very hot as it spilled in my lap entering my car. Damn Dave slow down, the riot will not start without you, I thought, as I wiped my pants off. In all reality there would be no problems until the results of the election came in and that would not be until 10 p.m. or so.

The one thing that we had in our favor is that the elections were held in the fall, a very cool time in Michigan and emotions were unlikely to flare up as easily as they may have on a hot August day. Any major riot in this country that took place in the 60's or 70's was during hot summer months, it's something about the heat that brings the worst out in folks.

I had never seen the parking lot of the Seventh Precinct so crowded, there had to be a hundred vehicles parked or attempting to park. I placed my car on the street adjacent to the station because of the lack of spots available. The station garage was jammed with blue uniforms that were waiting for roll call to begin; our squad room could not accommodate all these cops, only an area as large as the garage offered adequate space. Cigarette smoke filled the air, as did the strong aroma of coffee coming from the hundreds of cups lying around. To the old-timers, this was just another day at the office, but for us young cops it was a day that had potential for action, something most working cops craved.

Ok guys, fall in and get your assignments, it was good old Sergeant Jacobs a man I learned to respect at least when he was sober. All of us guys with less than ten years on the job knew we would be receiving a voting post for an assignment, most of the posts were located in public schools, police stations or some other city government building. Only seniority could assure a scout car assignment today.

I was one of the last to receive an assignment, just when I thought the sergeant forgot me he blurted out "Stealth, you have

Kettering High, pick up your voting equipment and use your private vehicle to get over there and by the way, there aren't enough radios to go around so don't get in any trouble." This is just great, no scout car and no radio, if the shit does hit the fan, not only is my car going to be torched, I won't even have a radio to let my peers know I am getting my brains kicked in.

Kettering High, located on the eastside of Detroit was a fairly new school and other then some sparse graffiti on the side of the building it was very attractive brick structure. I was positioned at the front entrance and would probably be the only white face seen at the school that evening due to the racial makeup of the area, which was primarily black.

My assignment was to assure that voters weren't tampered with and to make sure the candidate workers stayed the proper distance from the school, which is required by law when handing out campaign information. Once the voting post was closed, I would wait for the voting officials to tally the votes and then return them to the precinct under lock and key, actually a very boring job.

To my surprise the evening was pretty much uneventful, everyone conducted themselves like complete ladies and gentlemen. I was unsure of how things at the other voting post were going due to my lack of communication. Hell, the entire city could be going up in flames and I wouldn't know it. However, I would later learn my post was a reflection of most of the city, with the exception of a few isolated voter violations that were dealt with without incident.

I returned to the precinct a little after 10 p.m., many officers were still out at their voting post, others had returned and were already at the local watering hole giving their opinion on the election results. Rumors were flying like wildfire and the black officers returning to the station sported a look of confidence on their face that I have never seen before. I overheard one brother explain, "I don't know if Young is winning citywide, but I can tell you this, he overwhelmingly won at my post, even the few whites I had chanted "Young for Mayor." I knew this could very well be true, because we had several white liberal classmates who attended college with a few of us and they undeniably supported Young and were going to vote accordingly. Their theory is that a predominantly black city needs to be led by a black mayor, a very small mindset, yet it was echoed in cities throughout this country.

Once my voter box was turned in, I joined my peers for a cold beer and a lesson in electoral education, which no doubt would be taught by the senior officers with their infinite wisdom. And, we could expect it to have a touch of good old racism tossed in for good measure. As I entered the bar I realized the mood of the officers was quite different than that of the black officers back at the station. The atmosphere was very somber compared to the usual jovial upbeat mood. The expressions around the room reflected a strong sense of uncertainty, which I'm sure was due to the reports of low voter turnout at many of the white poll sites. Surely there was nothing to be concerned with, after all a majority of the media reports predicted Nichols to win.

The old-timers were definitely troubled and had no problem expressing the fact they would never work for a black mayor. Now I myself did not disagree with having a competent black mayor. However, I did strongly disagree with electing a person based on race rather than competency. I certainly did not want Young as mayor, a man who openly played the race card and in my opinion would cause a white exodus to the suburbs due to his apparent "black will reign" attitude. Whatever the outcome, we were only a short time away from witnessing a historical moment in Detroit.

It was now approaching the 11p.m. and suddenly the jukebox was turned down and all patrons swarmed around the large TV located over the bar. The 11: 00 o'clock news would be coming on any moment now, and it was certain that the election would dominate the broadcasts. But, unlike previous broadcast, this one would not be based on speculation and rumors; it would be based on results. "Good evening Detroit. It looks like our city is not only going to have a new mayor; it looks like we will be joining many other major cities around the country by electing our first black mayor." These words, coming from a WXYZ news anchorman, were devastating to most of us.

How could Young have won? The polls indicated Nichols camp was ahead.

"Fuck this, my white ass is out of here. I'm not working for some racist nigger mayor. The ass-hole will have all the brothers in scout cars and us snowflakes walking beats." This bigoted old-timer was well over his 25 years' service required for retirement, so he had an option unlike us young guys. I must tell you, I felt like someone hit me in the stomach with a Volkswagen. What the hell was going to happen now, this guy already said he was going to eliminate bureaus like S.T.R.E.S.S., which were made up of primarily white officers. This meant they would be coming back to the precincts and with their seniority, at minimum I would go back to walking a beat. Everything was just fine yesterday and now my world is being turned upside-down.

As I walked through the front door, my wife whose expression said volumes, cautiously approached me with the bad news and a beer in hand. Her apprehension was based on the anxiety I displayed because of the election results as well as concern for our future. I attempted to comfort her with some reassuring words, "Look, it is what it is and we can't change the results. We will take it a day at a time, and if push comes to shove, I will apply for a job in the suburbs." Now, I knew as well as she did that there was no way in hell I wanted to work out in the suburbs, my heart was in Detroit, I loved the action. Suburban departments would hire Detroit cops in a minute; it was like getting someone that served in war. We have typically seen more action in one year then most suburb cops would see in their entire career.

We talked to the wee hours of the morning as I depleted our beer inventory, with each beer I slowly felt like I was incredibly close to solving the world's problems. My wife just sat there patiently listening to me babble on, how disgusting it must be to soberly watch and attempt to understand a person who is intoxicated and drowning in self-pity. Being a cop's wife, in some cases, is like serving hard time, you get three meals and a cot, yet the environment is less than pleasant at times.

After what seemed like hours, I finally fell asleep with thoughts of what tomorrow had in store. I knew there would be no immediate fallout other than some razzing from the black officers and the local NAACP. The big change would come on January 1st when Coleman Young officially took office.

The morning news, as I expected, was primarily focused on Young's triumph over Nichols, with his victory speech being aired over and over, a speech I personally found very annoying because it gave the impression it was directed to the black population of Detroit and appeared to suggest a "You better straighten up or get out of town" overtone for white officers. I was somewhat confident that the city would now be taking off the high alert status because the black citizens had won and as of yet the only threats of violence had come from sources in the black community.

As I walked through the garage of the 7th precinct I was sure I would be greeted by taunting black officers really putting it in our faces, but to the contrary, most were taking care of business as usual and conducted themselves in a professional manner, a trait that very frankly I'm not so sure would have been displayed by white officers, should the results have turned out differently.

I spoke too soon, as I entered the squad room I was greeted by sounds of laughter in the locker-room, it was Kenwall being his loud obnoxious self. "Yea, Brother Coleman is driving now, and he said if whiteys don't like it they can get off the bus. It is our city now, and if they don't like it they can kiss my black ass." Naturally everything was being said loud enough so the white officers in the squad room could overhear it. What an ass hole!

Like clockwork the doors opened and in came the bosses, led by Lt Chimes "Alright guys fall in we got a lot to go over before you hit the streets" As we fell into our normal two ranks, Kenwall and a few other brothers exited the locker room and positioned themselves in the rear of the formation. The lieutenant just began giving out the assignments when Kenwall and the other brothers began giggling like a bunch of schoolgirls.

"Excuse me Officer Kenwall is there something you would like to share with us all?" "No sir, we were just talking about the election results". Well, the elections are over and so is the screwing around, is that understood Mr. Kenwall?" "Sir, yes Sir," said with a very condescending attitude. Immediately Byron Kane, one of the older white officers spoke up and said "Fucking Charles is already getting uppity" "Charles" is one of the expressions used by white officers to describe blacks. Oh shit, here we go I thought to myself. Fortunately

Lieutenant Chimes spoke up in a very angry tone "God Damn it knock off the bullshit and I mean now. There are enough ass holes out there in the streets for all you tough guys, but I will not have this nonsense in my precinct. I thought to myself, this is just the beginning, what would it be like come January?

I was never so glad to hit the street. Who the hell would they have called if us cops started going after each other? I'm not sure what the future of this city is and furthermore, I wasn't so sure I want to be part of it. "Let's get a coffee, Jim, before all our felons' wakeup." As we pulled into the Click restaurant I couldn't help but laugh to myself, there were six police cars and only one citizen's car. I wondered who was watching the city.

Inside, the conversations were going hot and heavy as we approached the twelve officers seated in a cluster of tables, and the topic was no surprise. Sergeant Jacobs was just beginning to share his perspective on the election results. "I was planning on giving it another two years, but with all this bullshit taking place, I'm out of here, it's time to retire." Now, the sarge had well over 25 years on the job so he had the option to leave whenever he chose, unlike most of us who had one or two options, which were to either resign or ride out the storm.

Jim and I being two of the younger officers had no alternative but to just sit back and listen to the veterans vent their anger. Cops are notorious for complaining, if they would hit the lotto, they would complain they had to pay the taxes. I knew most of these threats and complaints were a knee-jerk

reaction to a situation that in the eyes of the old regime appeared to be the demise of the Detroit Police Department as
we knew it.

Let's get out of here Jim, this is going nowhere quick, we
could be hear all night listening to all of this belly-aching.
Tomorrow is another day." "Your right Dave, I'm depressed
enough."

The following day for whatever reason was quite slow, I
guess I really expected it to be busy as hell due to Coleman
Young's victory. Once on the street, Jim just sat there silent,
looking out the passenger window deep in thought, "What's
up Jimmy Boy, you are awful quiet?" "Oh, I don't know
Dave; I just see how concerned you and the other guys are
over this black invasion and I just wonder what the hell is
going to happen to a rookie like me." "Look Jimmy, I would
be lying if I told you I am not fearful of what the future
holds for us, but I do believe we are blowing this way out of
proportion. First of all, nothing is going to take place until
January and secondly, they cannot just start firing us because
we're white or giving blacks all the preferred jobs, the DPOA
would not stand for it." Jim appeared to display a little less
anxiety following my few words of wisdom, I'm glad he feels
better, because deep within I still had huge reservations of
the transition, concerns that could only be answered in time!

"DETROIT'S FIRST BLACK MAYOR": UNITED OR DIVIDED?

WELL, JANUARY CAME AND GONE AND the transition of the new administration was underway. Coleman Young had come in strong and confident, making changes in all city government with a particular emphasis on the police department, which was his strongest campaign promise. The police commissioner post was eliminated and replaced with a new job title of chief of police, a position that would be required to report directly to the mayor.

Mayor Young, predictably, appointed a black chief of police, a gentleman by the name of William Hart who was a well-respected command officer that came up through the ranks. This would be one of the few decisions Young would make in his twenty years as mayor that I truly agreed with. Chief Hart was a kind yet professional man who loved police officers, especially undercover officers. I attribute this respect to the years he spent assigned to various covert operations. Little did I know at that time, but the majority of my career would be spent as an undercover officer, working under the tenure of this chief.

As promised, S.T.R.E.S.S. had been disbanded, with most of the officers being reassigned to specialized bureaus, such as homicide, vice and the tactical mobile unit. Young also got rid of the infamous precinct "Big Four" or "Cruiser," which was an unmarked police vehicle, usually black in color manned by four officers. These officers were normally considered the top cops in the precinct, often being huge men, hence the name "The Big Four." Three of the officers were in plainclothes and the driver was always in full uniform. The Cruiser would only receive priority runs such as robberies in progress, shootings, rapes, and breaking and entering in progress.

You can ask any old-timer, black or white from Detroit, about "The Big Four" and their answer will usually be, those guys were no-nonsense cops. If you were loitering on a corner and they told you to move on, you better vacate the area immediately, because if you didn't there would be a serious ass-beating coming upon their return. Was it respect or fear? I'm not sure but it appeared to work. However, this is the primary reason they, too, were out. Young apparently didn't appreciate their heavy-handed enforcement tactics, which he recalled from his younger days on the streets of Detroit.

The upper echelon of the Department was scrambling for position, with some being demoted while others were being promoted. For those that supported Nichols, it was time to pay the piper! The hammer didn't fall as heavy at the precinct level, due to the protection provided by our unions, the Lieutenants and Sargent Association and the Detroit Police Officers Association. There was no doubt that there would be a ton of revisions in our department policies, especially concerning arrest procedures, but a transition of this magnitude would not happen overnight.

The tension among the troops remained high, not only due to the new mayor, but also because of the Affirmative Action Policy implemented. This would mean minorities (especially blacks) would receive preferential consideration when it came to promotions and job placement. Needless to say this didn't set well with any of us white officers. Why should any person black or white who is less qualified receive a position or additional points on a promotional exam merely because of their race? Yet, the government had already implemented Affirmative Action policies, so, yes, it was a very clear and present concern.

Black officers for the most part, agreed with Affirmative Action, believing that the white establishment for years had abused them and this was just a small compensation to which they were entitled. There were a few black officers that declared they didn't want anything they didn't earn, including a promotion, and would turn down any advancement that was not based on actual test scores. Now, these men in my opinion could absolutely declare, "Say it loud, I'm Black and I'm Proud."

As if the Department didn't have enough controversy to

deal with, we were hearing strong rumors that our recruiting policy was being totally revised making it minority-friendly. The buzz was that we were lowering the required score for the entry examination; in addition the height and weight requirement was being eliminated and the command was actually considering assigning female officers to the street patrol.

Historically Detroit has always had women serving, but only in the

Women's Division "W.D.," which was used primarily for investigative work with juveniles and sex crimes. The thoughts of having women making police runs in the tough streets of Detroit was preposterous, how could a 125 pound lady arrest some 225-pound three-time loser who would rather die than go back to the "Big House". Affirmative Action was a real and here to stay, unless the appeal courts rule differently. But this ludicrous proposal of putting female officers on the street must have been some desk jockey's idea of a joke!

The old white guys were submitting their retirement papers in record numbers. Many of these veterans had plans of hanging on for a few years longer for financial reasons, especially those that had a gravy job that kept them off the street and out of harm's way. However, the general consensus was the city was going to hell in a hand basket and they were not going to be the last one out, left with the task of shutting the lights off.

Coleman Young immediately developed his security unit, which was the largest in Detroit history and, unsurprisingly, the majority were black, needless to say if you weren't a supporter of Young he didn't want you guarding his life, which is only logical. The risk factor for Coleman Young having some white supremacist or nut job out there making an attempt on his life were far greater than his predecessor's. So it was quite obvious his bodyguards would be earning their money, with duties such as protecting him from would be assassins, the news media, which would be a constant pain during his political tenure, as well as keeping away nosey Fed's or anyone associated with those agencies.

Mayor Young's frustration with the news media grew with each interview or story as his tolerance lessened. It was not uncommon for him to blow up and begin using foul language right on camera, or walk off an interview when he felt they were attempting to discredit him. Without question he was not the most polished man, but it can never be said he laid down and rolled over for anyone, to the contrary he was probably one of the most defiant arrogant men I have ever known.

In my opinion Young was his own worst enemy; he had a habit of making outrageous statements directed towards the surrounding suburban communities, many of which had unmistakable racial overtones. If any white public official had made remarks such as the Mayor had expressed, they would be crucified, declared an outright racist and ask to resign immediately or else!

One of Young's most controversial quotes after taking office was: "I issue a warning to all those pushers, to all rip-off artists, to all muggers, it's time to leave Detroit; hit Eight Mile Road! And I don't give a damn if they are black or white, or if they wear Super-fly suits or blue uniforms with silver badges. Hit the road." With this statement, Young offended everyone but Mother Teresa, good thing she was not in town. The suburban mayors were outraged and let it be known publicly, stating Young had no right to tell the criminals "To hit Eight Mile" indicating they better come to suburban communities to commit their crimes because it would no longer be tolerated in Detroit. Young's statement also suggested that police officers were also involved in Detroit's crime, and I assure you this was a gross exaggeration.

Can you imagine a white suburban mayor making such a statement, advising the criminal element to do their dirty work in Detroit? All hell would have broken loose and the NAACP would have a field day! A statement like that, in my opinion, was the catalyst for the white flight from Detroit to the suburbs. I also believe this was not Coleman Young's intention, he would not deliberately hurt the City of Detroit, he loved the city, I suggest that he really didn't understand the enormous consequences of his inflammatory statements and at the time didn't give a damn. I'm sure he thought if they want to leave our city well then get the hell out.

However, with each departing family, Detroit lost tax revenue not to mention one less resident in the city population count, which is used by the federal government census to determine Detroit's eligibility for financial assistance.

Much of Young's confidence came from his past, he was quite active in the labor movement within the automobile industry leading blacks as well as whites in the struggle for worker's rights with monstrous companies such as the Ford Motor Company. He would later be drafted during WWII making the rank of lieutenant while assigned with the legendary Tuskegee Airman, a unit that I salute and certainly earned their respectable place in history. Upon being honorably discharged from the service, Young became a target for the U.S. Government during the 50's with insinuations that he was associated with the Communist Party, a suggestion that was found without merit. Taking these credentials into account, one can certainly see why this man was seen as a fighter, arrogant as he may be.

The city was being littered with signs reading "Coleman A Young, Mayor of Detroit" They were everywhere, city benches, city vehicles, billboards and even the huge water tank in front of the Detroit Zoo. If you didn't know Coleman Young was the new mayor of Detroit, you would certainly realize it by time you drove through the city. I'm surprised he didn't have a gigantic sign placed on the waterfront facing Canada informing our good neighbors who was running Detroit now.

Detroit was going through a major transformation and like it or not we were all part of it for better or worst. Attitudes of the white officers had calmed down considerably; they had lived through the stroke of midnight January first, and found themselves still gainfully employed. There was no talk of drastic changes at the precinct level so it was pretty much business as usual, other than the tension between the black and white officers, which was becoming more obvious with each passing day.

The current concern was that Internal Affairs (I.A.) had been increased in numbers as well as in their agenda, adding a Residency Unit and a Professional Standards Unit. The Residency Unit was responsible for enforcing the residency ordinance, which required all city employees to reside within Detroit city limits. Most white officers whole-heartedly disagreed with this ordinance; their contention is the city has no right to dictate where their families should reside. They are employed by the city, not their families. These officers enjoyed working in the city, but argued they would appreciate the option of owning a nice home in the suburbs where they and their families could enjoy safer neighborhoods and more proficient schools for their children.

Whereas many black officials maintained one should reside in and support the city in which they are employed. If there was anything positive that could be expressed about the residency requirement, is that it would insure that several areas of Detroit would remain pleasant, safe and well maintained communities. These areas were commonly referred to as "Copper Canyons," insinuating that the majority of the homes were occupied by city employees, most of whom were white policemen and firefighters.

Young's new controversial Professional Standards Unit was designed to investigate police officers who violated department policy as well as allegations of unprofessional behavior. This Unit handled any misconduct that was less then criminal. Those found guilty by a Department Trial Board could receive sentences ranging from a verbal reprimand to dismissal. The changes in Internal Affairs, as much as they may have appeared to be warranted, were disturbing to most due to the fear of selective enforcement.

The majority of cops considered the Professional Standards Unit as an entity of Internal Affairs that was designed to target officers for petty department violations such as, observing officers getting out of their patrol car without their hat on or having their jacket unzipped. Many considered this as a deliberate attempt to harass white officers to the point they would resign from the department.

The fact of the matter is that Internal Affairs is a necessary unit, the police must be policed and if we are going to be scrutinized I would certainly prefer my own analyze me as opposed to John Q citizen. When being investigated by an officer, one could expect an objective investigation by a professional that has walked in your shoes.

As far as the Professional Standard Unit is concerned, in theory it was a good idea, but not very practical, especially when you consider that existing supervisors were already responsible for enforcing the same department policies that this new unit was now imposing, a very redundant move in my opinion. Did they actually believe that when I was in pursuit of some scumbag with a gun that I would be concerned whether or not my uniform adhered to department policy, please!

I assure you in those intense situations the last thing on my mind was my appearance. I would have challenged anyone of those paper pushers to jump out of a moving scout car in pursuit of an armed felon and see if they would actually be concerned with the fact their hat was on properly or their jacket was zipped up.

Now, if you were one of those guys who continually brought in prisoners that were beat to hell, oh well, you put yourself in that situation and far as I was concerned, I.A. could have at ya. Officers like this just made it difficult for those of us who would got into a legitimate battle where we were actually fighting for our lives. I, too, have brought in bloody prisoners who I had to fight like hell with and, believe me, I could care less what I had to do to overpower those clowns; we aren't payed to take a beating from some street thug! But, there is a fine line between affecting a forceful arrest and intentionally beating the hell out of a suspect because you can.

Mayor Young had a lot of mental scars from events that had taken place in his lifetime and unfortunately many of them involved police, white police. This is probably the driving force behind his advocacy for the black citizens of Detroit, certainly for those that have felt the extreme pain of discrimination.

Young was raised in the "Black Bottom," an area located

off Jefferson Ave on the lower East side of Detroit. The Black Bottom was segregated when William Young, the father of Coleman Young, moved his family up from Tuscaloosa, Alabama in the 1920's. The neighborhood was comprised of blacks, many of whom had relocated from the South with hopes of being employed in the automobile industry. That no doubt is where Coleman had his run in with the renowned "Big Four" or Cruiser. Little did those officers know back then, but their demeanor with Coleman Young on that day would be the catalyst for the demise of the "Big Four" some 30 years later, how ironic!

Coleman Young was in charge now, and it was time to set things straight. His recent termination of units and bureaus that had been traditional for decades, as well as the implementation of his new policies that were viewed by numerous whites as radical changes coming from a man motivated by racism.

Policemen in general do not like changes of any kind, for whatever reason, referring to the good old days as: "This is the way we have always done it kid." When I would hear this, I would always envision a caveman complaining about fire, stating: "I remember when we used to eat our meat raw, now you want to cook it with fire." I guess progress can be considered an enemy to the complacent. Now, when you take attitudes like this and mix them with drastic changes coming from a newly elected black mayor, you have a recipe for anarchy.

Young had restructured the entire city government placing

a large amount of the power into a newly developed city council, which would be responsible for running city business under the direction of Mayor Young. The premise of developing a city council seemed excellent at the time; this would allow the nine-member panel, which was racially diverse, to make

city decisions by voting, instead of solely leaving these matters in the mayors hands. However, as the council members matured they began to challenge the mayor on a number of issues and even vetoed some of his

proposals. Needless to say this didn't set well with Mr. Young at all, he was outraged. How could a council that he initiated dare challenge his authority? This would be the launching of an enormous tug of war battle for absolute power that would last for decades.

One of Young's more controversial moves was to appoint a number of civilian Deputy Chiefs whose job was to monitor police behavior as well as to suggest solutions for policy changes to Chief Hart and Mayor Young. The principle behind this move was to allow impartial civilian's to penetrate and regulate the Detroit Police Department, which was considered a good old boy network that traditionally resisted changes and practiced the infamous code of silence. The appointment of these civilian chiefs obviously was less than favorable for the vast number of DPD officers. These newly designed civilian positions were looked upon as an opportunity to charge and terminate white officers who were attempting to keep control of a crime-ridden city, and just another move by Young to stir the pot of dissension among the troops.

In Young's mind, the DPD was an organization that had a stronghold on the city and could only be policed from the outside with people that have experienced the bitter taste of discrimination. These civilian chiefs would show up at the most inopportune times, such as a street disturbance or a narcotic raid, any place where large crowds and police came in contact.

They would lurk in the crowd observing us like some overzealous warden anticipating a criminal act with our every move. The concern was that we had already been prejudged, found guilty and they were just waiting for the overt act to take place, no doubt in the form of excessive force or by re-acting improperly to a heated and often-unstable situation.

The most common argument within the ranks concerning Young's new watchdogs was that most officers believed the only people that could judge a cop fairly and impartially was someone that has worn a badge at some point in their life. They would understand and take into consideration the complainant making the charge as well as the surrounding circumstances, which vary with each arrest. These commissioners, for the most part, had no law enforcement background and any contact they have had with police in the past most likely came in a negative form. One would think these negative experiences support the need for reform and I agree. I have never said the machine is not broken, what I have said, is that we should not all be painted with such a wide brush and those policing the police should, at minimum, be familiar with the system and come bearing no personal revenge agenda.

Civilians cannot possibly understand the frustrations and anxieties that officers experience on a daily basis and, yes, I realize this is why we make the big bucks. However, the ordinary citizen being put into a situation that we would categorize as an average everyday event, would either soil their pants or faint. It's imperative that officers take charge of a situation immediately by whatever legal means necessary, because if an officer hesitates in the least, street predators often perceive it as weakness and this can turn a loud crowd into a hostile mob in an instant.

As controversial as Coleman Young's ideas were, many of them held water and would certainly improve the city if implemented and practiced in the manner in which they were designed. But, every change came with enormous opposition from the anti-black mayor faction, as well as some black leaders and managers who had benefited from the ways of the previous administration. To them it was about money and power, nothing to do with black and white. This opposition was met with welcoming arms, Young has fought for causes all his life and this was just another day at the office. Some close to him said it was almost like he feeds off controversy; it strengthened his determination to stay the course defiantly.

Mayor Young's campaign promises to revitalize the

downtown area, including the Detroit River waterfront, was already in the planning stages and as history would attest many of these dreams would come true. Each project initiation was a struggle, being delayed by opposition, ordinances, and funding. It was quite apparent the rebirth of Detroit, if feasible, was not going to be an easy task and would require outside funding, funding that just wasn't available in the city budget.

The Detroit downtown region 50 years earlier was a cluster of vibrant businesses and manufacturers supplying a healthy living for many of Detroit's residents. You had everything from small mom & pop restaurants and saloons to huge corporations such as the J.L. Hudson department store and Uni-Royal Tire Company, which was located directly on the riverfront and offered a spectacular view of beautiful Belle Isle.

Belle Isle was the Lower Peninsula's answer to the fabulous Mackinac Island located in northern Michigan. Taking a ride on Belle Isle was like stepping back in time, the winding roads took you into a paradise that had small herds of deer running free, ponds and streams that presented a perfect wildlife sitting for the many ducks and geese. There were canoe and bike rentals as well as horseback riding, not to mention the shores around the island offered year-round fishing. Yes, Detroit's quite a beautiful city and the streets of downtown were alive with pedestrians until the late hours of the evening.

One may ask, what the hell happened? Shortly after the

1967 riots, the streets of downtown Detroit began to fold up by 6 p.m. in most of the business district areas. Beautiful Belle Isle was not a place you would want to be found after dark. The riverfront district began to look like something you would find in a third world country, with vacant buildings vandalized to the point that many appeared un-repairable and often became a haven for vagrants and dope dealers.

There are those that have blamed the mass exodus from Detroit on the black criminal element that was perceived to be responsible for committing crimes against the cities businesses and patrons. But, I would suggest it is much more compli-cated than that. It is a combination of crime, racism and the fact that the suburbs offered a much safer atmosphere for all around living, which lured white and black residents as well as businesses from the city grasp. Whatever the reason, it is quite clear that in order for Detroit to shine again it must be a combined effort of blacks, and whites, as well as the local businesses to make a difference. Mr. Young certainly had his work cut out for him, he now had the difficult task of uniting two races that have historically opposed one another and have been imbedded with a strong since of distrust?

One thing was becoming quite apparent; the city even though going through an enormous amount of changes was not going to fall as Rome did. All the rhetoric by us pessimists predicting the downfall of the city under Mayor Coleman Young's administration within the first year was highly un-likely. Our paychecks were still coming in on time and most of the city's streetlights continued to come on nightly. I guess it was time to get over it, deal with it and move on.

Tensions were certainly running high, especially when arrests were made by white officers who found it necessary to use force to effect the arrest. Black officers were starting to speak up when they felt a prisoner's injuries were questionable and, believe me, this wasn't looked on favorably by the white officers. They considered any interference by an officer black or white, an act of treason against the blue brotherhood. Times were changing rapidly, and it was quite apparent that the days' of ruling by force were over for the most part.

A new injured prisoner policy that required the arresting officer to transport his prisoner to the hospital instead of to the precinct was not well accepted. The injuries that in the past would just have to be mentioned in the preliminary report now generated an ungodly amount of paperwork. This in and of itself was a deterrent for those who practiced heavy-handed tactics, or just enjoyed beating prisoners and I assure you, people like this were definitely in the minority.

This new intolerance attitude displayed by black officers was beginning to be practiced citywide, the election of Coleman Young appeared to unleash a new sense of courage combined with defiance. Black officers were now doing something that historically was rarely done, they were turning fellow police officers in for what they determined to be indiscriminate acts of police violence, or advising citizens to get badge numbers and names and make an official complaint with Internal Affairs. This was considered crossing the Thin Blue Line and entitled you to the name of "Snitch." Snitches were typically black-balled from fraternizing with other officers, not to mention the possibility of receiving little if any backup when you experienced a problem on the street. Can you imagine calling for help and having officers that are only a few blocks away ignore your plea for assistance and drive in the opposite direction?

These possible consequences had little influence on the black officers that chose to practice these informant type tactics; their contention was that rarely did they receive backup from white officers anyway, especially the ones they considered racist. And as far as being branded a "Snitch," they could care less; this is one of the kinder names they have been referred to as. To the folks in the black community these rebellious officers were often looked on as heroes and local leaders of the civil rights movement. They were considered a liaison to a system that traditionally ignored them.

The strategy being employed by these black officers in theory held some merit, because no person should ever be degraded, insulted or brutalized because of their race. However, this approach would backfire and be used by the unlawful, and dishonest, as well as those with a personal agenda.

It wasn't long before the criminal element realized they could get out of a legal predicament by simply making an official complaint, a complaint that was often a complete fabrication, but never-the-less would remove the light of suspicion from them and cast it on the officer. This simple allegation would initiate a lengthy inquisition as well as a mountain of paperwork.

Narcotic dealers were notorious for this tactic, they knew their complaint would initiate an immediate investigation and the accused officers were usually ordered to avoid the complainant during the inquiry. Consequently, the establishment had given the dope man a license to sell drugs during the period of the investigation, because any contact with the suspect during this period would be construed as a form of harassment.

Unfortunately, some of the mediocre cops were intentionally avoiding high drug traffic areas out of fear of false accusations. Once again the system had given birth to a new problem by attempting to solve another, bureaucracy at its best, the system wins and the citizens loose!

I have always considered myself a no-nonsense cop and I have been known to send a thug or two to the hospital when they would resist arrest or attempted to hurt me or one of mine. Have I lost my temper and went too far? Absolutely, and that is where a good partner comes in, by making you aware you have or are about to cross the line. But I and those I am associated with never beat a man unjustifiably just to see him bleed. That would be like putting a muzzle on a chained dog and then kicking it unconscious. That is not manly, that is man-less and in my opinion those who engage in such practices are not only a disgrace to the badge, they make it difficult for the next cop that attempts to arrest this guy. How would you like to have to live with the fact that because of your cowardly, unethical acts you created a cop killer? If a dog knows he's going to receive a beating even when complying, why shouldn't he aggressively attack first?

Spring was fast approaching and the anticipation of another hot violent summer was on everyone's mind. White officers were hesitantly accepting the reality that Coleman Young was indeed the mayor and would remain so for at least the next four years. Other than a few derogatory remarks, things were at least tolerable in the precinct. The brothers stayed to themselves as did the white guys, and worked together only when manpower offered no other alternative. The bosses knew that for the most part, whites preferred working with whites and blacks preferred working with their own, this was a tradition the department was reluctant to change. I guess you could say it was a form of acceptable discrimination. As small-minded as it may sound one typically has more in common with a person of the same race, which helps immensely when you are confined to the same scout car for eight hours.

Many stories exist in the department of incidents from years past concerning cruel behavior toward black officers when supervisors arbitrarily assigned them with senior white officers. One account shared with me was an incident where a white senior officer's partner called in sick, giving the lieutenant no alternative other than to assign the only available officer who incidentally was black, with the old-timer. The senior white officer was so disturbed over this decision he placed a partition made of cardboard in the scout car between the driver and passenger seats. He then advised the black officer, "I may have to work with your black ass, but I damn sure don't have to look at you or talk to you."

It was also common knowledge in those days that if a black officer witnessed excessive force being used, he was expected to practice the code of silence or else! The reprisal for reporting a white officer could initiate actions ranging from the silent treatment, physical violence, to malicious destruction of property, i.e., vandalism to the officer's vehicle or personal property. As disturbing as these reports are, I assure you they did take place and can be confirmed by many of the white and black officers of that era.

This type of mindset displayed by the old regime put the black officers of that day in quite an awkward position. Unlike today, there were only a handful of black officers on the force and their demeanor on the street was quite often the deciding factor on whether they were declared "A good old color boy" or an "uppity nigger." Their white counterparts were constantly scrutinizing their every move, so, consequently, some of the black officers would intentionally be twice as aggressive with black citizens as a way to gain acceptance and a reputation as a tough no-nonsense black cop or a "good old boy" that could be trusted.

Many stories have been shared about a legendary black officer by the name of "Rotation Slim," I'm sure some are true and others extremely embellished, if not outright fabricated.

Rotation Slim walked a foot beat in the infamous Black Bottom and was known to enforce the law by some very unorthodox means. He was known for his pearl-handled .38 caliber revolver that he sported on his side, along with his violent treatment of black folks that failed to comply with his sometime self-imposed laws. He was said to clear a corner of youths by simply telling them if any of them are found on the corner upon his return, they were going to the hospital. This was no idle threat, Slim, reportedly on numerous occasions was responsible for sending men to the hospital or leaving them lying in the street beaten to a bloody pulp with his trademark pistol.

Another story described that, on one occasion, Rotation Slim was reportedly walking a beat with a new black rookie right out of the Police Academy. Several hours into the shift, the young officer began to complain to Slim that he expected a lot more action on the street. Slim, after hearing this complaint repeatedly, allegedly said, "You want action I'll show you action," at which time he pulled the young rookie into a nearby alley, pulled out his pearl-handled .38 and shot the overzealous kid in the leg. Not quite the role model for any officer black or white.

As you may imagine "Rotation Slim" was accepted and admired by the veteran cops of that era, because he mimicked many white officers in their heavy-handed enforcement tactics. He also displayed an attitude held by numerous old-timers, which was that the majority of blacks were nothing more than primates who were incapable of reasoning and could only be dealt with aggressively.

The sad thing was that some blacks gave the impression that this mindset was acceptable, believing that they were inferior to whites and that is just a fact of life. I imagine if you are told every day of your life that you are substandard to others, you eventually begin to believe it. One can only wonder how many slipped through the cracks because of little if any self-esteem due to insecure attitudes and lack of self-confidence derived through mental abuse.

This type of abuse is exactly what Coleman Young has promised to eliminate during his tenure in office, which is understandable to any clear-thinking individual. Although I must say his methods and attitude toward whites in general, especially white officers were often perceived to be racist in nature and filled with vengeance. I found it very interesting that the very mayor, who promised to eliminate the racist non-compassionate white old-timers from the department, displayed many of the same traits he accused them of.

The two recognized police unions: the Detroit Police Officer Association (DPOA) and the Lieutenants & Sergeants Association (L&S) were overwhelmed with grievances from their membership for unfair labor practices toward the department and the city. Each grievance generated an investigation that could take months, and in some cases years, to resolve.

The department under the Coleman Young administration, seemed to adopt a premise that new polices would be implemented whether they were against the union contract or not and if grieved, they would deal with it one case at a time knowing quite well that the grievance procedure could and most likely would be very lengthy.

This was the beginning of a confrontation between the unions and city that would last the entire Coleman Young era and beyond. Young was quite an adversary for the unions, because of his experiences representing auto workers, he knew all the tricks of the trade, believe me. He used them to his advantage in everyday business as well as in contract negotiations.

It was becoming quite clear that this was Coleman Young's town now and he was making up the rules as he went along. It was not uncommon for him to attack tradition just to prove a point. I'm sure he believed tradition is one of the main reasons there was a lack of progress within the black culture. It was obvious that if city workers wanted pay increases and/or benefit packages it was going to be an upward battle all the way, because the "Old Man" was not giving us anything without a fight and it didn't matter whether you were black or white, this was simply about economics.

It was often said that when it came to money Young was colorblind and treated every city employee equally. If cutbacks or concessions were found to be necessary there was no favoritism displayed. It affected all of us no matter what your race. This arrogant regime inferred if you don't like it you could quit or file a grievance, there was little room for diplomatic compromise. It was apparent this was Coleman A. Young's World and we were just renting a space until we retired!

CHAPTER "YEAR OF THE WOMEN" 7

WELL HERE WE ARE, 1975 HAS arrived and having women patrolling the streets of the "Murder Capital of the World" is no longer a rumor. They're here and here to stay. Two precincts were designated as the pilot precincts for women patrol officers: the Twelfth Precinct on the Westside of the city and the Seventh Precinct on the Eastside.

To say that emotions were running high within the department was an understatement. Most officers proclaimed publicly that they did not want to work with split tails, a term used for women within the ranks. A much larger concern was the effect it was already having within the households of male officers. The wives were livid over the thought of their significant others working in the confinement of a police vehicle for eight hours with another women. My wife was a slight more civil and understanding; she indicated as long as it remained on a professional level she understood. However, should it ever escalate to a personal level, she would blow my damn head off with a shotgun while I slept. What a lady!

The day the ladies arrived the precinct took on a carnival like atmosphere, male officers from the midnight shift that typically leave as soon as they were relieved are suddenly in no hurry to depart. All these officers decided to congregate in the garage laughing like school kids along with the day shift as they awaited the arrival of the new rookies, officers that would be equipped with more than a sidearm and handcuffs and yes there were plenty of handcuff jokes going around.

As the ladies arrived in the parking lot silence prevailed, to the point you could hear the officer next to you breathing while we gawked like a bunch of voyeurs. They varied in size and race, although the majority of the women assigned to the Seventh Precinct were white. Their uniforms were much like ours other than the few modifications to accommodate the female anatomy. As they entered the garage two and three at a time, for precautionary reasons I'm sure, the schoolboy taunting began in attempts to embarrass the ladies as well as making them aware of our disapproval of women officers on the street. "Hey baby you want to see my gun?" "I can't wait to get you on midnights." "You take care of me baby and I'll take care of you on the street." And: "When the shit hits the fan you are on your own bitch." These were just a few of the vicarious macho remarks made by our brave boy's in blue.

The lady officers ignored the cruel comments as though they didn't even hear them, a technique taught to women at an early age. Their educators who were quite often mothers, would advise the young ladies to ignore their prey as if they didn't exist, knowing quite well this would intrigue the male species, causing them to do exactly what the female expected, pursue them and eventually believe they conquered their victim as she agreed to a date proposition, yea right!

Suddenly, the garage door opened and in walked another cluster of ladies and I must say this group was stunning; three were brunettes with long hair that was tied up in buns and bodies that were to die for. The fourth was a blonde with beautiful blue eyes, a chest that Dolly Parton would be proud of, not to mention a fragrance that silenced as well as aroused those in the immediate area. Within moments, I witnessed strong fearless cops that were quite capable of determining whether an individual lives or dies, revert to their boyhood days with hormones raging and priorities all shot to hell, all over the scent of a women.

Oh yea, there was a storm brewing on the horizon of the Seventh Precinct and it didn't take a meteorologist to forecast huge problems in the near future. Men and women have worked side by side in the corporate world for years with limited incidents. However, I would suggest they were not subjected to being in such close proximity for such long periods, day after day and to complicate matters further, they would share the adrenalin rush one feels in life and death situations quite often giving partners an intimacy that most marriages will never experience.

The precinct inspector welcomed the new officers and I must say it was quite a sight. It was hilarious to see him tripping over his tongue, while attempting to be so accommodating to the ladies. I never observed the man smile so much; actually, to be very frank, I wasn't sure if he had teeth until that day. The only time I ever saw the inspector as a rookie was when he was walking to his vehicle at the end of his shift. The over-obliging and double standards had begun.

After receiving their assignments to their prospective shifts, the ladies were advised to report for duty the following day, making their first day on the job a very short one. This kind gesture by the inspector was appreciated by the female officer's, but unfortunately opened the door for an enormous amount of criticism from the senior guys who witnessed it.

As the women exited the precinct, one of the desk personnel made his displeasure quite obvious with a remark that was intended to be over heard and it was. " Ain't this a bitch, no pun intended, I've been a cop for eight years and never got off early and these bitches walk in and get off after working only three hours. I guess all you need is a set of tits to get special treatment around here." I thought to myself, are you just finding this out today, what a revelation? This guy was either never married or dwelled in a cave far removed from the opposite gender.

The new arrivals were needless to say the hot topic in every scout car that day and would continue at choir practice that evening, with vows of unity between the partners, swearing never to display preferential treatment toward female officers. As I listened to these hollow promises I couldn't help but think of the episode on the original Little Rascal comedy series which aired many years ago, where Spanky and Alfalfa founded the "Women Haters Club" swearing to never let women interfere with their male bond. It, too, fell like a deck of cards when the rubber hit the road.

The clock was fast approaching 2 a.m. and believe it or not all the great minds present at Z's bar tonight were unable to resolve any of the world issues, go figure! "I'm out of here guy's, I've got court in the morning and 7a.m. is going to sneak up on me awfully fast, I'll see you ladies tomorrow." My sarcastic remark failed to get the reaction I expected from my intoxicated colleagues and it was probably just as well, it could have re-ignited the fire that was fought earlier in the evening.

The next morning came without warning as the alarm blurted out with its annoying buzzer. Today history was being made as women hit the streets of Detroit as full-fledged patrol officers. I could smell the coffee brewing down stairs as I entered the shower in a semi-comatose state. The hot water pouring down over my body eased the pain of my morning headache, which was becoming a familiar occurrence. Suddenly the bathroom door opened; through the steam of the shower I could detect an image of my wife placing my coffee on the sink. "Is everything alright in there honey? You sure are taking an unordinary amount of time in there today; you would think you are preparing for a date or something." I anticipated some cynical comments; I just didn't expect them to start so soon. "So what's your point? You know damn well

I take long showers and you are also quite aware of my stance on these women!" "Calm down officer I'm just joking," said with an air of sarcasm, which told me she was getting her point across in a way only a wife can.

As I made my descent down the stairs, the odor of bacon and eggs cooking coming from the kitchen was over whelming and any other day would have been inviting, but this morning my stomach was doing the tango and without me. She was preparing breakfast for our son Dave Jr., who was involved in his morning ritual of watching the Power Ranger cartoons prior to school. "No breakfast for me, I have to pick up Bob, his car is in the shop." "Say bye-bye to daddy son, he's off to see all the girls." "Please let it go, the only thing I want to see out there is criminals." I could see my wife had that obvious smirk on her face, a smirk that says, yea right; you can attempt to sell those goods elsewhere. "Have a good day honey, please be careful and don't forget who butters your bread." As irritating as her comments were, I certainly could understand her apprehension concerning the women. I know if the circumstances were reversed, I would be beside myself.

When I pulled in front of Bob's house, I could see he, too, was having a bonding conversation with his wife Judy on the front porch and it didn't appear as though he was contributing a lot, he was definitely the listener. As he observed me pull up, his expression appeared to cry out, Thank God you're here, I am so tired of hearing about women on the job. I honked the horn, in an attempt to shorten his sermon as well as keeping us on our timetable. As Bob entered the car, his frustration said volumes. "Good morning Bob, are you OK?" "Do I look OK? All I have heard since I woke up this morning is, police women this and police women that. I haven't even met these bitches yet, and I am catching hell already."

By the time we reached the Precinct, I had devised a plan to embarrass the new female rookies as well as get a laugh from my male coworkers. As we entered the locker room, which had been crudely divided to accommodate privacy for the ladies, I observed through the open door approximately six female officers in full uniform standing in a cluster in the squad room. There was a lone brunette near the coke machine talking with Hinders one of the black officers on the shift. Now I'm not sure if they were just having idle chit chat or he was making his move on the new recruit, but either way, the white guy's would perceive his conversation as an advancement on a white woman and, as the black officers were quite aware, this drove many insane. As one black officer explained "White men have taken our women out of our arms for hundreds of years, just because they could, and now that we can legitimately sleep with white women who are more than willing, you insecure white men can't handle it. It's called pay back!"

The locker room, which typically smelled like a high school gym, now sported the pleasant odor of female cologne and, wait, there's a second aroma, I'll be damn, its cheap after-shave, the same guy's that had taken vows of celibacy less than 12 hours ago are now concerned with their scent. So much for the infamous "Women Hater Club", the women have won the war and we had not even had our first battle, men are such wimps when it comes to the female species.

It was 7.45 a.m. and roll call was about to begin. As I peeked out the door of the locker room, I noticed something very peculiar; we now had three distinct groups, the whites, blacks and now the females, how much more divided could we be? I attempted to keep myself concealed until roll call began and the ranks were formed. Suddenly I heard "Alright fall in" at which point I hurriedly exited the locker room and joined the rear rank of the formation squeezing in-between two of the new female officers. I was clad in my full uniform minus my pants. Yes, there I stood with all my leather ware, boots, shirt and hat, yet nude from my waist down; however, my shirttails covered my business. I wanted to make a statement while not being totally obscene.

As the lieutenant began handing out the assignments, the entire rear row began to release their restrained laughter, which the lieutenant found very annoying. "All right folks knock it off, I have one hell of a headache today and I don't need any problems." Oh this is wonderful I thought, the day I pick to be a clown, the boss is ill, just great. By this time, the front rank including the remainder of the women, were laughing hysterically. The lieutenant walked around the formation and observed me standing there pant less, shaking his head he simply stated "Stealth, you have totally lost it, I don't even know how to write this one up." Fortunately, he had a good sense of humor and ignored my child like behavior while completing roll call with a grin on his face the entire time.

Assignments for that day were definitely designed around the ladies. Several of us were separated from are usual partners and assigned a rookie female, while others were assigned a lady as a third person on the car. This was a logical but untypical move by management, who, I'm sure, were concerned about liability. However, it was clearly a double standard that left many of us with an uncomfortable thought: Was this an indication of the administration's stance on equality? If so it was transparent as hell and one-sided, ostensibly saying, "Treat female officers as equals, but regardless of the circumstances let no harm come to them."

My partner for the day was Officer Jenny Hawes, a cute little blonde, but I must say my emphasis was focused more on her size than her looks, she couldn't have weighed more than 110 pounds soaking wet and stood about 5'2", not very intimidating. This was quite a contrast from my usual partners, who are guys that go well over 200 pounds and are threatening just by their mere presence. I could only imagine the outcome if the ca ca hits the fan, I most likely would be fighting for two, as opposed to just holding my own. The other men on the shift shared my concerns, so we agreed to back one another up far more than we were accustomed to.

"Hi! I guess you're stuck with me today, the name's

Dave." "I'm Jenny and it's more like you got stuck with me." Her introduction was accompanied by a pleasant smile and a tone that was almost apologetic. "Jenny why don't you follow the guys and sign out a prep radio, I'll get the shotgun and meet you out at the car." "Sure thing Dave" As she walked away I couldn't help but to notice her voluptuous body as did every other officer gifted with sight. On any other day, I would be dreaming of having her in my vehicle, but as a partner in a life and death situation, the jury was still out and only time would tell.

Guys in the precinct were walking around with a smirk on their face that was reminiscent of kids at an amusement park waiting in line to ride the roller coaster for the first time. They were intrigued yet frightened of the unknown. But one thing was becoming quite apparent, many of my macho counterparts who swore they would never cater to the ladies were losing their edge in record time, smiling like kids in a candy store and were so over-accommodating I wanted to gag. I was waiting for them to open the scout car door for the ladies as if they were on a date. I was not such a pessimist that I would insinuate women officers would never be effective on the street, however, there were many issues that needed to be addressed and the learning curve could be devastating.

Shortly after pulling off the ramp, my temporary partner found the courage to speak up, "Dave I realize or I should say we realize, you guys don't want us on the street, but all I ask for is a chance and if I fail then your opinion will be justified."

Her voice was not that of a pleading woman, it was stern and matter-of-fact, immediately it brought to mind the request I asked of Jerome, the Malcolm-X wannabe, to accept me on performance not on perception.

This little lady definitely appeared to have character. "Look Jenny I'm not going to whitewash this, I do not like the idea of a woman replacing my male partner, who without question, is capable of handling most of the situations we will encounter. Nevertheless, you have a valid point, so I will attempt to remain open-minded until the facts prove otherwise, is that fair enough? "Absolutely Dave, I can't ask for anymore then that" "Ok Jenny, how about a coffee before we get our hands dirty?"

As we entered the Click restaurant, all eyes turned toward us, this was not out of the ordinary because cops usually arouse interest wherever they go, I think it's a combination of the uniform, gun and the obvious authority that accompanies the title. Nevertheless, this time a new novelty came into play, a female in uniform! The patrons thoughts were oh so transparent behind the condescending grins they wore that articulated: What in the hell is she going to do? Who in the hell is she going to scare? I wouldn't want her as a partner, but I sure would like to see her in the leather gear minus the uniform! Should I go on? I don't think it's necessary you get my point.

It wasn't long before a few other units, two of which were gender mixed, joined us. Roger was assigned with a little redheaded officer and Robbie was with a little lady named Linda. My heart went out to the officer assigned with Roger, because her day would be filled with stories of his heroic acts and how he and he alone keeps the Seventh Precinct safe from all the heathens. The irony is that he actually is a very courageous man; if he could only lose the chip on his shoulder and his cynical outlook he could actually be a decent mentor.

The atmosphere at the table was anything but normal today, the crude remarks concerning the waitresses and what services could be provided for them were absent, as well as much of the foul language . The polite request of "Please pass the cream" was also uncharacteristic. It was comparable to a night out with our significant others, with everyone on their best behavior.

Well, this thought was blown out of the water real quick, as Roger spoke up as only he could with his words of wisdom. "So, you ladies think you can handle these fucking animals out here? This is the real thing, not the academy where you play act!" The entire table just looked at each other lost for words, the women held an expression that screamed, "Where in the hell did this come from?" "Come on Rodge not today, not now, let's enjoy our coffee." "Robbie, I just want to know if they think they can handle the street, we're all thinking it, I'm just the one with enough balls to ask the question." Goofy had a point; we were all wondering how they would perform under duress. Even so, as usual, his delivery was less then elegant. Jenny, spoke up, "Only time will tell Roger, we are quite aware we're rookies and aren't declaring ourselves as cops yet, that's just our goal." Her remarks were a slight less authoritative as they were with me earlier; nonetheless, they were not only excellent they actually shut Roger up, that in and of itself was quite an accomplishment.

"7-5, west of Chene, north of Warren in the alley three men striping a blue ford van" Jenny's look was almost laughable, it seemed to say," Why us, can't they assign that run to someone else?" "Jenny, you have the radio, just say, on the way radio 7-5." She seemed to snap out of it as she notified the dispatcher that we received the information and were in route. Her reaction was very typical of a rookie, it is your first police run in a hopefully long career and you just want your performance to be acceptable and professional. "Dave we will back you up." "Thanks, Robbie why don't you come in from the south and we'll come in from the north side." Rodge also indicated he would join us; an offer that typically would have been welcomed. Yet, my concerns today were that he might go overboard in attempts of impressing the new female officers.

As usual, in our haste we left our coffee cups half-full, this is a common occurrence in our business, you're not on an authorized break and must remain in service. It seems more often than not you will get a radio run as soon as your coffee is served. Our waitress Judy, yelled out "Hey guy's you want us to keep the coffee hot?" "No thanks Judy, we're not sure when we will be back." What Judy really meant, is Robbie returning? It was common knowledge that Judy was attracted to Robbie and she had no problem letting the world in on it. Robbie was a handsome man, with a great built and could charm the pants off most any lady and usually did, but he considered Judy just a little too substantial for his taste.

"Now look Jenny, when we pull in the alley these idiots are going to take off like a bat out of hell so be ready to run. Robbie will be coming in from the other direction, so no shooting, you might hit one of the good guys. There is nothing out here worth dying for except saving your partner or the helpless, ok? Punks and Crime will be here long after we are gone." "Got it Dave, thanks."

Our tires squealed as we pulled into the alley, probably just low on air, nonetheless it gave our adversaries a few seconds warning that wasn't intended. There were four black males who immediately took off in typical fashion, four different directions, a technique that minimizes arrest, and no doubt had been discussed as well as rehearsed. Before I could open my mouth, Jenny was out of the car and running like a deer pursuing one of the suspects. "Radio 7-5, my partner is on foot west in the alley north of Warren chasing a black male, 6', 180 lbs. wearing black pants and a grey sweatshirt." Communication is an officer's ally on the street, it allows other officers to find and assist you as opposed to searching for you blindly.

I pulled around the stripped vehicle with intentions of going west around the block and corralling the thug Jenny was chasing. Unfortunately, Robbie's scout car was unoccupied, with doors open and blocking the alley, Murphy's Law was coming into play. I immediately went to plan B, which was activating my vehicles emergency equipment as I traveled against traffic on Warren to get to my partner as fast as possible. Jenny was not responding to my request for her location and status, which indicated one or two situations were occurring: she was in trouble or she was not monitoring her prep-radio. As I turned the corner, I had a pleasant surprise, my new partner had the suspect spread eagle on the ground, standing over him in a combat stance with her gun pointed directly at his back. I'll be damned not only can she run, she has moxie as well!

"Radio, 7-5, my partner has one suspect in custody, make us out of service to the station with an arrest." "10-4 you are busy with your arrest 7-5." "Jenny I would ask you if I could give you a hand but it sure appears you have this situation under control." "Dave I have not searched or read him his rights." I noticed her hands were beginning to tremble and her voice sounded a slight bit shaky. She obviously was experiencing a little post-arrest syndrome; a condition that appears with some when one realizes what just happened or what may have happened. "Good job kid, everything is going to be fine, put your gun away and I'll take it from here."

The suspect received a minor facial injury during the pursuit and arrest, nothing of a serious nature just a small abrasion, but an injury never the less that would have to be explained. "What happened to your face man?" "That bitch beat me for nothing that's what the hell happened." "Brother, let me make sure I understand this, you are saying this little lady chased you down, a man who stands approximately 6'2," weighing somewhere around 200-lbs. and then assaulted you? I'm not so sure I would want my buddies to hear that story." My sarcasm didn't affect this clown at all, he was determined to use any means necessary including making false accusations against Jenny to minimize the severity of his crime while placing the attention on the arresting officers.

Jenny was silent until we were a block or so from the precinct when she suddenly turned around and glared at the prisoner with that look, the look only a mother or angered women is capable of delivering. The stare that tells most men, we have just crossed the line! "You black bastard, you know damn well your lying, I never laid a hand on you!" Woe! This little lady was hot and apparently harnessed some thoughts concerning blacks or at least black criminals. "Calm down Jenny, don't take it personally, this ass hole is quite aware that a complaint will take the heat off of him. Your job is to write it up like it happened and move on." "I'm sure you're right Dave, I just detest having false accusations being brought against me."

"Well Jenny, you sure chose the wrong profession if you don't like false accusations, because in today's world false accusations are merely part of the defense system."

The word spread like wild fire that Jenny made her first

arrest and naturally the rumor had her beating the hell out of the defendant, which was a total fabrication. Yet, there were those on both sides who found this account very useful in their hateful agenda. Some blacks believed it was a rite of passage, which allowed her acceptance by the "Good Old White Boy Club," a club some believed, existed with the sole purpose of brutalizing blacks. On the other hand there would be those whites that would say, "That girl is alright, she beat the shit out of a big tough brother." Then there were those that just said she did what she's paid to do and did it right. All in all Jenny accepted the teasing very well and was quick to squash any versions that were unrelated to the truth, which I found very admirable for a rookie.

Once the prisoner was processed, I suggested we take our code 9330 (lunch) at a restaurant where we would be unlikely to run into any of our colleagues, this would give us an opportunity to reevaluate the arrest and get Jenny's reaction on all the hoopla. We sat down at Patsy place, a small Tavern that serves a great kielbasa sandwich and was located in a small city within the borders of Detroit and is largely populated by Polish immigrants.

Patsy was a tall attractive blonde with gorgeous eyes and was very well endowed. She was one of the kindest ladies I have ever known. Anytime a cop was in trouble she was there, sponsoring a benefit to raise money or at minimum, making a generous donation. Patsy was also known for her bar antics and unsavory language. If angered, she could make a sailor blush with her choice of four-letter words.

When introduced to new rookies, this lady would have them squirming in their pants within seconds, she would either grab them by the crotch asking them to dance or pull up her blouse revealing her huge breasts which she would place inches from their face. Patsy found great pleasure in their embarrassing reaction.

"Patsy this is Jenny, she's one of our new officers" "Hi! Jenny, how in the fuck are ya?" Fortunately, I had enlightened Jenny concerning Patsy and the possibility of her using less then appropriate language for the shock factor. "Nice meeting you Patsy, I have heard a lot about you and yes, it was all good." She smiled and invited Jenny to come up on a payday night and party. Payday for cops are like a holiday, everyone has money and bars like hers were always filled with girls that for some reason were attracted to cops.

After placing our order, Jenny and I enjoyed some small talk, but it was obvious she had much more on her mind as I did. "So Jenny, how's it feel to have your first arrest under your belt?" "It feels great Dave, I can't express the rush I received chasing and catching that idiot, it's like nothing I have ever experienced before." "It's better than sex, hey?" "No, I won't go that far, but pretty damn close." "Well, I want you to know you did ok out there today, but, be aware that all arrests will not be that easy. It could have gotten really ugly if that big sucker wanted to fight, or tried to get your gun. By the way where did the statement "You black bastard" come from? Do I detect a little prejudice in you officer?" said with a smile. "Dave, I'm from Georgia and was raised around some real bigots where the word nigger was commonly used. No, I don't believe in the mixing of races, but I think I have matured enough to realize that you have blacks and then you have niggers," a statement as we have discussed is frequently used by those who were attempting to justify their hidden bigotry.

The more she tried to explain her statement used during the arrest, the deeper the hole she dug. I attempted to comfort Jenny by informing her that I too had Southern roots and have used less than appropriate terms to describe the opposite race during my life. "Jenny, just try to control your instilled feelings, these are words used in the past and that is where they need to remain." She nodded in agreement; apparently realizing how severe the consequences could be from a statement made in the heat of a moment. "No harm done Jenny, just be careful and please don't mimic any of our resident bigots, black or white, they are so filled with hate they detest everyone, including themselves."

By the end of the shift Jenny and I had become very familiar with one another, she revealed her entire life story as well as making it very clear she and her husband were not doing so well, way more information then was required or needed. As we put the equipment away I was tempted to invite my momentary partner to join us at the bar, however, fears of the invitation being taken out of context prevented me from doing so. Not to mention, rookies are never invited to stop until they prove themselves on the street, which sometime takes months.

I had a few calls to make at the precinct prior to joining the fellows for that well deserved drink, which I'm sure would be accompanied by numerous accounts of the females first day on the street, which at minimum promised many laughs. This is one day the entire shift would be stopping and I was no exception.

Upon arriving at Z's I found it curious that there were an abnormal amount of vehicles parked around the tavern, a thought that I would soon have answered. As I entered the bar I could not believe my eyes, standing with the guys were at least eight of the rookie ladies, including Jenny. It was quite apparent that the rules had changed, at least when it came to spit tails. Inviting a rookie out for a drink on the first day is unheard of and totally went against tradition. I'm sure my expression supported my surprise.

"Hi! Dave, long-time no see." said with a half smirk. "Hey Jenny I didn't expect to see you ladies up here." "Obviously Dave, you look like you've seen a ghost. Sarah was invited to stop for a drink by her partner, unlike me, (said with sarcasm), so she asked a few of us girls to join her, that's not a problem is it?" I could feel my face turning red, and a sensation similar to that of a man being discovered in a compromising situation came over me. "Uh, not at all Jenny, it's a free country and after today I'm sure you could use a drink or two."

Soon the sexes were shoulder to shoulder with some engaged in deep conversations while others laughed hysterically over crude cop jokes. The bar had taken on the atmosphere of a nightclub pick up joint. All indications pointed to big time trouble on home fronts. Opposite genders can remain professional in a work environment, even ours. However, when you spend eight hours in close proximity with one of the opposite sex and then continue this relationship off duty in a drinking setting, well, situations will arise.

It wasn't long before one of the fellows raised his glass in a show of endorsement for Jenny's arrest as he initiated the chant: "Here's to Jenny raise your glass, here's to Jenny she's a horses ass." Jenny, who was feeling no pain became quite embarrassed, which made her even more attractive. It was quite apparent the boys and girls were playing well together.

Once again Z was screaming last call and advising us to get the hell out so he could retire. On this particular night, everyone left separately, just like the ladies and gentlemen we were. Unfortunately, this pattern would not last for long, it was quite apparent that many of us tonight were just one drink away from initiating an affair. Tomorrow was another day, many of us had court and we all certainly had a never-ending honey-do list that our spouses waited patiently to be completed. For many of us, everything became secondary to the police work, even are home life.

It wasn't long before the girls began to frequent our drinking establishments on a nightly basis and partnerships were

starting to develop on and off the job. I was witnessing insep-
arable partnerships falling apart due to newfound infatuation
between one of the male partners and a female officer. It was
also crossing over into the racial sector. A few black officers
were becoming very friendly with several of the white female
officers and, believe me, their flirting drove some white officers out of their minds and the brothers were quite aware of
the effect it had on them.

Dating or even flirting with one of the opposite race
was considered taboo by numerous whites and blacks. If a
lady of either race had an affair she was considered tainted
goods by many men and not worthy of a genuine relationship.
However, some might say the actual reason was they were not
sure if they could follow the brother's act in bed. Whites for
years have heard the fable of the black man's lower anatomy
superiority, to the point some feel threatened or inferior. Now
I have been around blacks all my life, and I can attest some
blacks have been blessed in that sense, while others were out
right robbed. Yet, the myth lives on.

One of the most revolting, cruel and insensitive incidents
I witnessed during my career took place within the first six
months of the females' arrival. It occurred shortly after a white
female on the shift began discretely dating one of the black
officers. Once her trust was gained and they were several
dates into the affair, the brother secretly placed a tape recorder
under the bed with intentions of recording her while having
sex. During this encounter the female officer was requested

to make flattering remarks concerning her new found black lover during their passionate love session. He later played the recording in the precinct locker room at full volume for the brothers, who laughed hysterically. Unfortunately, they were not the only audience; white officers also heard it as well as the female victim who was dressing with her female counterparts in the adjoining locker room.

The female, needless to say was totally distraught due to the enormous level of humiliation she experienced by this heinous act of betrayal. She was now caught between the two worlds, the white men wanted nothing to do with her and she was a standing joke in the black community. The level of anxiety she experienced was so high she nearly had a nervous breakdown and subsequently transferred to a different precinct. Unfortunately, tales of the incident transferred with her.

Several months after the females' arrival, management began assigning two females alone in a scout car. In these cases we would attempt to back them up when they received runs of a serious nature. Although, several incidents had occurred recently that gave reason for concern as well as to lending to the argument of whether women should work alone or not.

The first incident occurred when a suspect refused to be hand cuffed. My partner and I were dispatched to assist 7-2 in an arrest, upon our arrival we found the two female officers in the backyard standing face to face with a suspect that appeared to be approximately 6 feet weighing about 200 pounds and obviously intoxicated. "What's the problem Kathy?" "Dave, we placed this gentleman under arrest, but he said no, he's not going to jail." "Kathy in the first place he is not a gentleman, if he was he would have let you escort him to jail properly. Secondly, you are the sheriff in town and this makes you responsible for preventing total chaos from erupting in our streets. Nobody and I do mean nobody informs you they are not going to jail even if it costs you an ass whipping or worst, arrest are non-negotiable!"

"Ok pal, here is the way it is, you are either going to jail or to the hospital and it doesn't matter to me what your choice is, so what will it be?" I began pulling my handcuffs out as I moved toward the suspect, the defiant look he had been sporting earlier suddenly disappeared as he dropped his head turned around placing his hands together behind his back in a very submissive fashion, this was clearly not his first rodeo. He was then placed in Kathy's rear seat for transportation.

"Dave, thanks a million; we didn't know how to handle this situation." "No problem Kathy, anytime. Just remember that badge doesn't run from anyone or anything. I don't care how scared you are, you must move forward and take control of the situation or die trying.

The second incident as I recall, took place when two female officers responded to a holdup alarm at a local party store. Holdup alarms are frequently found to be bogus, being tripped unknowingly by an employee or even weather conditions can activate a system. These mishaps unfortunately often cause the responding officers to expect a false alarm, which consequently makes them take the dispatch less than serious, this could be a deadly mistake!

When the dispatched vehicle arrived, they found the two female officers sitting on the stairs of the party store crying. Apparently, when they entered the business the holdup men disarmed the ladies of their side-arms as well as a 12 gauge shotgun, how embarrassing. This is not to insinuate that male officers have not been disarmed, because they have, but the crying on the stairs is a bit much. These were two lucky cops; a habitual criminal may have killed both of them with their own weapon.

All and all, I must say the females were merely committing rookie mistakes; gender wasn't really relevant at all. Regrettably, in the world of law enforcement, mistakes are a form of education. We learn from our sisters and brothers who have sacrificed sometimes with their lives!

Yes, the first year of the women had proven to be very interesting, six divorces had taken place and many new relationships have begun, you talk about a Peyton Place, there were wild parties every night, parties that would have made Sodom & Gomorrah blush. No, I wasn't exempt from the casualties, I wasn't divorced yet, however, while attending a birthday party for Mary Ann, one of our most attractive lady officers, I met a beautiful little Italian lady by the name of Penny, who I would fall deeply in love with, marry and eventually be gifted with a gorgeous daughter.

What became quite clear is that females had earned the

right to join our ranks. Not only did they earn the respect they deserved, many became regarded as excellent cops who, without a doubt, would lay their life down for fellow officers. Welcome aboard brave ladies in blue!

"MY BEST FRIEND, A RACIST?" 8

THIS DAY THAT STARTED OUT LIKE any other, would turn out to be anything but normal. I was assigned to work Scout 7-3 with Officer Bob Field, which was a pleasure in and of itself, he was the most diligent officer I had ever met and led the shift in arrest, felonies and misdemeanors. Working with Bob always assured one of an interesting evening. Dispatch advised all cars that we had a backlog of 25 police runs and each car was receiving two runs at a time while requesting us to get back into service as soon as possible. This was going to be a crazy night, I could just sense it.

Bob and I have become quite close over the years. It's difficult not to become close to a person that shares so many of your values, we both had very high work ethics accompanied by a great sense of humor. He is a man with a heart the size of Texas but also a force to be reckoned with when angered, the epitome of a "cop." Yet, there were those who disliked Bob, they were typically the do nothing or average cops, whose outstanding trait was laziness. They would continuously complain Bob was "Trying to kill the job," a phrase used by slackers, which simply implied you need to slow your production down because you're making us look bad. Bob would simply laugh and say, "They don't need my assistance; they're doing a decent job looking bad on their own."

Young working cops are often tattooed "Hot Dogs" by the sandbaggers or old-timers who have had their day in the sun and are just dog-tired. Real cops pay no attention to this gibberish and tenaciously continue enforcing the law. Because in reality these clowns are envious and just do not possess the right stuff to be a decent cop. There are those that work for their paycheck and those who just collect it.

There were also a few radical black officers' who detested Bob, labeling him a racist that loved to beat brothers. There could not be anything further from the truth. The fact of the matter is that when you search out the most violent offenders of the law as he does, then the likelihood of having a confrontation with a defendant who resists arrest doubles. It's really a no-brainier, the more arrests you make, especially of violent offenders, the odds of an altercation increase accordingly. Dah!

Bob is a large burly man who wears his cop face around the clock, disappearing only on the occasions when he is laughing. It is easy to understand why brothers or just people in general would interpret his expression as one of anger or even hatred. I can assure you that look prevented more altercations then it has ignited.

"7-3 East Grand Blvd. and Gratiot man with a gun at the bus stop, description is as follows: Black Male 6'2" 180 lbs. wearing a red hooded sweatshirt and blue jeans." "10-4 radio 7-3 on the way." Bob was driving and I was jumping, which meant if this run is valid, it would be my responsibility to catch this character should he grow wings.

Traffic was heavy and it took a few creative maneuvers by Bob to get through traffic, we didn't want to turn the toys on (siren and lights) in fear of alerting the suspect of our presence. One more light and we would have the location in view. As we approached we could not believe our eyes, at the bus stop were six black males all wearing red hooded sweatshirts. "I don't believe this shit, I couldn't help but wonder, is this a set-up or what? "Be careful Dave I don't like the looks of this." To make matters worse, there was an elderly lady with a small child setting on the bus stop bench, which made shooting a real concern.

Bob pulled approximately 15 feet short of the bus stop as a precautionary measure, should a gun battle erupt we would have ample distance between the shooter and us. We immediately ordered all the men to take their hands out of their pockets and step over to the scout car. As they were complying I observed one of the men discard what appeared to be a blue steel revolver on the ground. We already had our guns drawn partially concealed behind our legs. "Bob, the tall one on your left just dropped a gun, everyone on the ground face down, NOW!" Bob could sense the anxiety in my voice and immediately went into a high alert mode, pointing his weapon directly at the suspects. I confiscated the gun, which turned out to be a blank starter pistol. "Bob, I got the gun it's a starter pistol" to which Bob replied "That doesn't mean there's not another one."

Excellent point, I cannot begin to tell you how many good cops have given their lives because of complacency, after finding a gun on a suspect and assuming there were no others, they were shot and killed with a second weapon they neglected to find on the criminal.

I cuffed my guy and then covered Bob while he began to search the suspects. A second gun was found on one of the knuckleheads and this one was no starter pistol, it was a nickel plated .32 caliber revolver fully loaded. A third suspect was found to be in possession of an illegal switchblade knife. Bob decided to place all six under arrest for suspicion of armed robbery due to the fact that half of them were found to be in possession of a weapon. The detectives can sort it out and at least identify these idiots that we no doubt will be running into again in the future.

We would later learn that all six were members of the Chene Gang, which was a very deadly bunch of young hooligans on the north end of the precinct, which explains the indistinguishable red hooded sweatshirts. When not sporting hoodies, they were known to wear dark gangster hats.

My prediction about this day being an interesting one was coming to pass, the shift had just begun and we already had six felony arrests and got two guns and a knife off the street. Yes, I consider the starter pistol a weapon also, because if a suspect in a dark alley is pointing it at you demanding your valuables, I can assure you it appears authentic enough that you would most likely comply.

"Dave, lets grab a coffee up at the Clock before we get our next lockup."

Suddenly the radio blared out: "All cars in seven we are getting officer down on the I-75 service drive and Clay, We are now getting officer shot." "Radio 7-3 is responding" "Ten-four 7-3, there are units at the scene, no information on status of the officer or description of suspect at this time." I activated the lights and siren, which is protocol when responding to an officer in trouble or officer down. Bob and I sat in silence both wondering if the officer was alive or not. God if we lose another one this year, enough is enough!

By the time we got to the scene the entire street was blocked with unoccupied scout cars, it looked like the precinct parking lot. As we approached the house all indications were bad news, officers were crying and heads were hung. Such a Solemn atmosphere can only mean one thing; it appeared our worst fear had come true, we had lost another officer.

As we approached the scene a sergeant was exiting the house with what appeared to be an evidence bag in hand. "Boss what's the situation?" "The officer is dead, one shot right to the heart; he's on the back stairs." We made our way to the rear of the house where we observed the corpse lying on the stairs. It was a black officer in plainclothes with a badge around his neck and his revolver lying about two feet from his hand; apparently he was pursuing the suspect who ran into the front door of this house and out the rear, when the officer exited the rear of the house in pursuit, the suspect was laying in await and shot the officer in the chest killing him instantly, a damn ambush!

I just kept staring at the lifeless officers body, thinking he was alive an hour ago, now look at him, it's over, he's never going home and he will never hold his love ones again, at least not in this world. I'm sure his family is not even aware he's dead yet. I just pray the good Lord gives them the strength to cope with the anguish that is at their threshold.

One cannot fathom the level of grief families endure following the death of an officer, which I attribute to the typical graphic and senseless manner in which they are killed. It's not as if they were taken by some incurable disease or even killed abruptly in an automobile accident. No, they are normally murdered by some habitual criminal who has no regard for laws or life.

As a DPD police officer and former infantry sergeant in the U.S. Army, I have viewed my share of corpses, but I have to admit, I'll never get acclimated to seeing my comrade's lying dead. I've heard far too many bag pipes playing Amazing Grace during my life time.

The entire area was now terribly congested with cops; we were actually stepping on one another, to the point the crime scene was in jeopardy of being compromised. The radio dispatcher made a general announcement to all officers, no other cars were needed at the location and any one not directly involved in the incident was to leave the area immediately per the commanding officer at the scene.

Lawmen are inquisitive creatures by nature, that's why we're cops. However, the overwhelming response to this scene and any other officer in trouble incident, is not merely because we are nosy or want to provide additional assistance, it's also designed to demonstrate to the other side (the criminal element) that we are a brotherhood which is deeply concerned about each other's well-being, assuring thugs we are a force to be reckoned with when confronting a hostile or threatening situation and we will use whatever force that is necessary to protect our own!

As we returned to our vehicle, I overheard a passing officer make one of the most appalling statements I have ever heard. A responding crew asks if the officer was dead and his despicable reply was, "Yea, he's dead but no biggie it's a black cop." Suddenly, I was sick to my stomach! How could anyone racist or not, make such an insensitive statement of an individual that is wearing the same badge and just gave the ultimate sacrifice while upholding the law? My God he is not a brother, he's a brother cop!

This man, this officer just sacrificed his life while attempting to arrest a piece of dirt that violated the law, a law that each and every one of us took an oath to uphold. I didn't know this black officer and maybe he, too, was an extremist, but I am sure of one thing, he died upholding justice and this small minded bigot has the audacity to make his extreme sacrifice something less then valiant is disgusting and inexcusable.

"Bob did you hear that piece of shit?" "Yea, I heard him Dave and he was totally out of line, but don't let him get your panties in a bunch. He's an ass-hole who was attempting to be cute." "Well, I don't find anything humorous about an officer dying, black or white!" "Slow down Dave, I'm on your side. That was an outrageous statement to make and the moron needs his ass beat, but do you really believe an ass beating will erase all his bigoted beliefs and hate? Well it won't and I thank God he doesn't represent the majority of us. I'm hurting for that officer's family as well as his partner, you are quite aware how I feel about any officer dying, but he's gone and we have to move on. That maggot's remarks are not worthy of repeating or dwelling on." As usual Bob's wisdom and compassion shines through, lending comfort to this situation and most any other.

Bob's IQ soared through the ceiling; he was so intelligent he could have had his choice of careers as well as salaries. Yet, he desired only to be a Detroit street cop, that's where his heart was and all else was secondary. The job was his life and his life was the job!

After several hours of uneventful dispatches we received a radio run that would prove to be interesting to say the least. "7-3 Chene and Lafayette in the parking lot investigate the suspicious blue Lincoln Town Car occupied by several black males possibly drinking." "On the way radio 7-3."

The Lincoln stood out like a sore thumb due to the white landau roof and white wall tires, appearing to have a number of occupants. As we approached the vehicle from behind I could observe a lot of abnormal movement going on inside of the vehicle. I advised Bob, who had taken up a position at the right rear of the vehicle. While shining my flashlight in the vehicle during my approach, I observed five large black males in the vehicle, three in the rear seat and two up front.

Upon slightly tapping on the driver's window to get his attention, the power window slowly came down with cigarette smoke bellowing out like the interior was on fire; the smoke was accompanied by a strong odor of alcohol, which is a repulsive smell if you are not partaking. "Excuse me sir may I see your operator's license and registration?" What took place next totally caught me off guard. "Hi! Officer, everything's cool, all of us are cops." "OK, could I see your ID officer?" The driver of the vehicle smiled and replied courteously "Yes sir, no problem." Suddenly, one of the rear passengers screamed out "Fuck these white mother-fuckers, the only reason they are checking us out is because they saw a car load of niggers minding their own business. We all got guns and badges, I wouldn't show that peckerwood a Goddamn thing." This jerk's negative racist attitude appeared to be communicable, two of the other occupants began shouting racial slurs indicating we were only investigating them because they were black and furthermore, we had no right to ask for a driver's license because the vehicle was not in motion.

The situation was beginning to turn ugly real quick. I advised the driver we were dispatched to this location by radio and if he didn't control his passengers I was going to summon a supervisor to the scene, which is protocol when investigating or arresting police officers. The driver who was complying immediately yelled out "Would y'all shut the fuck up, the man is doing his job, he got a run here because someone made a complaint! Officer I'm sorry they been drinking tonight, one of our friends was shot and killed earlier today." Obviously the officer we visited on the rear stairs.

In light of their loss and the drivers redeeming attitude, Bob and I, against our better judgment decided not to involve a supervisor and let the fellows go on their way with a warning. Although, I did make them aware that the dead officer was also a brother of ours and their inappropriate attitude was less then acceptable, even if they didn't think they were doing anything out of line. Obviously someone was concerned enough to report them to the police. I could hear the loud mouths in the rear seat mumbling something, which I chose to ignore because it was obvious these guys weren't showing the love.

This day could not become any more bizarre, we had six felony arrests, witnessed the body of a fallen officer shot and killed, came in contact with an insensitive white bigoted officer and now a car load of hateful black racist cops and the day is not even half over! You wonder why we drink.

The remainder of the shift was rather kind to us; it consisted of an accident report, a couple domestic dispute runs and a stolen car report. Other than that it was all over but the crying. It was finally "Miller Time" and boy was that beer going to taste fantastic!

Once at the Goodyear bar, Bob and I related our stories of the day's events to a few of our peers, who thankfully agreed that the white, bigoted cop's insensitive statement were outrageous concerning the fallen officer. Bob's theory is that idiots like that cop as well as the black militant officers drinking in their car do not represent the vast majority of our society, who in general are far more compassionate then we sometimes realize. You see police officers, more times than not, interact with an element of society that the public fears and would rather not deal with; consequently we sometimes forget that there are civilized God-fearing folks out there.

The Bar was packed; drinks were going down like water and old Art was in no hurry to go home, a combination that could be dangerous; this had the makings for one long night. The tavern's owner Art would gladly stay open as long as police stories were being told. He was infatuated with anything relating to law enforcement, we often jokingly told Art in his previous life he was a sheriff in the Old Wild West.

This was one of those rare nights where there was no other place you would rather be than with your fellow lawmen drinking and telling war stories. Most of us called our better half's advising them of our intention to just have a couple more, which they knew in reality meant 5-10 more and for those who neglected to call their spouse, oh well they will have to deal with them when they get home. There was no hanky-panky that night, at least not in the bar, just drinks, laughs and lies.

We had drunk the girls pretty and ourselves sober. Art was sleeping with his head on the bar, snoring like a bear in hibernation, leaving us to serve ourselves, trusting us to pay on the honor system. We walked out with the morning sun rising and birds chirping, thank God I didn't have court this morning, I could at least get four to five hours sleep before returning to work. The everyday Joe would have called in sick after a night like this, but not us, we were afraid of missing the action.

My reasoning for returning this afternoon went beyond my love for the job, or fear of missing the action; it was because once again I was assigned to work with Bob Field an opportunity I didn't take lightly.

Three-thirty and all were present and accounted for, waiting for roll call to begin. Everyone appeared fatigued and hangovers were obvious with some, messed up hair, pale faces and eyes that appeared to be hemorrhaging. It's hard to believe we put our bodies through this on a daily basis. When you take into consideration the drinking, excessive stress levels and lack of sleep, there is no wonder that the aging process for cops is accelerated far beyond most professions.

Jenny Hawes walked silently into the squad room wearing

sunglasses, head hung low with her hair brushed down across her face, damn, she must have one hell of a hangover! Her silence was totally out of character; ordinarily she is very perky, even when hung over or tired.

I approached her with intentions of consoling her; by making her aware that hangovers are temporary and will get better as the day goes along. "You ok kid? You look like shit!" "Thanks Dave, you always know how to comfort a girl. I'm fine; I just took a bad fall." It was at this point I realized this girl had more than a hangover, someone had beat the crap out of her, the left side of her face was black and blue and her right lower lip was swollen twice the side. "Jenny, who in the hell did this to you, was it because you got in so late, was it your husband?" Her answer was swift and convincing "No, Dave my husband has never laid a hand on me." "Well, then that only leaves Dick." Dick is a real nut case cop that is assigned to an adjacent precinct, who has been dating Jenny for a while. Her head dropped, and she began to weep uncontrollably, at which point I escorted her into an unoccupied office so she could re-group and pull herself back together, as we were departing Bob's expression indicated that I should do what I had to do and he would cover for us at roll call.

I didn't even get the door closed and Jenny began confessing, opening up revealing everything concerning the relationship with Dick. She indicated that this was not the first beating; he had abused her on several occasions one of which was because he observed Jenny talking to me at the saloon and became enraged with jealousy. She apparently has been telling her husband these injuries were all work related. What came out of her mouth next astounded me, " Dave please don't say or do anything this must be kept confidential, I love him so much, it's not his fault, he has a terrible temper which he has a difficult time controlling. It's my fault because I say and do things that upset him." I could not believe my ears, this girl, this officer, has all the signs of the battered-woman syndrome. She was actually blaming herself for the mental and physical abuse this piece of garbage was inflicting upon her. The irony of this situation is they both were married and had children, go figure!

"Jenny don't worry, I will keep it hush-hush, but I would be remiss if I failed to give you my opinion, which is, lose this guy and lose him quick. Once a cowardly woman beater always a woman beater! Leave this dirt-bag before he kills you!"

I learned a long time ago you can't help someone who refuses to help themselves; some folks are just born to be victims. As we left the room the shift was coming out from roll call, which gave us an opportunity to just blend into the crowd, our timing was impeccable, no one even noticed.

Bob didn't say a word as we pulled off the ramp; he just began checking vehicles on the hot sheet, which is a print out of cars' license plate numbers that are reported stolen or wanted in relationship to a felony. Bob, let's keep an eye on Jenny tonight, she's not doing so well." "Anything you want to talk about?" "Actually, I would love to talk about it but I gave my word to keep quiet, sorry." "No problem, your word is more important than information." Wow, what a guy. He not only preaches, he practices what he preaches!

"Did I miss anything at roll call Bob?" "Not really just the usual, except they gave out the funeral arrangements for the plainclothes officer. He will be laid out at Swanson's Funeral Home this Wednesday and Thursday with the burial on Friday. We're both off on Friday do you want me to pick you up?" "Yea, that sounds good Bob, afterwards we can stop for a couple pops." Which was normal procedure following the burial of a fellow officer.

I couldn't help but think to myself that this is the guy that a number of black officers at the precinct have labeled a brother-beating racist. Yet on his day off and his own time, he is attending the funeral of an honorable officer, not a black officer, not a white officer, simply a fallen officer who is worthy of respect.

As luck would have it, Bob got a hit off the hot sheet (A printout of all wanted vehicles) right after we pulled off the ramp. "Dave, the black Buick Electra two cars up is stolen." "I got it Bob, I'll wait for it to stop at the next light then we'll take him down. " Radio 7-3" "Go ahead 7-3" "We are following KBD-263 north on Gratiot and are going to attempt to stop the vehicle at Gratiot and East Grand Blvd." "Ten four 7-3, we have that car stolen out of the Fifth Precinct. All cars in seven, 7-3 is attempting to pull over KBD-263 at Gratiot & East Grand Blvd."

We stopped the car without incident, which I would attribute to the fact we waited until the vehicle was blocked in by traffic, extracting the thieves from the vehicle in record time with our guns screwed in their ears. It sure beats getting into a high-speed chase! The two occupants were taken into custody and transported back to the precinct along with the vehicle that appeared only to have damage to the steering wheel column from the ignition being punched out. The passenger was only fourteen but as luck would have it the driver was nineteen and would be charged with grand theft auto. Not bad, ten minutes out of the chute and we already had one recovered stolen vehicle, one felony arrest and a juvenile detained.

We were back on the street in no time at all due to Bob's superb typing skills. He was fantastic at writing reports, he typed with just two fingers, but at record speed with little if any typing errors, whereas with me, report writing and spelling was not my forte. Bob would often say "Dave you're one hell of a street cop, but you couldn't spell your way out of a bag." Needless to say, Bob did a majority of the paperwork.

After a quick cup of coffee at the Click Restaurant, we decided to attempt to begin the day with a narcotic arrest, which in the Seventh Precinct was not a difficult task. We drove to Mack and Concord, which is a high volume heroin trafficking area and positioned our scout car kiddy-corner across the street down an alley where we had an excellent view of the corner. This location also offered ample cover for our marked scout car. Within five minutes, we observed a black male in a brown jacket and black pants standing on the corner involved in four suspected narcotic transactions. He appeared to be getting his narcotics from a windowsill nearby. This was like taking candy from a baby, so I thought.

We had enough probable cause to effect the arrest of this clown, so we decided to drive around the block in an attempt to approach him from his blindside, which in theory may have been successful if it was not for a group of prostitutes across the street that alerted him with an obvious prearranged signal. Our suspect didn't even attempt to visually locate us; he just took off running like a bat out of hell and guess whose job it was to catch this jackal? "Let me out here Bob, you go around the block." The chase was on and our boy had the advantage of a head start as well as his familiarity with the neighborhood and residence. There were a thousand and one places this clown could be headed for, and it was up to us to figure it out.

Bob, fortunately, had enough foresight to stop long enough to confiscate the evidence from the windowsill before circling the block in an attempt to cut the suspect off. If he had not retrieved the heroin, the prostitutes would have had a lot of free fixes and we would have a suspect with no evidence, not a good thing!

I have never lost a suspect in a foot chase and I was damn determined this was not going to be my first. The suspect was apparently becoming fatigued; every fence he jumped, his pace would slow down a little more. "Stop or I'll blow your fucking head off." An idle threat and the suspect knew it. He was quite aware that this was not a shootable offense. The next fence almost changed that. The thug stopped running, placed his hands over his head in an obvious act of surrender, thank God!

"Don't move and keep your damn hands up." With my revolver pointed at the suspect, I used the other hand to retrieve my radio and advise dispatch of my location and the fact the suspect was in custody, a report that I would find was premature and not entirely accurate. While climbing the fence my pant leg became entangled in the mesh fencing, causing me to lose my balance and fall, which left me hanging upside down with my leg caught. To make matters worse during my fall I lost the grip of my gun which went flying in between the suspect and me. What a predicament, this was certainly an "Oh-shit moment!"

After a brief struggle attempting to release my pants from the fence, they ripped, causing me to plummet to the ground. Damn the pants at least I was free. Upon looking up I observed the suspect just peering at me as if he was analyzing my dilemma. Shockingly, he got this eerie evil smirk on his face and to my amazement suddenly started moving toward my gun. I cannot believe this; everything was going in slow motion at this point and all I could think of is that I'm going to get shot with my own gun! Each of us had approximately ten feet to travel before reaching my pistol and I knew I had to get there first or die trying. I dove in the air and came down right on top of my weapon with the suspect colliding a half a second later on top of me, at which point he franticly began grabbing for my pistol. Fortunately I already had it in hand. Gathering all the strength I could muster I rolled the asshole off me and struck him across the face with my pistol, splitting his head wide open causing blood to fly everywhere.

I've lost my temper before, but never like this, I went crazy on this character. I'm sure what was only seconds seemed like hours as we exchanged blows, and, I must tell you, I won hands down, which confirms just how dangerous a frightened man can be. This individual who I would have now been totally justified in shooting, will think twice next time he attempts to kill a cop or fight him for his weapon.

"Dave slow down, he's had enough." The suspect appeared to give up when he heard Bobs voice, he didn't want to dance with both of us .Once again Bob was there to prevent me from going overboard. "Thanks partner, this son-of-a-bitch tried to get my gun when I got tied up in the fence, he was going to shoot me I know it!" "I believe you Dave, but you know as well as I do when this dirt bag comes to his senses, he will have a totally different version from the actual event. I want you to place your pants on evidence when we get back to the precinct; they will support your account of getting stuck in the fence and falling. Do you have a second pair in your locker?" "Yea, but it's a damn shame we have to jump through all these hoops to dispute an outright lie from a guy who just tried to kill me!"

Scout 7-4 conveyed our prisoner to Detroit General Hospital where he was listed in serious condition. Bob and I went back to the precinct and completed our report of the incident, charging the suspect with Violation of the Controlled Substance Act (VCSA) for the possession of the heroin and Assault and Battery of a Police Officer, a charge that no doubt would be dropped because his injuries were far worse than mine.

Officer Kenmore was standing at the front desk conversing with a second officer as I turned in our report. I just knew he would have some derogatory remark to make and, as usual he didn't disappointment me. "Hey Stealth, I hear you and Field put another brother in the hospital, is that right?" "Yea, that's right I did, but Field had nothing to do with it. Truth be told, the asshole should be lying on a slab down at the morgue, but unlike you I have compassion for all people black or white!" I don't know why I wasted my breath by dignifying this jerk with a response; his only purpose in life is to cause dissension between the two races.

Once back on patrol, Bob could see I was deep in thought. "Are you alright partner?" "Yea, I guess the reality of almost getting wasted tonight by that scumbag is setting in. I can accept dying Bob, however, I can't accept dying with my own gun, that's just totally unacceptable." "You're right Dave, just try to shake it off; we will take a slower pace the rest of the shift." It was a kind gesture, but Bob knew as well as I did that idle was a speed that neither one of us possessed. If anything I needed another incident to put this one behind me.

The silence was deafening as we drove around, I guess we were both thinking that this night could have ended up being a nightmare if that idiot would have got to my gun first. One of our worst fears was notifying the love ones that one of us was not coming home.

Suddenly, I observed a car parked in the alley about a half a block down with its lights out, if occupied, they were motionless, it was difficult to discern at night from this distance. "Did you see it Bob?" "Yea, I saw it, I'm going around the block so we can come up from behind." We slowly pulled behind the vehicle with our lights out; a silhouette of an individual's upper torso was visible through the fogged windows coming up then down with a forward motion. It didn't take a mental giant to realize what was going on, the severity of which was yet to be determined. We slowly exited our scout car leaving our doors ajar as we approached the vehicle cautiously with are flashlights off and guns drawn due to the possibility this could be a rape in progress.

Once we were both positioned at the drivers and passengers doors, we shinned our flashlights in the car simultaneously which illuminated the inside, there they were going at it hot and heavy with the male on top. Believe it or not they were totally oblivious to our presence and continued on, never missing a beat. The woman was entirely nude and the male on top had his trousers down to his knees.

Bob gave me the nod and we knocked on the windows with our flashlights announcing, "Police officers open the doors." They both almost jumped out of their skin. We then ordered the male out on the driver's side and advised the female to put her clothes on and exit the vehicle. The black male was very nervous and justifiably, he indicated this was his 19-year-old babysitter and if his wife ever found out about this indiscretion she would kill the two of them.

Bob interviewed the lady and ascertained she was indeed a 19-year-old adult. In this type of a case, we ordinarily give them a warning or write them a ticket for performing a lewd and indecent act in public. We have also taken the man's telephone number advising him if he was found involved in hanky-panky in our precinct in the future, he could be assured his wife would be receiving a call from us. This tactic would typically scare the unfaithful husband straight. "What are we going to do Bob?" "Let's just.........."

"Radio 7-7 needs assistance, East Grand Blvd and Warren" "That's Kenmore and Anderson" "Let's go Dave, give this pervert his ID we have an officer in trouble." I tossed the folks their ID in their car window as we speed off with lights and siren going. This was that guy's lucky day. However, his future is uncertain to say the least, there is a good chance the babysitter will inform his wife of the affair when he attempts to end the relationship; young girls can be very vengeful when ditched!

As we approached the scene we could see a crowd fighting like hell on the front lawn. Our car was the first on the scene, however many sirens could be heard coming our way off in the distance. Bob and I immediately jumped in the middle of the crowd and went to work pulling these savages off Kenmore and his partner. Within minutes, 20 scout cars had arrived and the situation was under control. Kenmore and Anderson were ruffed up a little but nothing that would require medical attention. Apparently Kenmore and his partner were attempting to make an arrest when the family intervened, escalating the situation into an outright brawl. Actually it happens quite often.

Kenmore wanted everyone arrested for interfering with a police officer during arrest. Bob and I advised him we would convey three of the twelve defendants into the precinct for him. "Thank you brother Dave and if these bitches give you any problem slap the shit out of them!" He then shook our hands and thanked us once again. Bob and I just stared at each other in astonishment "Do you believe this Bob? He actually shook our hands, called us brothers and gave us permission to assault his black prisoners, unbelievable!" "Fear will do strange things to a man Dave, I guess that's called selective racism! It's ok to abuse blacks if he gives us permission, how convenient!"

The night was finally coming to an end and I must tell you none too soon. I was exhausted this has been one emotional day. I was almost too tired to stop for a drink, Yea right, if there was ever a night to stop for a drink it was tonight. Besides I only had one more day to work with Bob and then my partner Jim returns, which is not to insinuate that was a bad thing, Jim was a good cop and we worked well together. It's just that I learned so much from working with Bob, and it was as if we had this mental telepathy thing going on when it came to criminals.

"Give us another one Art," "You sure Dave? The guys have two backed up?" "You're right Art, so just give me one." They were going down exceptionally well tonight and I knew I would suffer the consequences come tomorrow morning, O well, I'll deal with that problem then. Rodge was in the middle of a bunch of the female officers, no doubt sharing some of his courageous war stories and how he alone prevents the City of Detroit from falling.

"Hey Dave, why didn't you kill that black bastard today?" I knew it was too good to be true and just a matter of time until he got into my business over that incident, just to impress the ladies. "Rodge, stick a sock in it, I'm enjoying my cold beer don't mess it up with your idiotic questions." "I'm just saying Dave, I would have blown that low-life, dope dealing, mother-fucker away if he even looked like he was going for my gun." "Yea, I'm sure you would Rodge, but that is the distinguishing difference between the bad guys and us. Dudes like him are supposed to be cold blooded murderers, we are not. Remember, we are the guy's with the white hats!" The girls chuckled, which embarrassed goofy; he will be silent for a while, at least until his small mind conjures up another asinine statement.

"Come on Bob, have one more." "No thanks Dave; it's

time we get out of here. Why don't you leave your car and I'll take you home?" Bob, in his infinite wisdom realized I was far to impaired to get behind the wheel. "OK, but you will have to pick me up tomorrow?" "No, problem buddy, let's get you something in your stomach first, then I'll get you home." It's a good thing I didn't attempt to drive home; I don't even remember being dropped off that night. I very well could have killed myself, or worst, killed some innocent citizen!

My ultimate nightmare is making some small child motherless or fatherless because of my over-indulgence of alcohol. The sad trait about an intoxicated person, especially a drunk cop, is that they believe whole heartily they are in control, which lends to that sense of arrogance and over-confidence, a combination that can be devastating.

Granted, the field of law enforcement holds the dubious distinction of being one of the few careers that have stress levels that soar off the charts! As I have stated on many occasions, I attribute this to us dealing with vulnerable victims and the lowest level of predators within our society on a daily basis. You're constantly on an emotional roller-coaster, feeling compassion for the helpless and unbelievable outrage for those who have the audacity to commit these blatant crimes. Now, you add in domestic problems and you have an ideal Segue into drinking, if not outright alcoholism. In no way am I justifying our alcohol abuse, I am merely stating we find drinking to be an antidote, a temporary remedy that often cost us our families, careers and occasionally our lives!

"Good morning tough guy, how do we feel this morning? As she placed my coffee on the bed stand, the aroma was oh so welcoming and very much needed. "Bob called, he's running a few minutes late." It took a minute to kick start my brain through the spider-webs in my head and then I recalled Bob had driven me home because of my drunken state. He was picking me up this morning and driving me to retrieve my car. This certainly worked to my benefit; I could use the extra time to attempt to come back from the dead.

Bob's arrival was welcomed; this was one morning I didn't want to have one of those husband and wife conversations where I'm told I need to slow down on my drinking, not today!

"The beer is in the cooler in the rear seat, he said with his half grin." "Hell no, I feel like I'm going to die, why did you let me drink so much last night?" You will be ok, all you need is to sweat it out, I'll see if I can get you into a foot chase today." "Oh yea, that's just what I need, you wouldn't have to worry about losing me, just follow my trail of vomit."

I would never let Bob know, but I sure was praying for a light day. I felt sick as hell and the thought of chasing or struggling with some thug made me want to hurl.

Three hours into the shift and as of yet, it had been a fairly uneventful day other than a few reports. This was certainly not due to a lack of trying on Bob's part; he was pulling over cars left and right, in an attempt to generate a decent arrest.

"Scout 7-3 at 1350 Townsend, we're getting a report of

a man beating a woman in the upstairs flat" "On the way Radio 7-3" Upon our arrival we could hear quite a disturbance coming from the upstairs. As we entered the residence we found this rather large black male holding a lady down on the couch with his hands around her neck screaming, "I'll kill you bitch, I'll choke the hell out of you." Bob and I grabbed his arms, forcing him to release his grip from her throat allowing her to catch her breath and jump to her feet, which proved to be a less than wise move. The lady who turns out was his girlfriend begins assaulting her lover with her fist, striking us far more then him, one must appreciate true love.

Finally, I was able to secure the lady and Bob appeared to have the boyfriend under control. The female was taken to the staircase where she began to scream "The Police is taking me to jail, Oh Jesus, please help me." Her cries for assistance did not go unnoticed; the entire clan from the lower flat came to her aid. Fortunately, Scout 7-4 arrived to assist us. "I have this one, check on Bob upstairs, he may need some assistance." 7-10 manned by Robbie & Dan also backed us up thankfully, I turned over the loud-mouth girlfriend to Robbie and requested she be conveyed to the precinct and we would transport the boyfriend.

I made my way up through the mob on the staircase where a black officer was facing the screaming crowd while protecting the entrance to the upstairs flat. As I gazed around the officer I observed Bob on the floor struggling with the boyfriend who was armed with a knife. My partner was literally fighting for his life. I instantly pushed the officer aside and drop kicked the boyfriend right in the chest, this momentarily took his breath away, causing him to release the knife, at which point we were able to effect the arrest and handcuff this potential cop killer!

I could not criticize the officer standing security at the door; this was not a black and white thing. The screaming was at such a level, it would have been difficult for anyone to hear the commotion coming from the inside of the residence and, in all fairness, I asked him to prevent anyone from entering and he did the job that was requested of him; however, he did it a little too well. An officer must learn to multi-task and always attempt to be fully aware of the entire surroundings. He will chastise himself enough; there is no need for me or anyone else to remind him how out of hand this situation had become and how tragic the outcome could have been.

After placing the bad guy in the scout car, Bob's expression seemed to imply he wanted to say something but couldn't find the words. Moments later he spoke up, "Dave, thank you buddy, that bastard was getting the best of me, if you wouldn't have come along...." "Well, I did come along and I did no more than you would have done for me. However, if you want to buy me a drink for saving your lousy life after work I'll accept it." "I thought you had a hangover?" "I did but like you said, I just needed to sweat it out and I've certainly done that."

Later that night at the bar, Bob asked me to become his

permanently scout car partner, which would mean I would have to leave Jim. I must say ordinarily this would have been a problematic decision, I certainly must take Jim's loyalty into consideration, but this was also a career move, and opportunities like this only come around so often. It was like a promotion. Jim was now a veteran by today's standards and was quite capable of having his own scout car; this would be a career advancement for him as well.

I accepted the opportunity without hesitation; finally I was going to work with the man that was considered an exceptional cop by the vast majority. Unbeknownst to me at the time, this was developing into much more than a partnership, this was the beginning of an intense bond that would not only last through our police careers, but also for the remainder of our lives.

Bob would not only become my best friend, he would also be my best man at my wedding and eventually become the Godfather of my lovely daughter.

"PERSEVERANCE PAYS OFF" 9

WHERE HAVE THE LAST SIX MONTHS gone? It seemed like yesterday that Bob and I teamed up and hit the street running! We have led the shift in arrests each of those months. A topic often discussed between us was how our production could soar if we weren't burdened with everyday police runs and reports. There is so much work to be done in this city, but as with any metropolitan city the bureaucracy often discourages or hinders officers from aggressively working the streets.

"7-3 to your station, you will be out of service." "On the way Radio 7-3."

A run like this is typically not encouraging, due to the fact it ordinarily is concerning a subject dispatch prefers not to transmit on the air, such as a serious family situation or emergency.

As we approached the front desk, Lieutenant De Cree stood up and said, "You two in my office right now!" Bob and I looked at each other with a puzzled expression on our faces. In one sense this was a relief because it obviously didn't concern our families, seeing as he brought us in together, but on the other hand it was apparent it was something of a serious nature that had to be discussed behind closed doors.

"Ok, guys here's the situation, 7- 6's scout car was broken into at Mt. Elliott and Forest and their 12 gauge shotgun was stolen from the rack. I need not tell you the mountain of paper work this will generate as well as one hell of an investigation by Internal Affairs, not to mention the possibility of our own gun being used against us! You guys are my best; can you get it back by the end of the shift?" Our answer was immediate and direct' "Lieu, we will give it one hell of a try; however, we need your word you will handle any complaints concerning our tactics." "Don't you worry about the complaints; I'll handle them and far as your tactics go, just don't kill anyone." "Lieu you know we can't make that promise, but we will promise you we won't shoot anyone that doesn't attempt to shoot us first."

The area in which the incident took place is the "Coney Ownies" territory, a rival gang of the Chene Gang. A notorious but not so bright gang, their name the "Coney Ownies" was derived from Francis Ford Coppola's "Godfather" film starring Marlin Brando and Al Pacino. They apparently were so impressed with the movie, they named their gang after "Don Corleone" the Godfather, although the spelling somehow was lost during the transition and Corleone became the Coney Ownies.

As luck would have it, three of the Coney Ownies boys

were walking in the area where the theft occurred, all of whom were dressed in black shirts and pants with a black wide brim gangster hat, which is always tilted slightly to the side in their typical gang garb fashion. A brief street interrogation accompanied with a promise that we fully intended to make their lives a living hell from that point on if we didn't get the shotgun back, got their attention immediately. Our expressions and tone conveyed a sense of urgency, making it quite apparent just how serious we considered this incident. We further offered them a once in-a-lifetime deal, total amnesty with no prosecution of this crime as long as we recovered the weapon immediately.

The oldest of the three was more than cooperative, not because he was striving to be a law-abiding citizen who was delighted to assist his local police department; to the contrary, he was simply aware that as an eighteen-year-old, he was the one that would be charged with a felony should we link him to this crime.

After having a serious eye-to-eye conversation with one another, they advised us that the word on the street was that the shotgun was concealed in a rolled up carpet in the attic of the red house on the corner of Mt. Elliot and Warren. A lot of information coming from someone who just heard it on the street, nevertheless, we gave our word, so we took their names and released them.

The information was solid, the red house stood out like a sore thumb, right on the corner as our newfound friends had indicated. Bob and I notified radio that we were entering the location for an investigation. As we approached the rear door of the residence, two black teenage females were exiting. "Do you ladies live here?" "No, we were coming to see Derrick." "Is Derrick home?" "No, there is no one home and I don't know anything else!" This told us she knew everything, including why we were there.

As we entered the back door we alerted the occupants by announcing: "Police, is anyone home?" After receiving no response we began our assent up the enclosed staircase of this dilapidated home which was probably built back in the 1930's and certainly was in need of much TLC. The old wood stairs squeaked like those found in a haunted house, there certainly could be no element of surprise. Once at the upper landing, we found the rolled up carpeting and just as specified, the fully loaded 12 gauge shotgun was concealed inside. People could be heard scurrying inside the second floor residence, however, this was not a concern of ours at this time, there would be no arrest, we got what we came for. The odds of arresting these little gangsters for future crimes at a later date was better than not.

"Radio 7-3." "Go ahead 7-3." "Radio please advise number 7 precinct desk we have recovered that property and we're returning to the station." Before Radio could respond, the lieutenant transmitted, "7- desk OK on that information Radio, tell them fantastic job and thank you so much!"

Needless to say the lieutenant and the crew that lost the

shotgun were elated over the recovery and I must say we felt pretty good as well. It was quite obvious in the lieutenant's eyes we could do no wrong; he had complete confidence in us and our ability to get the job done.

At the completion of off duty roll call, Lieutenant De Cree requested that Bob and I remain behind after the shifts release. "What's up Lieu?" "I want you guy's to know I really appreciate what you did today and now I want to do something for you two, starting tomorrow you guys are working a booster car in plainclothes on the power shift 7p.m. till 3.am. shift." We could not believe our ears, this is an assignment that all aggressive working cops aspire for and we just received it. We both shook the lieu's hand, thanking him for the opportunity and assuring him we would not let him down.

The Booster car or B & E (Breaking and Entering) car as it is sometimes referred to, meaning its crew targets individuals who lurk in the shadows breaking and entering into homes and businesses stealing valuables. This is considered a preferred assignment and typically held by cops who have been around for a while, proving to their supervisors and peers that they have exceptional skills, talents that allow us to think like the creatures we hunt.

The positive aspect of this assignment is that you do not receive police runs from dispatch. Although, you do have the luxury to respond to any of those you choose. You are expected to make numerous felony arrests per month, a task that we found intriguing rather than threatening.

The anticipation of our first day in plainclothes was killing me, I wanted to get this day in motion. Bob on the other hand was not one to get excited very easily, and God forbid he shows some emotion through his rough exterior. It was my turn to drive and I was about 15 minutes early. Judy appeared at the front door and waved me in. "He'll be out in a moment. Well, Dave you guys finally got what you wanted, I'm so happy for you, just please be careful, I've got four babies to raise and I don't want to do it alone!" "Don't you worry sweetie, I promise there's nothing going to happen to the big boy that doesn't happen to me first." About that time the bathroom door opened and out came Bob dressed in blue jeans and a white t-shirt finally ready to go. "Let's go kid, we don't want to be late for roll call." Oh yea, who's the one that's been waiting.

The Special Operations shift (7p.m. to 3a.m. shift) had a roll call much different than the uniform shifts. It was very informal with everyone sitting around with his or her feet up on the desk. The bosses informed us of the areas that were experiencing high levels of crime and we were to patrol accordingly. This unit was designed to target the hardened criminals during the peak hours as well as covering the street during shift change.

There were two existing plainclothes crews, one black and one white, along with a number of uniform crews which were considered the eighty series. The entire shift welcomed us, which in of itself was extremely different behavior then we were accustomed to on the swing shift. Black and white officers were sitting together actually carrying on civilized conversations, I could learn to like this assignment!

We hit the street in our blue jeans and unmarked Plymouth sedan, which in theory is intended to make us inconspicuous, veiling us from the criminal element, but in reality every citizen black or white in the city of Detroit knew who we were. Yet, when using the right techniques you can still have an edge however slight on law violators.

It felt very strange riding around in civilian attire after wearing the uniform for the past few years, a very good sensation, almost like and advancement within the ranks. I made myself a pledge that I would never return to uniform and finish my career in plainclothes if at all possible, a vow that would be substantiated through time.

Oddly enough, the wrong doers appeared to respect or maybe even fear plainclothes officers more than those in uniform. I would say this is because they believe we were either more experienced or very aggressive, which in most cases was accurate. However, there are uniform officers who are absolutely terrific cops and just choose to work the uniform division, declining all offers concerning plainclothes assignment; it's a matter of personal preference.

Unlike uniform police officers, plainclothes investigators aren't confined to specific scout car districts; you have the luxury of patrolling the entire precinct, which for a working cop translates into freedom and opportunity.

"Dave what do ya say we hit the south end and see if we can get a gun or two?" "Sounds good to me, let's start with the Methadone Clinic." A treatment center, which is designed to assist addicts in withdrawing from heroin addiction by administering methadone, at regulated intervals. The clinic was a haven for low- life's that take advantage of the weaknesses of those who are addicted. As with most experimental cures or alternative medicines, there are consequences, in this case it was rip offs.

The junkies would receive their methadone, conceal it from the staff and subsequently smuggle it outside, where the drug would then be sold to other addicts who were often white suburban kids. The sellers of the methadone would then take the proceeds and purchase their drug of choice, heroin. Once again, a system that was designed to eradicate a problem cultivates a much more severe dilemma.

Unfortunately, the hard-core hooligans found junkies and kids to be easy prey, especially the white suburban kids who often arrived in nice cars sporting designer clothes, jewelry as well as hard cash. All of which they would gladly surrender should a gun be put in their face, after all it wasn't theirs, mommy & daddy bought it for them. These crimes, quite often went unreported because the victims refused to bring the incident and the fact they are using drugs to their parents' attention. Parents, who in many cases believe drug abuse is an inner-city problem and it only affects the black society, well, talk about walking around with blinders on!

As we turned into the clinic parking lot it was not about who, it was about how many we wanted to arrest. There were so many addicts it was like shooting fish in a barrel, not that I have ever experienced that, but that would certainly be a good analogy. The white kids were notorious for fronting their money, a term meaning to give the suspect your money prior to receiving the drugs. Once the perpetrator received the money, he assured the naive purchaser or "Mark" that he would return shortly with the product, which is like leaving the porch light on for Jimmy Hoffa, it isn't going to happen!

That was the best-case scenario, because the only thing they lost was their money. Whereas, if the suspect asked the Mark to drive him to a secondary location to pick up the drugs and they are dense enough to agree, they are endanger of a much more heinous outcome, such as rape, losing their vehicle, and maybe even their life, and they just keep coming back for more, unbelievable!

The one target that caught our eye was a large black male dressed like a homeless person leaning into a late model vehicle occupied by a young white couple. A transaction was taking place right before our eyes, the black male accepted currency from the kids and, in return, reached in his coat pocket and pulled out a clear vial containing a pink liquid, possibly methadone which he handed to the buyers.

No sooner than the transaction was completed, the suspect spotted us and attempted to hastily walk away in an easterly direction across the parking lot toward the alley. Bob pulled the car between the suspect and the alley ordering him up against the scout car, while I approached the other suspects in the car on foot. Suddenly, the young driver threw the car in reverse almost striking my leg in an attempt to escape, I immediately moved to the driver's side and identified myself as an officer pointing my gun at the suspects head while ordering him to put the vehicle in park, to which he complied.

Seconds later, Bob yelled out that his suspect was armed with a gun and in custody. "Get out of the damn car now and don't touch anything, lady you keep your hands on the dash and don't move." Once I secured the occupants of the vehicle, both of whom soiled their pants, I recovered the suspected vial of methadone on the front seat, it did not appear to be the real thing because of the lack of labeling as well as the size of the vial, which was not the customary bottle used by the clinic.

Bob's suspect advised us that the vial contained Kool Aid and nothing more, it was a typical suburban burn pack, meaning it was a substance that was disguised to appear as a narcotic, to be used in a fraudulent transaction, in other words a burn. The kids advised us that the suspect attempted to get them to drive him to an unknown location, fortunately they declined; a decision that most likely prevented them from experiencing a far more severe fate.

Taking into consideration police officers are not chemists and methadone is a substance that cannot be easily field-tested in the street, all three suspects were arrested and charged with possession of suspected narcotics, as well as a charge of carrying a concealed weapon for the black male. This was one time that the parents of these two kids would have to face reality as they read the revealing police report, which can't be denied, only disputed. After all we certainly didn't drive them down to the inner-city methadone clinic!

Two weeks have now passed and Bob and I are feeling very comfortable in our new plainclothes assignment. Each night brings new challenges, encounters that are not only welcomed but essential in making good officers better cops. We have almost doubled our arrests, a direct result of not being burdened with radio runs and having a free reign of the entire precinct.

The night had just begun and we decided to check out the Eastern Farmers Market District where there had been reports of truck-drivers being robbed while waiting to make their deliveries of livestock and produce. As we were cruising down Gratiot Avenue we observed a lone black male walking in front of Joe Muer's Restaurant. "Damn that guy looks familiar Dave, turn around let's talk to him." I drove down about a block so I wouldn't spook the man, assuming Bob's intuition was correct, which was usually the case. The man had that deer in the headlights expression as we pulled up to investigate him, a very good indication he had something to hide.

"Step over to the car partner and break out some identification please." "I ain't got any ID officer and what the fuck did I do anyway?" a reply that was less than sociable and certainly put us on guard. "Where do you live sir?" "I stay with my aunties on Russell Street and I don't know the address." This suspect was conveniently ignorant, answering all of our questions in a very vague fashion, which generally implies guilt of some sort.

Bob insisted he recognized the suspect, but couldn't quite put his finger on where, however, you could be certain it was related to crime. Possibly, from a mug book of wanted felons he reviewed while temporarily assigned out to a taskforce, a unit whose sole purpose was to locate and arrest suspects who were wanted for serious felonies such as robbery, rape or homicide.

Unfortunately, this assignment had taken place several months' back, which certainly didn't help his memory any. "All right buddy, you're going to have to come with us until we get this straightened out." "This is bullshit, you know damn well you are just fucking with me because I'm black and I'm going to have your fucking badges for this. You white mother fucker's have picked on the wrong nigger this time." This clown kept up his idle threats all the way to the precinct, which was a positive indication that Bob was once again spot on.

Once we placed the suspect in the lockup, we approached the lieutenant to enlighten him on our incarceration as well as the extenuating circumstances. Regrettably, the supervisor on duty was Lieutenant Shall, who was black and very radical in his beliefs, which he shared with anyone who cared to listen, white or black.

"Lieu, here's what we have, I recognize this suspect and know he is wanted, but it's going to take me a minute to research it." "So, let me get this straight Field, you know this brother is wanted for a crime, but you don't know what crime he's wanted for, is that right?" "Sir, this is not merely a hunch, I assure you he is wanted on a warrant and I will prove it, if given the opportunity." "Ok Field, have this gentleman's prints checked through the Identification Bureau, I'll give you guy's to the end of the shift to convince me he's wanted and if not the brother goes free." I had no problem with the lieutenant's decision, however, I did have a problem with him referring to the suspect as a brother, he was a suspect and race had nothing to do with it, or did it?

We drove directly over to the Felony Task Force which was located on Belle Isle where we received permission to review the mug books of Detroit's most wanted. You talk about searching for a needle in a Haystack. After reviewing what seemed to be two hundred photos, Bob turned a page in the third book and there was our suspect staring up at us big as life. He had three outstanding warrants for rape, for which he had been positively identified. Mr. Innocent was also a prime suspect in six other sexual assaults; we had a real serial rapist. In each case the woman was brutally beat during the attack, this guy was a real piece of work!"

We immediately returned to the precinct to advise Lieutenant Shall that the "brother" was indeed a wanted sex offender and thanks to Bob's keen eye and photographic memory he was now in custody. "Here you go Lieu, our guy is a real predator." As Bob slid the photo in front of him, Shall, got this strange look on his face as he studied the mug shot, which left no doubt this was the perpetrator. The lieutenant slowly lifted his head avoiding any direct eye contact with either one of us, which is not a promising sign. As he tossed the photo back to us he explained, "You guys are a little too late, I released him about 30 minutes ago." "What the hell do you mean you released him? You said you would hold him until his prints cleared and give us to the end of the shift, did his prints clear?" "You better watch your tone Stealth, you're talking to a lieutenant. You cannot just go around locking up brother's because you think they may have done something and besides he gave us his address." "This is bullshit lieu that was no brother, that was a brutal rapist and you need to learn to separate the two, just because they are black doesn't mean they are innocent! We work in a precinct that is predominantly black, which means black violators are going to be arrested, not because they are black, because they're criminals. Your radical beliefs superseded common sense and you let him walk out that door after he gave you some bogus address, just because you thought the "brother's" rights were being violated, what about the rights of the victims he raped?"

Bob inconspicuously attempted to silent me by kicking my leg to the point I wanted to scream. My partner knew that any attempt to convince the boss he was making inappropriate decisions based on his bigoted beliefs would be totally ineffective. It's difficult to persuade an individual that he or she is on the wrong track when they find comfort in their distorted self-serving beliefs.

As we expected, the suspect prints did come back positively identifying him and revealing, in fact, that he was wanted for numerous home invasions followed by brutal rapes. However, the lieutenant was so convinced that we were railroading a black man that he negligently failed to review the results of the suspect's prints, which verified he was indeed a very dangerous individual.

I cannot believe the arrogance of this man, he deliberately released this dirt bag because in his small mind he believed the suspect was being abused by a white Jim Crow system that intentionally seeks out defenseless black citizens for the sole purpose of persecution, or he was merely attempting to make a statement to Bob and me that he would not tolerate the mistreatment of his brothers.

We could have reported the lieutenant to his superiors; however, supervision would be reluctant to give anything more than a verbal reprimand out of fear of receiving a discrimination complaint that could wreck their careers. More importantly, this would leave him free to pursue revenge, no thanks; the repercussions would be far greater than any discipline he would receive. Once again incompetence and poor judgment will be excused because of one's race and the fear of being labeled a bigot!

"You know Dave, here is another example of a person

flagrantly making a decision based on their one-sided beliefs, which typically harms the victim and allows the violator to walk. This is just another example of protecting the criminal's rights and ignoring the victims, where did our society get de-railed?" "Let it go partner, it's just another speed bump in the road, let's just keep on driving forward. If we allow idiots like this who are hell-bent on practicing selective enforcement prevent us from doing our job, then they have won, and we might as well turn the torch over and move on to another career."

Even after giving Bob my version of "Mom and apple pie" his disappointment and resentment for Lieutenant Shall was more than outright blatant. "Damn that bastard, what the hell are we supposed to do just lock up white people? Three of this savage's victims that he raped and beat half to death were black ladies, why doesn't he explain to them why he let the sexual predator walk? I'm sure they would understand when he makes clear he felt this low life may have been a casualty of indiscriminant police profiling.

The remainder of the day was spent attempting to find our released rape suspect, a search that was fruitless; he no doubt was long gone. I'm sure he is very thankful for the ethical courteousness extended by Lieutenant Shall, but this was too close for comfort and it was time to get out of Dodge. God willing, some other crew will be fortunate enough to investigate and arrest this assailant before he claims another oblivious target.

Fate can be very rewarding as well as unpredictable. Two days later Bob and I were on Gratiot Avenue heading down to Police Headquarters with narcotic evidence we confiscated on an earlier arrest. Bob was so intent on our conversation he failed to notice our rape suspect from the other night walking north on Gratiot. The suspect on the other hand, damn sure observed us as we passed, which was obvious through my side mirror where I could see him turn around and visually follow us as we drove away. "Bob, don't hit the brake, just look in the rear view mirror, it's our rapist that Shall let go the other night. He's watching us, so drive down to the next block slowly and make a right, we can circle and come back around and come up from behind." Bob knew if he accelerated in the least or varied in his driving this guy would be gone like a turkey through the corn.

This was too good to be true, a second chance and we didn't want to blow it. Our hearts were pounding as we made our way back to Gratiot in anticipation of the suspect vanishing once again. To our amazement the rapist was nonchalantly continuing north on Gratiot oblivious to anyone approaching from behind, I'm sure he was at ease and chuckling to himself about the two dumb cops who just passed by.

We pulled up and had this guy cuffed so fast he didn't have time to consider running, but he did find time to play his race card. "I'll have your Goddamn badges, the brother lieutenant let me go, he said he knew what ya'll had did to me just cause I was black." "You can let it go brother, the lieutenant won't help you this time, we have confirmed you are wanted on several rape warrants." You would have thought this character had an off switch; he shut up as if his parents were scolding him. After advising the suspect of his rights and placing him in the rear of the scout car, Bob and I gave each other a high five over the hood of the scout car. Our enthusiasm was two-fold, we got a dangerous thug off the street and we would have the satisfaction of surrendering him to Lieutenant Shall for the second time.

Our timing was impeccable; we entered the precinct with our arrest just as Lieutenant Shall took charge of the front desk. "Lieutenant we have our rapist again, what would you have us do with him? My sarcasm was more than transparent and I loved it. "What do you usually do with your arrest Officer Stealth? Knock off the bullshit and just process your prisoner." It's not easy eating crow, but the lieutenant did it oh so elegantly, which supports the theory that practice makes perfect. Maybe next time he won't be so quick to generalize and review the situation impartially based on the facts, leaving his bias beliefs at the door.

The true reward was that this brutal rapist would eventually be convicted of first degree rape on three of his assaults and most likely would be sentenced to 25-40 years hard time for these ungodly acts.

From that day forward our relationship with Lieutenant Shall took a 360, at least during working hours, our arrests were never questioned and what we said was gospel. It was kind of a mutual respect, he realized now that we weren't out to mistreat the black race, our only intent was to do the job we were paid to do and do it well. If one of our prisoners were to play the race card, Lieutenant Shall would tell them to either validate their grievance or shut up. It appears we all have been enlightened from the incident.

Lieutenant Shall came to realize that most cop's, black or white, are simply professionals, interested in doing their job with no ulterior motive. We on the other hand learned that Shall could look beyond his personal beliefs, working at a proficient level while not compromising his own ideals. What a unique concept, working in harmony!

"7-3 and units in Seven, East Grand Blvd north of Warren, we are getting multiple calls on shots fired, three men lying in the street." This is one of those rare occasions when you find yourself in the right place at the right time. We were just a block away and definitely heard several shots being fired. "Radio 7-23 we are responding to 7-3's run, and shots are being fired from that area." "All units in seven, shots fired in that area of East Grand Blvd. and Warren have been confirmed by 7-23 who is responding, use extreme caution as you approach."

Typically when there are numerous calls on the same reported incident there is a high probability to its legitimacy. When you factor in officers hearing the shots, now we have a situation!

As we rounded the corner I observed a dark vehicle several

blocks away traveling at a high rate of speed, we could also see three men lying in the street. "Bob, I have a feeling the shooters are in that car." "Make a call Dave, do we go after the car or remain at the scene?" Sometimes, you have to listen to your sixth sense and this was one of those occasions, either the shooters were hiding in the area or the vehicle speeding away from the scene was, indeed, involved. "Radio 7-23." "Go ahead 7-23" "Radio advise 7-3 there are three suspected shooting victims lying in the street. We are pursuing possible suspects involved in the shooting north on Van Dyke from Warren in a dark Ford, unable to obtain a plate at this time."

We finally caught up with the vehicle at Mack and Van Dyke and to our surprise the driver complied with are orders to pull over. "Radio 7-23 has the suspect vehicle, license # LHB 359 with numerous occupants, pulled over on Van Dyke just North of Mack, request backup." "Bob they're doing a lot of moving around in the back seat." "Yea, I see, watch your ass!"

We approached the vehicle very cautiously with guns drawn. Many officers leave their guns holstered until they see an overt act, due to the fear of a citizen's complaint, which quite often leads to some sort of discipline by their unnerved superiors. Bob and I on the other hand, always approached vehicles and suspects with our guns un-holstered, usually partially concealed alongside of our leg. Our theory was the hell with department policy; we would rather deal with a complaint than face the consequences of notifying our families that one of us died because we were being considerate of not offending a suspect.

I ordered the driver and front seat passengers out of the vehicle one at a time while advising the occupants in the rear seat to remain seated with their hands raised until given orders to exit. This prevents a lot of confusion as well as a safer environment. After all, six passengers were extracted from the vehicle and placed under the watchful eye of my cohort, I approached the vehicle and to my delight, I observed a blue steel 357 Magnum revolver lying on the front passenger floor. "Bob, we got a gun." My statement immediately placed my partner into a high alert mode, ordering everyone on the ground in a prone position with their hands on top their head. His command voice carried a no-nonsense tone with a definite sense of urgency.

My hunch paid off big time; we ended up confiscating six handguns from the occupants and vehicle. Thank God they didn't decide to shoot it out, because we were certainly out-gunned. The two women were snitching out the male occupants as the shooters of the three men before we could even place cuffs on them. 7-3 advised us that two out of the three men shot were dead upon arrival. So our shooters now became murder suspects. Not bad police work, if we could say so ourselves. Arresting a person in possession of a concealed weapon (CCW), is considered a preferred arrest by most lawmen, but when you get six guns and six arrests out of one car, that's almost unheard of.

We would later learn from detectives at Homicide that these murders were a direct result of flirting between one of the deceased and the shooter's girlfriend. Not quite a worthy reason for taking a life, then again for those with no respect for life itself, it's very easy to justify, another indication of the deterioration of morals in today's society.

During my career in law enforcement, I have witnessed numerous homicides and other than the few that were obviously self-defense cases, the majority were committed for petty reasons, everything from jealousy to taking an uninvited bite of a peanut butter sandwich.

The people who were typically involved had little regard, if any, for life and more often than not alcohol or drugs were found to be a factor. Another common denominator is income; the crime rate in the low-income areas or ghettos is much higher than that in the suburbs. This is not to insinuate that all low-income folks are black or white trash, certainly that is not the case.

My theory is simply this: those who have less find themselves envious of those who have more, which consequently leads to a state of depression and where you find the depressed; you find depressants i.e. Alcohol and Drugs. And as we all know, substance abuse eventually leads to tragedy.

I by no means am attempting to justify this unorthodox behavior; there is no excuse for breaking the law or taking a life, other than self-defense. If you don't have what the Jones' have, go out and work for it legitimately. There are no short cuts in life. I would much rather have less, than face a life of incarceration or worse, death! Don't get mad, get educated. You may not be able to change your zip code, but you can change your attitude for no cost at all!

As time passed, Bob and I would come up with more innovative methods to outwit the bad guys. It was like a chess game in life; the criminals would figure out our MO (Modus Operandi) and change their method of criminal activity. We then would adapt to their MO with a counter. It was a vicious-circle that brought challenges to both sides.

It's been said a city never sleeps. Even after most residential lights are turned off and the empty streets are calm, there remains an element that roams the city in hopes of taking advantage of those who rest in their supposedly secure homes. So often while we sleep, predators stalk out would be victims under the shroud of darkness, with the sole purpose of taking what is not theirs and harming those who are unaware or helpless.

This would be one of those evenings. We would learn the next day that while we slept, one of ours, an off duty Wayne County Sheriff's deputy was shot and killed after a robbery attempt in the parking lot of the Tip Motel located on Gratiot just south of Mack Ave. Apparently, he and his companion were walking to their vehicle when the murderer who was hiding, suddenly jumped out and attempted to rob them. After a brief struggle, the gunman shot and killed the sheriff's deputy and then ran off into the night empty-handed, what a waste. If there is a silver lining to this tragedy, it's that the lady was unharmed and we now had an eyewitness, a witness who stated the deceased identified himself as a lawman prior to being executed.

Armed robberies at the Tip Motel have become all too common in the last two months. There have been three reported parking lot robberies not to mention the ones that went unreported. Crimes of this nature quite often go unreported to the authorities because the victims fear their extracurricular social activities may be exposed to their loved ones. They realize they should be home with their wife and family instead of frequenting some sleaze bag Motel with Mrs. Jones. The robbery becomes secondary; the victims are simply elated to escape with their lives and anonymity.

In all of the reported motel robberies, it appeared to be the same described suspect using the same (MO). He would lurk in the parking lot awaiting the motel customers to exit and attempt to enter their vehicle, at which time the suspect would then approach the unaware victims armed with a blue steel revolver demanding all valuables.

In this incident our suspect graduated from a typical holdup man, to a cold-blooded murderer and worse, a cop killer. Now, I will not attempt to convince you that law enforcement agencies do not prioritize cases where an officer is killed compared to John Doe citizen, because they do. Not totally because they killed a brother officer, but rather for the reason that when criminals are flagrant enough to knowingly kill a protector of peace then God only knows what kind of heinous crime they are capable of committing to citizens in the future.

Most criminals will tell you they don't want any part of killing a lawman, not because they respect us, but rather because of the repercussion or wrath of punishment that would most likely follow. However, there is that minute segment of mutants in today's world that takes pride in killing a cop and afterwards they flagrantly wear the evil deed as if it was a badge of honor. Often being admired or feared by their demented constituents who recognize this as a huge taboo.

From this point on, the Tip Motel would be receiving a lot of special attention from our crew, at least until this maggot was behind bars or became fertilizer, the choice was his and his alone. This is one case where the defendant will have a difficult time interjecting race as a factor in his ruin, because the deputy he murdered was black as well.

There are those who believe that if you kill a cop, it is an automatic death sentence: if the arresting cops do not assassinate you, our judicial system will. I assure you this is not the case, are there some rogue cops and random questionable incidents, absolutely! But, the vast majority of law enforcement does their upmost to incarcerate the suspect without incident, only to see our judicial system take immeasurable and sometimes embarrassing lengths to assure the defendant gets a fair trial, leaving the officers' actions in question.

It has been two weeks since the deputy was executed and no other reported robberies have taken place in the parking lot of the motel. Did this guy feel the heat from all the media coverage and move on to a different target? I think not, my sixth sense told me he was a local who lived in the immediate area and found this location to be convenient geographically as well as comfortable to his limited intelligence.

Bob was off today and my partner for the evening was Karen Defott. Karen was one tough little cookie who would fight at the drop of a hat. We made our normal rounds checking our traps for guns and dope to no avail. This could be a very quiet evening, I thought to myself. We are going to have to work for an arrest tonight, but no way was I going to let Bob return and find there had been no arrest for the last two days, it was a matter of pride.

It was now around 2a.m., which was a good time to check out the parking lot at the Tip Motel. All of the reported robberies had taken place between midnight and 4a.m. When time allowed, we attempted to set up a fixed surveillance on the motel or, at minimum, drive through the parking lot three or four times each night. We really wanted to get this guy off the streets.

As we pulled in the lot, I observed a person wearing a black, hooded sweatshirt crouched down between two cars. He apparently heard our vehicle approaching because he took off like a bat out of hell. "Karen, there's our guy" before I could finish my sentence, she was out of the car gun in hand chasing this idiot down the dark alley. I pulled out of the alley with my tires squealing like I was in a NASCAR race, my thoughts were if he continues running in the same direction Karen would chase him right into my arms.

"Radio, 7-23, my partner is on foot chasing an armed robbery suspect east in the alley from the Tip Motel Parking lot. The suspect is described as a black male 5'10"180 lbs. wearing a black hooded sweatshirt. The suspect may be armed and wanted for questioning in the homicide of a Wayne County Sheriff's deputy." Upon turning the corner, I observed my partner in the street kneeling down behind a vehicle parked at the curb with her attention directed on the corner house. She explained as she exited the alley in pursuit of the suspect, she observed the door slam shut on the corner house off the alley, but was unable to identify who entered the house.

Karen was not entirely convinced this was the same individual she was chasing through the alley, however, we now had an idea of the house or at least the vicinity in which our holdup man dwelled. We then decided to complete a report of this incident and forwarded a copy to the Homicide Division and Major Crime Mobile Unit.

Two days later, four of our detectives from Headquarters Major Crime Mobile Unit obtained a search warrant for the residence where we believed the suspect entered. Upon arriving at the residence the detectives knocked and announced the fact that they were the police and had a search warrant. Within seconds they heard a loud gunshot come from inside the dwelling. The crew immediately took cover alongside the house and behind their vehicle.

The sergeant in charge of the crew, a tall rather husky good looking fellow by the name of John, declared a barricaded gunman situation, which entailed bringing in the upper brass who usually takes on the role of negotiator. In theory, they will bring stability to the volatile circumstance. If the criminal surrenders the command officer becomes an instant hero, but if the outcome is less than desirable, the sergeant is typically held accountable while the command officer silently disappears into the night.

After approximately two hours with no communication with the suspect, the order was given to gain entry by forcing the front door in. A large officer by the name of Dick Janson approached the door armed with a huge metal ram followed by six of us. Dick was quite a Cop, shot numerous times during a raid approximately three years ago. He refused a retirement and was now back with a vengeance, displaying a no-nonsense attitude like only he could.

The command officer aided by a loud speaker, announced "Police open the door" one last time and when answered by silence, he gave the signal for our entry team to enter, while the remainder of the officers assigned to outside security took cover in anticipation of a shootout with the suspect.

Dick hit the door with such force it exploded, giving way for the entry team which entered cautiously. We found the house eerily quiet, no TV's, no radios just dead silence. The smell reminded me of damp soiled clothes that might be found in a wet, rat-infested basement. There were no lights on which just magnified the unnerving atmosphere.

As we began clearing the first floor, I remember thinking this idiot is going to pop out from behind some door and just start shooting, why not take a couple more cops with you? One dead cop or three dead cops, in Gods eyes it won't matter you're going to hell anyway. The kitchen had roaches crawling over dirty dishes with un-eaten food stuck to them stacked on the sink and kitchen table. This place was definitely a breeding ground for disease.

Suddenly, a noise came from behind a door off the kitchen; we all looked at each other as we positioned ourselves on either side of door in anticipation of a full-fledged confrontation. The nod was given and the door was opened, revealing a steep set of stairs leading down to a dark damp basement, where water could be heard dripping. Once at the bottom of the stairs our flashlights and weapons scanned the basement revealing our culprits, rats the size of small house cats were scampering across the shelves and floor. This entire setting was right out of a Stephen King film.

The first floor and basement were now clear, only one level left and that was the bedrooms on the second floor, he had to be there. As we rounded the upstairs railing, the floors squeaked, alerting any occupants we were approaching. The anxiety among the entry team was at an extreme level, it wasn't a matter of if he was up there, just a matter of where he was and what he intended to do when we came face to face.

All of our questions were answered as we entered the first bedroom off the stairs; there was the suspect lying on the floor with a gun in hand, a pistol that ballistics would later confirm was indeed the weapon that was used to kill the deputy sheriff. One shot to the head let him escape the police for the final time. The shot we heard earlier was a man having his own trial without jury, finding himself guilty of murder, receiving the death penalty, a verdict that he alone would carry out. Whether it was performed out of fear or guilt, we will never know and frankly I don't give a damn. Thanks to his cowardly escape, there would be no technicality issues to deal with or claims of mistreatment and the shooting of a black man prior to a fair trial. I only had one thought as I left the premises and that was: Rest well my brother in blue, justice has prevailed!

CHAPTER 10

1975 LIVERNOIS AND FENKEL "RIOT OR DISTURBANCE?"

SUMMER WAS UPON US AND THIS night started out fairly typical. The sergeant informed us of all the crimes committed in the city over the last 24 hours along with areas in which we were to provide special attention. Roll call was followed by the usual word of caution advising us to be careful: "It's a hot July night out there, so watch your asses." Little did the sergeant realize, but this night was going to be the hottest night since the 1967 Detroit Riot.

I knew by Bob's expression, something was on his mind; he was engaged in our conversation yet wasn't hearing a word. "What's up Bob? You are way to quiet." "Dave, I was just thinking how much I love this job and how if it was physically possible I would work around the clock without pay." Now, to most this would sound insane, but Bob was very enthusiastic when it came to law enforcement and to say he is passionate concerning his career would be a gross understatement. He loved his brother cops and, if needed, was willing to give his life without hesitation. Locking up criminals was his life, second only to sex, and at times sex took a back seat.

We were totally unaware that while we were involved in this discussion, a very volatile situation was beginning to unravel across the city. We always speculated how it would have been to be involved in the 1967 Riot. Well, our question was about to be answered.

"Radio, 7-23 to the station right away." "On the way radio, 7-23." Again, an unknown crisis awaited, damn I hated that kind of call. Once again we had to wonder, what had happened and did it involve one of our families? "Bob, I can't understand why they don't just tell us what the problem is?" "Dave, are you sure you want them to broadcast your business city wide?" "You're, right, it's just the unknown that kills me."

Once at the station, we were pleased to hear our families were not the reason we were summoned. There was apparently a large disturbance on the Westside of the city at the intersection of Fenkell and Livernois, an area I was totally familiar with due to the fact I was raised in this very same neighborhood prior to enlisting in the U.S. Army.

The preliminary briefing indicated that a white bar owner in the area shot and killed a black youth that reportedly was breaking into his establishment. As a result, a large angry mob had formed and was vandalizing his bar along with other businesses in the vicinity. This was going to be a long, hot night!

The mayor was taking no chances, immediately placing

the city on the highest state of alert with all vacations and leaves canceled for first responders. Every available cop in the city was being called in to address the problem before it got out of hand.

The brass wasted no time getting officers equipped properly and in route to the Westside. Bob and I would remain in plainclothes and in our unmarked police vehicle, most likely to be used as a recon unit to observe the crowd's movement and actions.

All forces gathered at the temporary staging area, which was a large fenced in parking lot off Livernois, not far from the Tenth Precinct. There were units from every precinct in the city, a show of force that was very impressive I must say.

Eventually the upper echelon released more specific information; apparently a white bar owner shot and killed an intruder who had broken into his business. The bar had apparently been broken into and robbed on numerous occasions and the owner, distraught and fed up, decided to take matters in his own hands to protect his property. He locked himself inside the bar and waited for the burglar to return.

It seems the young black youth forcibly broke into the establishment at which time he was shot and killed by the owner, who had laid in wait. Supposedly, the youth was shot after an altercation took place once inside, an account that will never be verified, because there were only two witnesses inside the bar that night and only one survived.

I will not insinuate for one minute that the youth was

murdered, only the owner knows whether he had to take the shot or not. I will say the proprietor had the right to protect his property from thugs no matter what age or color and if the intruder made him fear for his life, then he did what he had to do.

However, our laws do not tolerate for one to lay in wait or bait a person with the intention of executing them. The law expects the property owner to allow the criminal the right to surrender and accept punishment for his crime within the judicial system. It has been argued that the criminal gives up his right when he knowingly breaks into a residence or business with intentions of doing harm or committing larceny of hard earned-property.

But, in our liberal society we must protect the rights of the cruelest criminals that walk the face of the earth, while putting the victim's rights often second. This defies logic, take it from me in the world of wrong doers it's a joke, criminals keep attorneys on a retainer for the next offense. Offenders laugh at us as they continue to commit crimes and manipulate the judicial system time and time again. It's not about how many crimes you have committed it's about how many times you beat the case.

As I expected we were assigned as a recon vehicle, which meant driving on the outskirts of the trouble area near the bar. We had strict orders not to make contact with the crowd and to only enforce the law in situations we deemed life threatening.

Many of the officers that were assigned closest to ground zero were black. This was by design, the management believed they would be able to relate better and their presence, considering the current situation, would be less offensive to the already hostile crowd.

I understood the premise of this decision; however, I must tell you it left me with a sense that the oath I had taken to protect and serve was a joke. This was the epitome of selective enforcement. Again we were catering to the radical element, which in many ways were blatantly breaking the law. There are people currently serving time in prison for committing the very same crimes, yet these thugs get a free get-out-of-jail card because they're doing it in the name of discrimination and injustice.

Once again this gives the criminals the green light to Loot, Burn, and Rob, with little if any punishment. The thugs were quite aware that all their criminal acts would be tolerated at the onset of the outburst, giving them a window of opportunity of approximately 24 to 48 hours to commit their ugly deeds before incarceration would become an issue. There unlawful actions were cloaked under the pretense of rebelling against a racist white society, when in reality it is merely an opportunity to commit despicable wrongdoings.

The looters complained that society, the white regime, restricted employment, opportunity and prevented them from obtaining the bare basics for survival: food and clothing. Yet the pillagers carts for the most part contained liquor, cigarettes, bicycles, stereo systems, furniture and weapons. Not quite the essentials needed for survival, but items that would yield a good buck on the street.

Once on the road, Bob and I reported large crowds of youths walking toward the incident scene. This hot summer night had almost taken on a circus atmosphere with crowds of people walking the streets, while others just sat on their porch watching the show. All the businesses in the area were locked up tight with some white owners guarding their livelihood with shotgun in hand. Other store owners painted, "BLACK OWNED" on their windows in an attempt to ward off the radicals and opportunists.

The crowd was getting larger and larger with each passing hour, yet the hundreds if not thousands of police officers remained in the Command Post parking lot. The fear of the upper echelon and mayor's office was that this could spread city-wide causing another 1967 riot, a concern that was warranted and had to be taken into consideration.

During this hot evening an unaware white motorist was driving through the area of the disturbance, a choice on this date that would prove to be deadly. He was attacked by the mob, pulled from his vehicle and beaten to death. His crime was being white in the wrong place at the wrong time. I'm sure there are those that will say a life for a life, you killed a black man and we killed a white man. I would suggest the distinct difference is the black youth was knowingly committing a felony, while the white, unwitting father was simply driving home to his loved ones, now you tell me who is the murderer?

The dawn was welcomed by all; we knew that the criminal element that roamed the streets realized that daylight would not offer them the anonymity that darkness provided. The crowds were lessening, which allowed more police presence in the area of concern. Whatever was to be done had to be done within the next 12-14 hours before nightfall returned.

Mayor Coleman A. Young had addressed the citizens of Detroit on all TV and radio stations in the metropolitan area with a plea for peace and stability. He also was scheduled to come down to ground zero and walk the streets in attempts to relate with the citizens face to face hearing their complaints first hand. If this did not work, it would be up to us. However, in the mayor's eyes, addressing this issue with force using local law enforcement was the very last option and the National Guard was not even on the table.

It was now the day after the initial uprising and a majority of the instigators and thieves were down for a few hours of sleep before they would return for another opportunity at disrupting the city for personal gain. It's this very element that impedes activists who are genuinely involved in a movement or cause. They could care less about the crusade or the rights of others, using chaos as a smoke screen to do their dirty deeds. But inevitably when apprehended they suddenly turn into icons of the civil rights movement.

I took advantage of this calm to take my partner on a tour of the old neighborhood in the Wyoming and Fenkell area. We patrolled street by street and with each turn, a story of my boyhood was told. Bob, who was less than entertained, was beginning to take on that expression that one sports when they're forced to sit and view reel after reel of old family movies at a relative's house.

What was once a middle-class neighborhood with a majority of white residents, had now transformed into an all-black neighborhood, with many of the homes neglected and badly in need of painting. There were homes abandoned and boarded up, no doubt from bank foreclosures and abandonment, where the owner or occupants just walked away, often vandalizing the home before vacating. I found it very sad, it was not the vibrant, clean neighborhood I remembered as a youth.

As we turned onto Indiana Street where my family once lived, memories began to shoot through my head. Suddenly, I remembered the names of the occupants of each house, that's where the Moore's lived, that's the Jenkins house and so on, as excited as I was, Bobs expression screamed shoot me now. All of a sudden, my house came into view. "Bob, right there the red brick bungalow, that's where I was raised." The structure seemed sound enough, but the landscaping was a real eyesore with the lawn and shrubs over-grown. The front screen door was barely hanging on with the screen half torn out and blowing in the wind. The front door window, which once had beautiful stained glass, now, had a piece of plywood over it. Thank God mom and dad weren't here to witness this.

I've seen enough Bob, let's get the hell out of here. As we

pulled away I observed a large crowd of black folks several doors down sitting on the front porch of what once was the home of Mrs. Dickson's, a fine black lady whose family was one of the first black families to move in the area. I remember a neighbor referring to them as "Block Busters," a term we were not familiar with back then.

The neighbor explained block-busters were the initial black family sent into all white areas to purchase a home, once they become homeowners, the white flight begins. The whites panic, and start selling their homes at bargain rates to other blacks waiting in the shadows to purchase. Thus, transforming the all-white neighborhood into a black community.

I am not about to concur or even entertain such an absurd premise today, but as a naïve teenager this ridiculous concept seemed like a logical conspiracy theory, a scheme not even the CIA could cultivate. Never the less, we should never disagree with our elders, or maybe we should? If there was ever a time to break the cycle, it was then. But ignorance and raw racism prevailed.

My neighbors never considered the fact that the Dickson's like any other family just wanted to escape from the crime-filled ghetto, to enjoy safe neighborhoods and the good life, isn't that the American dream?

Now, I will say my observations in the metropolitan Detroit area support the thought that many of the run down areas of Detroit are occupied by blacks and have a far greater crime rate then their suburban neighbors. I will even explore the theory that there is a conspiracy that economically restricts blacks, intentionally holding them back. That is an argument for another time, and frankly I'm not qualified enough to speak to the subject, not to mention the fact that I find merit in both arguments.

However, I would suggest, Mr. and Mrs. Dickson's had no ulterior motive, they simply wanted to move into a clean, crime free neighborhood and give their family the best they could provide. Actually, Mrs. Dickson's became the self-appointed neighborhood watch. I remember how she would sit on the porch for hours watching the children play in the streets and should a car come down the street at a speed that she determined put the children's safety in question, this protective lady would place her hands on her hips and walk directly toward the street glaring at the driver like only an irate mother could. Now, I'm telling you as a law enforcement officer, she put more fear into those careless drivers then I could have in full uniform!

As we rolled up in front of the well-groomed home, all the individuals on the porch stared at us defiantly, as if to say what are you white bastards doing in our neighborhood? A look we were all too familiar with. Even though we were in an unmarked Plymouth and in plainclothes, all those that looked on knew quite well we were the police. Not too many white males would be driving in a predominately all-black neighborhood, taking into consideration the current situation and, if they were, they certainly would not be driving at such a slow speed. We, as law enforcement officers, could not and would not allow fear to show in such a tense situation, so we would have the perpetual stare down.

I noticed the crowd was surrounding a short heavyset lady who was sitting in a chair; she, too, was not looking very pleased by our existence. Even with the slight presence of gray hair now appearing, there was no mistaking this lady, it was Mrs. Dickson's. "Bob, I know this lady." I brought the vehicle to an abrupt stop and exited before Bob knew what was going on. "Dave what the hell are you doing?" "I know her Bob, it's OK."

As I exited the vehicle, those who weren't already standing on the porch suddenly stood up, as if to say you aren't taking anyone of us without a fight. "Mrs. Dickson?" The lady in the chair leaned forward somewhat squinting her eyes as she stared at me with a puzzled expression. "Yes, I'm Mrs. Dickson." I smiled, which to some extent defused the animosity that was oh so prevalent. "I'm Dave, Dave Stealth, we use to live two doors down," pointing to the house. By now, Bob had exited the car and was right behind me, and I know he was once again thinking, what the hell is this kid doing now? Yet, he had my back as always, just like a good partner is expected to do. Mrs. Dickson, now smiling from ear to ear, jumped up and wrapped her arms around me saying, "Lord have mercy honey, I would have never recognized you, you have grown so big." The embrace was welcomed and seemed to last forever.

The atmosphere totally changed, making my partner extremely pleased and the crowd for the most part was now sporting smiles because of the reunion, letting all know it was OK and a temporary truce was in place.

Mrs. Dickson and I sat there discussing old times and the present situation that had brought us together, while bringing one another up to date on the status of our families, interrupted only by transmissions on my radio. She expressed her disappointment about the current situation in the area and her fear the police and soldiers would return as they did before (referring to the 1967 riots). "They will treat all of us like animals Dave, like we are out robbing and burning and it just ain't so. I keep my family nearby so they don't get shot, we can't help what others do, that's not us!" Although her words were few, they were filled with wisdom and unfortunately scarred by terrifying past experiences. What words could I use to comfort a woman who made a career out of looking after others, no matter what color they were?

"Mrs. Dickson, I am so sorry and I promise you we will look in on you while we are working on this side of town." Her dark brown eyes seemed to be taking on a bewildered look as she stared at me, "Child, that is so sweet and I appreciate it, but unless you plan to take this problem back on your side of town it will remain here after you leave." Again simple words that said volumes, my temporary fix would not help anything; the change had to be nationwide. But, recognizing the compassion and understanding between me and this sweet lady left a glimmer of hope for all of us, she was one fine lady whose memories and wisdom will remain with me forever.

For the next few days, we often drove by Mrs. Dickson's home, giving her special attention when time allowed. This was not only done for her, it was for me as well. I felt terrible leaving her in this mess, I remember feeling so helpless, I wished I could have change things for she and her family. But, this wasn't about economics or the haves and have not's, this was about inhumane treatment.

Mrs. Dickson wasn't asking for the entire world, just a small place on Gods earth, where her family could live in harmony. She was quite content living in her neighborhood and was merely asking to be treated civil and not viewed as a criminal because of the color of her skin or the location in which she resides.

None of us assigned in the area made any arrest, we were advised to turn a blind eye unless it was a flagrant violation of the law. The brass from the mayor down was very concerned about something re-igniting the disturbance. I understood their theory, but I must tell you it didn't set well with those of us that considered ourselves good cops.

The mayor's promise to have a full scale investigation of the young black man's death accompanied by his walks among the folks at ground zero had a very positive effect. The number of protesters began to decrease with each passing day, leaving only the thugs and criminal opportunists on the street.

Once again, we had a minority of race-batters that wanted this disturbance to continue and eventually escalate into a full-blown riot. Then and only then do these hate mongers find they can use their dissension tools effectively, spreading hateful racist ideas to the already volatile crowd. How sad that one can only find themselves within such an ugly environment.

I have more respect for the common criminal who takes advantage of disorder to loot and steal, at least these characters are transparent and do not attempt to conceal their ugly actions behind a cause, a movement they conveniently support because it's a vehicle to obtain notoriety, fame and financing.

Four days later, we were advised that the situation had calmed to a level that the officers assigned to the area could police their community effectively, so us reinforcements were released and ordered to return to our assigned precincts. This was great news for most. Change is good, but not knowing the bad guys and geography of the precinct was uncomfortable to say the least, it was like starting out as a rookie again.

As we returned to the eastside my thoughts were bitter-sweet. One side of me regretted not experiencing the tactics used to defuse a full scale riot. The other, more logical side, thanked God no others were hurt and the incident was controlled. I also was leaving with a sense of gratification, for the life lesson a little unassuming lady named Mrs. Dickson had taught me. In all her innocence she had affected me with her wise reassuring words. Yet, I know for a fact, this was not her objective, not at all, she was simply stating in her non-wavering fashion what was the truth and asking others to do what was only righteous. A lady most will never know, yet one I will never forget.

CHAPTER 11

SUMMER OF 77
TIME TO MOVE ON

THINGS AT THE SEVENTH PRECINCT HAD not changed for the better in the last five years, the whites still avoided the black officers and vice versa. The power shift was still the lesser of the two evils, with black and white officers backing one another up on runs, yet the race divide was still very prevalent and getting older with each passing day.

There were rumors that the Precinct Narcotic Units (PNU) were going to be disbanded and consolidated into a Central Narcotic Division, a large unit with over 200 men and women under the direction of a new inspector, which would be responsible for narcotic enforcement throughout the entire city.

The old-timers in PNU were less then pleased by this move. They were quite content with their little world that consisted of a quaint five-man crew with only a sergeant to answer to. The buzz was that the powers to be were looking for new blood, cops that would be required to purchase narcotics themselves rather than using informants. There is no stronger case in court then a hand-to-hand drug transaction with an undercover officer.

Many of the older guys had become complacent in their efforts of narcotic enforcement, for this lack of determination they were to be eliminated. PNU traditionally consisted of guys with seniority that were sponsored by a member of the crew, a crew which is usually very tight and hush, hush. What happened between the crew, stayed with the crew, a model practiced by many within the blue ranks.

I approached Bob concerning the two of us transferring to Central Narcotics and, to my surprise, he displayed very little interest in the move. Eighty percent of our arrests were drug-related in one respect or another, hell, majority of crime is drug-related. Robberies, burglaries, writing bad checks, prostitution were all crimes committed by addicts to finance their habit. So, in all reality, we would be doing exactly what we were doing now, just citywide.

Now, you have to understand, Bob is one of those people who are quite satisfied with the status quo, the less change in his life the more content he is. Yet, once he experiences a new endeavor, he adapts to it quite well. I guess it's just that old cop line of thinking: "It has been done that way for years why change it?" In my opinion, this line of thinking can dwarf an organization's progress and keep it in the dark ages.

The city was on the brink of change and the Detroit Police Department, as we knew it, was going to have to bend with it.

The conversion would need new blood that would be willing to work through the stagnancy of their predecessors. I wanted to be part of this revitalization; change quite often encourages positive growth. Bob, the epitome of procrastination, finally agreed and our applications to the revised Central Narcotics Division were submitted. Our work record spoke for itself; it was just a matter of passing the oral board.

I found something very exciting about becoming a NARC, the idea of the cloak and dagger thing really intrigued me. To become the animal, you hunt, to see how we are perceived from the criminal side. I would have to change my identity, maybe an earring or two, long hair or even a beard. What most cops fail to realize, is that in the attempt to disguise their identity as a cop, they often become obvious and very transparent to the criminal element.

Five days later there we were at police headquarters sitting in the hall with 50 or more applicants from around the city, many of whom we recognized as aggressive cops who we'd seen in court daily. This was the first day out of a week of scheduled interviews. We heard there were going to be over 500 applying for the positions and only 200 would be accepted.

What kind of questions do you think they will ask us Bob? He looked at me with somewhat of a frown on his face, as if I annoyed him with the question. "What the hell you worried about? We work our asses off and we're honest as the day is long, I'm sure they will ask the typical integrity questions. Just be straight-forward and answer direct, it will be fine."

Many of the people in the hall were dressed like they were already accepted for the position, a little presumptuous if you ask me. There were those in motorcycle attire, others dressed like pimps and some just looked like homeless people. Bob and I had on sport coats, due to an earlier court case.

After about an hour, the large oak door leading into the Narcotics Division opened, an older gentleman stepped out. He was tanned and very distinguished looking, a real player with white wavy hair, wearing a dark shiny blue suit with blue shoes, an ensemble that cost more than my entire wardrobe. He appeared to be sizing up the candidates while glancing around the hallway.

Suddenly, he spoke up, "Stealth, Dave." Oh great, I thought, all these cops and I'm the one they interview first. Well here goes nothing. As I stood up and walked toward the gentleman, it appeared that his expression said, "You got to be kidding me, this kid wants to be a narc." "Come on in officer."

The Panel was made up of two black and three white officers, one being the distinguished gentleman who I found out later was a lieutenant by the name of James, code name "Cowboy." I was directed to an old wood chair in the middle of the room, positioned right in front of the panel. I now understood how defendants being questioned felt; the only thing missing was the large bright light hanging over my head. The first question was predictable. "So what makes you think you can be a NARC?" "Well, sir I have worked plainclothes for a while now and feel I'm much more effective out of uniform."

This answer just ignited a flurry of difficult questions. "Do you realize you will be required to purchase narcotics? Are you a religious man? Do you or have you ever used the word Nigger? Have you ever taken anything that did not belong to you? Would you turn your partner in if he or she were stealing? Have you ever used weed or any other drugs?" Wow, what a firestorm.

The Interviewers were looking for a reaction as well as an answer. I would later learn to appreciate this. If I could not handle the pressure of rapid fire questioning from fellow officers, how would I react to a dope dealer holding a gun to my head accusing me of being the Poe-Poe (Police Officer)?

The Panel asked me to stand out in the hallway until summoned. I'm sure I was only out there for moments, but it seemed like eternity. I recall thinking to myself, I don't need this damn job anyway. Who the hell do these guys think they are. I'm a hell of a cop and I don't need this shit. The door opened once again and I was asked to come back in and have a seat. It seemed like hours before anyone spoke. God I could hear the old office clock hanging on the smoke-stained wall ticking.

I must have done something right, because the panel looked at one another, nodded in agreement allowing a slight smile to appear on their faces. The lieutenant stood up extending his hand, "Welcome to narcotics Dave, we believe you will be a good fit. You come highly recommended, and I'm sure you will make us proud."

My partner had his interview shortly after mine, but Bob's

would be a real slam-dunk, his reputation as a great cop definitely preceded him. They would be fools not to accept him, talent like his only comes by every so often. He too received good news and was invited to join the new unit.

One week later we found ourselves sitting in the auditorium of the Centennial Building located at East Jefferson and Chene, the new home of the Narcotics Division. You talk about a humbling situation; here I sat in the company of the top cops of Detroit. They came from across the city; most had worked precinct Booster cars, Vice, Mobile Crime's Unit and the recently disbanded Stress Unit. You talk about egos, we were the cream of the crop and we knew it.

The first speaker to address the audience was the new commander, a well-dressed man who we would soon find out, supported his men to the fullest as long as they were honest and acted in good faith. He also had a love for being in front of news cameras, which was a humorous trait that would follow him throughout his career. His message was quite simple and to the point, we were declaring war on drug trafficking in Detroit and he would ensure we had the proper tools to do so. His emphasis was on integrity and assured us he would not tolerate corruption at any level, those that were involved in the slightest fashion would be prosecuted to the fullest extent.

After addressing all issues and expectations, the Inspector introduced the executive officer and the remaining command staff. He then said "Now, that I got that out of the way, let me introduce you to a living legend, Mr. Narcotics himself,

Sergeant Donald "Cobra" Burton." The entire room stood up in a standing ovation. Even the few officers that were not familiar with Cobra, followed suit, for the simple reason if this audience respected him to this level he had to be something very special.

Burton, embarrassed by this introduction and the audience reaction, reluctantly stood up and addressed the Narcotics Division in his normal Cobra fashion. "The Inspector is correct; we are going after these fucking drug dealers and we're targeting them honestly and with a vengeance. We are a team of one, so if you have a problem working with blacks or you brothers have a problem working with whites, you can get up and walk the fuck out the door right now. We are family and we will watch each other's back, our goal is to get drugs off the street without having any of ours killed." The crowd once again came to their feet. These weren't idle words; Cobra truly loved his narcs and would literally do anything for them, including giving his life if necessary.

I remember looking around the hall at this elite group thinking, we are going to war and there is no question there would be losses, the question is who would be the casualties. Our ranks comprised of Blacks, Whites, Hispanics, Asians, Male and Females all of whom were quite aware of the imminent danger we all faced in the war against drugs. Little did I know, it wouldn't take long before we would realize the Dope Dealer was an equal opportunity killer and could care less about the race, creed or gender.

Each officer was required to select a code name prior to hitting the street. This code name would be your radio call sign and eventually take the place of the officer's actual name. I decided on "Hillbilly" due to my southern roots. A few of the many code names that I would like to recognize were; Mistral, Meatball, Bear, Spiderman, Batman, Ironman, Bush, Woody, Bronco, Doc, Rock, Big Bird, Lucky, Too-sweet, Spook, King, Gypsy, Hawkeye, Star, Jap, Spoon, Budda, Jaws, Chico, Eagle, Banjo, Diver, Lion, Gitmo, Cowboy, Bushwhacker, Lips, Tiger, Animal, Popeye, Playboy, Stumpy, Dumpy, Snow White, Roadrunner, Skitter, Rapper, Fiq, Stallion, Hollywood, Mouse, Spartan, Whip, Curly and Bomber. I could go on and on, but I think you get the idea. The names were as diverse as the individuals and would stick with these heroes for the rest of our lives.

Bob was assigned to the Surveillance Unit, whose primary function is to follow and protect the UC (Undercover Officer) as well as shadow targets (defendants/suspects). Whereas, I was placed on a Narcotics Enforcement Unit, which consisted of five to seven police officers and a sergeant. Our job was to buy street level narcotics, heroin, cocaine and any other illegal controlled substance.

This assignment suited me just fine. Prior to coming to Narcotics I purchased cocaine from a scum bag at the Eastern Market, located in downtown Detroit. I will never forget the rush I got; just the fact that I could deceive a low life into actually selling me, a cop, narcotics was intriguing. Not to mention the fact that a hand-to-hand purchase involving a police officer is a very solid case, unlike the typical possession case.

My crew consisted of two white males, one white female and three black males, one of whom was our immediate supervisor, Sergeant Tyler. It wasn't long before we begun to form a team of one, we all knew our partners had are back. Initially the blacks did all the narcotic purchasing and the whites did the arresting and raiding. Not because the whites were opposed to buying, it was just the fact that most of the areas we went into on the eastside were black and the thought was: blacks were more easily accepted. However, we would soon learn that whites could cop (buy drugs) in black neighborhoods as well. Sometimes it required a little more persuasion to convince them you weren't the man (police), but in the end greed and money prevailed.

Our crew, as with most in the Narcotics Division, became family, we ate, slept, and partied together daily. Now when I say party, I mean extreme partying. We worked hard and partied harder. This obviously was back before Mothers Against Drunk Divers (MAD) was prevalent and before most of us displayed common sense, knowing when to say when. Narcotic officers were initially known for frequenting the Old Shillelagh bar, a small Irish establishment located a couple blocks from police headquarters in downtown Detroit. Everyday citizens who would walk in would have quite a shock; their expressions often said, "What the hell have we walked into?" The pub appeared to be occupied by pimps, ladies of the evening, bikers and bums, when in reality they were Detroit's Finest, the Narcotics Division.

The entire unit laughed and cried together; we were definitely a family. This is the kind of police department I always imagined and wanted to be part of. Now I'm not going to blow smoke and attempt to convince you I found the promised land, however, I am saying that blacks and whites alike, not only worked together we genuinely cared and looked out for one and other.

One partner I became very close to was Jamar, a small-framed, light-skinned black gentleman. Jamar was one brave man and a hell of a partner. When you talk about buying dope, this kid owned the city. We often joked with him, chanting, "Jamar, Jamar the light skinned star." A joke that really carried a great deal of merit and could easily be verified by his hundreds of narcotic buys. After a purchase, Jamar who was still on his "copping high" (purchasing high) would boast, "Dave, I can buy dope from the Pope."

Before I go any further, let me clarify my previous statement for those of you that are not from the world of an undercover narcotics officer. When I say Jamar was still on a "copping high", please let me explain. This is merely the adrenaline sensation one receives after purchasing drugs. Contrary to popular belief, narcotic officers were not allowed to take any controlled substance when making a purchase. Out of the hundreds of narcs I worked with, I am not aware of one ever consuming drugs.

Consider this, we undercover officers step into a world that is dark and ugly to say the least, with characters that would kill you in a New York second if they even suspected you were a cop. Therefore, we do our job in such a fashion that we not only convince the dirt bags we are not cops, they actually sell us narcotics. As cool as we may portray ourselves during a purchase, I can tell you this, our pucker factor can be off the chart at times and when we get back into friendly territory among our own, we are not only relieved, we are high on victory. So, now you understand what a "copping high" is, I trust.

Jamar may have been slight in stature, but I assure you he was fearless. There are two incidents that come to mind where he displayed exceptional courage. The first was on a raid in the Eleventh Precinct, upon entering the residence, two armed gunmen and I became engaged in a gun battle, the problem was there were several young children in the dining room between me and the assailants. With bullets flying everywhere, my daring partner Jamar, with total disregard for his own safety ran to the children's aid, extracting them all. Remarkably, not one bullet hit any of them, lucky? I think not. I would say one courageous cop and angels are the reason those innocent children survived.

The second incident occurred when Jamar and I entered a large Wayne County jail cell referred to as the "Bull Pen" occupied by approximately 25 inmates who were primarily black. Jamar and I entered the Bull Pen to extract a loud mouth brother who was enticing his cellmates to riot. We were unarmed and back-to-back, but in the end we accomplished our goal removing the mouthpiece, which, as we expected, became a whimpering coward when separated from the population.

Our unauthorized entrance into the jail cell caused quite a commotion with the sheriff deputies and supervision. Quite frankly, it was an irresponsible if not stupid thing to do; we could have created a hostage situation or even worse, we could have been over-powered and killed without much effort. I really believe the only reason we are here today, is that the inmates thought this salt and pepper team was out of their damn minds and now that I think back, we may have been experiencing just a little temporary insanity.

My point is that Jamar, as poor as my decision may have been, stood by my side knowing quite well the odds were against us and the consequences we faced looked pretty bleak. Our unconditional loyalty was not a trait unique to the Narcotics Division. What was unique is the fact that race was never an issue. When we walked into that cell we walked in as a team and the fact that the inmates were black never entered our minds.

Over the next several years the Narcotics Division had many triumphs, but not without cost. We had a number of our officers shot, two of whom were Killed in Action (KIA). These find heroes were Jack "Meatball" Buffa and Charles "Maestro" Beasley. The others were seriously wounded, some to the point that they were required to retire. Countless officers were assaulted while undercover, one of whom was thrown out a three-story window. Each incident created a stronger bond within the unit, making us that much more determined to put our enemy, dope dealers out of business.

Hospitals around the metropolitan area became acutely aware that when a narcotic officer was injured and conveyed to their facility, they needed to make provisions for a hundred or so concerned narcotic officers. You talk about networking, when one of ours was shot, it didn't matter if you were on leave or off shift, the majority rushed to the hospital.

Typically the hospitals would set up a couple of rooms where we could congregate and support our fallen comrade. Our Chaplin, code name "Moses," would lead us in prayer followed by silence; you could hear the proverbial pin drop, as we all waited for the condition of our colleague. In the unfortunate case we lost one of ours, the room would be filled with grief and tears, coming from the toughest guys and gals that the city of Detroit had to offer.

Our Inspector, who was always on site, would make sure that at least two officers would stand security for the injured officer 24/7 until released. Assigning officers to this detail was not an issue, there was always an abundance of volunteers, this was one of ours and we would look after our own.

On duty misfortunes were not our only casualties; many of us were suffering on the home-front as well, due to the long hours and the longer hours in the bars. Four of us went through divorces at the same time; our wives retaining the same attorney, which lends to the joke that our four wives got a group rate. I can't speak for the other officers, but I was the problem in my marriage, when you put your family second to a job and partying, divorce is imminent.

Narcotics had several watering holes (saloons) The Irish Pub, Kim's Lounge and the infamous Clemens. It was never a question of if we were going to stop for a drink; the question was what time we would get there. Each crew worked separately, so the arrival time was based on the amount of arrests you made and how proficient your crew was with the paperwork.

Every night was like a Friday, plenty of drinks, laughs and tales of accomplishments and close calls. We had our share of ladies that would stop by to see the crazy narc's, the stories being told about our antics were spreading like wildfire. I guess their curiosity got to them and they wanted a firsthand look, we had ladies visiting from the entire metropolitan area even from our neighboring country Canada. The jukebox never stopped and was loaded with good old Motown music. We would often make a gauntlet of narcs dancing our way between the lines one by one making our steps up as we went along, many of us looked like we were having muscle spasms, but it was all good.

I think back now and wonder how we kept such a schedule, we would go to court during the day, work in the afternoon, close the bar and start all over the next day. This brutal cycle never stopped during the 16 years I would spend in Narcotics. My God, how did I do it?

There were secondary bars that many of us would occasionally stop by as well. We had the Precinct Bar, Brewery Tavern and Tip Pub, which were white bars, and Wanda's on the westside, a black bar. If I, as a white man would walk into a black tavern alone, not only would heads turn as silence fell over the room, I would most likely have a hell of a fight on my hands. But, if I walked in with one of our black undercover officers no one would pay attention to the white man being accompanied by the brother. This same concept worked in white bar's when a black entered, if you were escorted by a white, it was assumed that you were ok and not there to cause a problem.

Another event that was very popular with the narcs in the summer was the payday hotdog roast on Belle Isle. The barbecue was usually organized by Animal, Stumpy and Lips a team commonly referred to as "TNT." It was three dollars a person for all the hot dogs you could eat and all the beer you could pour down your throat and believe me our guys could put away some beer.

The Narcotics barbecues were supported by both white and black officers, an occasional group of young black knuckleheads would attempt to crash the party, which was usually a move they would come to regret.

Even with all the work and play, the men and women of the Narcotics Division attempted to find time for their families. The men had an annual Father and Son canoe outing. Each year, we would pick a river in Michigan and for three days we would canoe the river camping each night under the stars. It was truly one time out of the year that we had uninterrupted time with our sons. What started out as three fathers and our sons eventually grew to approximately 90 men and boys with 40 canoes, 7 of which were filled with supplies.

We would often receive some pretty suspicious looks from the northern Michigan population who weren't accustomed to seeing families of blacks and whites coming down a northern river in harmony. In the initial trips you could see a slight skepticism between the black and white children, but by days end, color faded and they all simply became boys having a great time in the wilderness, a lesson that could be learned by all. These were memories in the making, memories that would be discussed for years to come.

It was not long before the Detroit Narcotics Division became the icon for Narcotics enforcement around the country, with a reputation of excellence not only in the U.S., but also with large Police Departments around the world. We had detectives from Germany as well as Japan visit the unit to observe our techniques and procedures. The Inspector had put the Narcotics Division on the map, giving the unit a sense of pride that was second to none.

The joke in the unit was that we undercover officers were buying more dope then the junkies on the streets. Everyone was making narcotic purchases, black and white alike. The dope man was constantly changing his MO to prevent from selling to a Narc. They would make a change and we would figure out a countermeasure.

One dealer we arrested made the statement, "That's it; I'm not selling shit to anymore white boy's." This was really not an option, because he knew as well as we did, that a good amount of Detroit's traffic was white suburbanites who would venture into the big city to buy their dope, often getting more than they bargained for.

Occasionally some white kid would drive down with his girlfriend to purchase his drugs; only to have a gun put to his head, losing his money, car and then being told to walk back to the suburbs. The girlfriend at times wasn't so lucky, she would be kidnapped and gang raped for days. If fortunate, she would eventually be released and advised to fend for herself, after being threatened with reprisals if she reported their ordeal to the authorities.

As time passed, there were those of us that became impatient with street buy after street buy, craving more. It was common knowledge that when we locked up a street dealer they would have a replacement on the same corner prior to the paperwork being completed. These aggravated Narcs wanted the supplier, the guy that brings the dope in and takes the money away. I, too, was one of the impatient ones!

One of the most tenacious narcs I would ever have the honor to work with was "Bronco." He was also one of those who wanted more than the dealer on the corner selling single packs of heroin. He wanted the person responsible for supplying the pusher. Bronco set his sights high and led the charge against the infamous YBI (Young Boys Incorporated), who, to date, had remained under our radar.

This notorious gang was responsible for supplying the majority of Detroit with heroin. However, that is not what brought them fame, it was the technique used to traffic the drugs. Juveniles as young as ten years old were recruited to transport and sell heroin on the corners of Detroit, hence the name "Young Boys Incorporated."

The YBI was quite familiar with the judicial system, after all this was their business. If they were not clear on a legal issue, they could seek advice from their pool of retained attorneys, some of which sold their conscience and integrity for blood money and extravagant gifts.

This organization used juveniles to sell there drugs and carry out their illegal acts, not because they worked for less, on the contrary, they paid them well, often earning more money than their parents were making legally. The YBI was quite aware that by using juveniles they could evade and manipulate the judicial system. Juveniles were not incarcerated like adults; they often needed to have three to six serious contacts before they would be considered to be a menace and confined to juvenile home. Even those who committed capital crimes such as murder were typically only held until they reached the age of 18 at which time they were released back into society, quite often showing no criminal history on their records.

So, more often than not, these kids who would shoot you at the drop of a hat, would be released and back on the corner dealing drugs before you got off shift. Those that were unfortunate enough to get locked up for long periods were assured by YBI that their parent(s) would be financially compensated during their absence.

Bronco, Spiderman, Spoon, and Buddha were four of the narcs that recognized this gang at the early stages for what they were: a dangerous, well-structured, criminal organization, with a chain of command second only to the military.

These fearless officers followed by the Narcotics Division declared war against the YBI. Enforcement crews would arrest the street dealers daily, most of whom were young kids. Rarely did these youngsters reveal any information; they were mentored by the best in the illicit world of narcotics.

Once the Narcotics Division realized the magnitude of the case, it was decided to bring in the Big Guns, the Drug Enforcement Administration (DEA), to join Detroit Narcotics in a cooperative investigation. Special Agent James Bing, code name "Kong," would take point and lead the effort to abolish the YBI. This endeavor was far larger than any undertaken by a law enforcement agency in Motown's history.

Success comes with a price. When you raid every night and make countless arrests, you inevitably will receive citizen and injured prisoner complaints. This was a tool that the dope dealers used frequently; knowing quite well that Internal Affairs (IA) would open an investigation. As I have indicated, when an investigation is initiated, the officer or crew is often discouraged from having further contact with the person who made the allegation, simply because continuous contact could be construed as police harassment. This now allowed the violator to deal his drugs uninterrupted, a simple, yet very effective ploy.

Many of our defendants at the time of arrest would advise us they would have our jobs stating, "That's all right, I'm calling IA and all you Motherfuckers will lose your jobs and then I'm suing the damn city." The populace of Detroit knew that IA would investigate every complaint and the city was quick to make monetary settlements out of court. I can't tell you how many low level dealers graduated to the big leagues of narcotics, thanks to the generosity of the Detroit City Law Department.

I'm not saying that IA should not exist, the unit is not only necessary it is vital in maintaining the highest-level of integrity, especially in larger agencies. My complaint was that the Detroit Police Department should have been more selective in their recruitment of investigators within the bureau.

To be fair, there were detectives who performed their investigations like professionals, but others we had interaction with, were self-centered amateurs, more concerned with their GQ appearance then justice. They believed that an allegation was proof of guilt and treated us like many of the criminals that made the complaints. You were considered guilty until you could prove your innocence. The investigators would take the word of a low-life murdering dope dealer before yours, a fellow officer.

This is not to say Internal Affairs should disregard an allegation because you are a brother in blue, not at all. It is of paramount importance that each and every complaint be investigated thoroughly and if you are proven guilty, you should receive no better treatment then the common criminal, and be prosecuted to the fullest extent. However, here's a thought, we should have the same rights as the people we lock up, innocent until proven guilty and should be treated accordingly until facts dictate otherwise.

The majority of the investigators we dealt with were black, but I can honestly say, I don't believe race in this particular case was the issue. Because the blacks assigned to Narcotics visited IA as much as the whites, we all worked together and all received complaints, so no one was exempt. Although racism most likely wasn't the driving force behind their investigation, discrimination was certainly a factor.

The complainant, often a low-life with ulterior motives was believed unconditionally, while we, the professionals, were made to feel like we were wearing orange county jail uniforms, even before we were interviewed.

Internal affairs were backed fully by the Coleman Young administration, which explained much of the arrogance. During his campaign he made the promise to the citizens of Detroit that the police department would be accountable for their actions. The police brutality he had personally experienced as a young man would never be tolerated again. He further promised that anyone exposed taking part in these despicable acts would be disciplined to the fullest extent.

I, along with the majority of my associates, had no problem with this pledge, because the crews in Narcotics had a reputation of being tough but fair on the street. You shoot us, we will shoot you back. If you assault us, we will assault you. Very elementary rules, but rules the people on the street understood, it kept us alive! With that said, excessive force by outsiders was not tolerated and, believe me, we policed our own. We weren't opposed to stopping other officers who felt they could get an unnecessary blow in on a suspect that was being apprehended or cuffed.

One incident comes to mind when I think of the worst example of verbal abuse I witnessed during my career. It happened during a raid of a heroin house in the Seventh Precinct off East Grand Boulevard. The house was occupied by at least 20 people; I remember how strong the stench of body odor was as we entered the residence, hygiene is not a priority among drug users it's all about the next fix. Among the occupants were junkies, the dope dealer and members of his family, which included a small black child by the name of Pete.

Pete, who couldn't have been any more than four years old, was understandably terrified by the forced entry. Once he settled down from witnessing a crew of armed officers barging in his home, he became very inquisitive, asking one question after the next. Our partner, "Sterling," a very attractive black narcotic officer compassionately sheltered him. After securing the prisoners, we let Pete walk around the house freely under "Sterling's" close observation, making sure he stayed clear of narcotics, weapons or anything else that might harm him. This was much more than his father, the dope dealer, ever did for him.

After handcuffing those under arrest, we requested the two uniform officers who accompanied us on this raid transport the defendants down to police headquarters. As they were leading the prisoners out, Pete asked a simple question of the escorting uniform officers, "Where y'all taking my Daddy?" To which one of the officers, an overweight white officer and, believe me, I'm being polite, he was an outright fat slob, with a uniform that was desperately in need of some soap and water, stated, "We are taking him out back and going to shoot him in the head." Pete immediately began screaming uncontrollably, pleading for his father's life. His daddy, who was a low life without question, was still the only father he had.

Well, I'm not quite sure who got to the officer first, but our entire crew was all over this creep. Sterling immediately calmed the child down while assuring him that no harm would come to his father, however, he would have to go to jail because he was selling drugs.

This innocent child was not a criminal and he certainly didn't choose to be reared in a home that freely used and sold drugs in front of children. He was merely a product of his environment, a fragile casualty of the drug world, with an escape to a better way of life highly unlikely. Pete was not only communicating with the police, he was relating with white police officers, which was a unique experience for him I'm sure. This could have been a great opportunity to leave a positive imprint concerning law enforcement.

Unfortunately, these sincere efforts by our crew were undone in one swift moment, with an insensitive statement by this tough guy, who instead of creating an ally, very well may have produced a future cop killer!

One of the life lessons we learned in Narcotics was the fact that just because you were found inside a dope house, did not necessarily mean you were involved in the illegal operation. The elderly, sick and children often found themselves prisoners in a world they had no means of escaping. When possible, we would attempt to comfort them by suggesting ways in which they could seek assistance. Just a kind word making them aware we realized they are not of the same makeup as the garbage we were taking to jail, offering them a slight taste of the self-esteem that they so desperately needed.

A good friend of mine, Officer Danny "Jaws" Baker, always said, "It doesn't cost a dime to be nice to a person" and believe me this Fin-lander was no pushover, he was one tough cookie. His simple words were not only profound; they have remained with me till this day. One kind word can pay huge dividends. Bullishness acts, like a bad storm, will fade away with time, but a kind deed will be remembered to one's final hours.

I cannot begin to tell you how many times being kind or treating someone with respect paid off immensely. We even had gang bangers give us information, not because they had seen the light, but because they didn't agree with the crime and knew we would follow up and treat the defendant fairly.

One of the BKs (Black Killers) once gave us information concerning a child molester, which we later apprehended and eventually was convicted. I will always remember the statement this gang member made after giving us the details. "Look man, I ain't no snitch, but no kid should be done like that. I know you guys are straight up and do the right thing. I also know you will still come after me for doing what I do and if you do catch me, it will be solid, not some bogus case you put on me." It was just an understanding developed through mutual respect from two men, one that lived by the rules of the street and the other who stood by the law of the land.

CHAPTER "THE BIG STORE" 12

AFTER TWO YEARS OF WORKING ON a Narcotics enforcement crew, I was fortunate enough to get involved in a case that would eventually give me an opportunity to work on a conspiracy crew. The Conspiracy Unit was viewed as the big time, where large amounts of narcotics were purchased, a chance to go after the main man, the head of the snake, an objective that all narcs aspire to.

However, the perception that conspiracy officers were somehow superior to street level undercover officers was not necessarily true. Simply because the street level enforcement undercover officer purchased illegal substances daily, keeping them alert while honing the skills that brings ones confidence to high levels. Whereas, conspiracy undercover officers, even though they purchase pounds and kilos, found their transactions and interaction with defendants far less frequent.

I will say this, working a conspiracy crew certainly opens numerous doors and allows the undercover officer assets that aren't available at the enforcement crew level. One of the main perks is that it exposes you to the federal agencies and their funding.

My new supervisor, Keith Mills, code name "Playboy," was a flamboyant individual, who was highly respected by those in the law enforcement field and admired by the ladies, hence his code name. He could also drink like a Viking and smoke more than me, which is a feat in and of itself, because during that period of my life, I was smoking four packs of cigarettes a day.

Our crew was outstanding when it came to moving surveillances, they could follow a target across the country without the suspect ever having a clue, not to mention they were all big time dope purchasers in their own right. If you were working a high level case, you couldn't have asked for a more experienced well-rounded team.

The case that brought me to my new assignment in the Conspiracy Unit was a criminal organization that referred to their group, as "The Family" The head of this Family was a small overconfident man of Italian origin by the name of "Mike." This organization, with connections in Florida, Texas and Mexico, was responsible for the manufacturing of PCP, trafficking of cocaine and stolen vehicles.

Overnight, I went from a street enforcement crew where I was driving a rusted out old Pontiac buying $12.00 packs of heroin off the streets of Detroit, to a conspiracy crew where I was given an exorbitant expense account, undercover apartment in a luxury high rise located in downtown Detroit, while driving a new luxurious Lincoln Mark IV. Life was good and I had all the toys to get the job done properly.

My meetings were often scheduled at my undercover apartment, where they were recorded and filmed. On one occasion, the equipment was malfunctioning, so our technician, a black officer, decided to hide in the closet and film the meeting manually. During this meeting the defendant, who was an outright bigot, began to talk in his normal chauvinistic fashion, saying nigger this and nigger that, every other word seemed to be nigger, I'm sure his KKK remarks were magnified because of the fact I was aware of my colleague's presence in the closet. I could only imagine how the black officer felt hearing these blatant racist remarks coming from this idiot.

After this particular meeting, I apologized to the technician, for his exposure to this ugly situation. I remember his reply to this very day, "Dave, it's no big thing, we know these things are being said when we are not in the room, this just confirms it. Bad guys aren't the only ones using these racist terms Dave, Cops use them as well, that's just the way life is."

As sad as his remarks were, I knew from personal experience they were based on fact. Although, I truly believe there had to be hurt and resentment locked up inside this logical man. I'm sure he's correct; you become callus to a certain extent after hearing the hate filled names time and time again. Nevertheless, I'm certain the scars that are left behind are everlasting for some, leaving a sense of distrust and bitterness.

One redeeming thought was that eventually this maggot

would become cognizant of the fact that his friend, me, who he had been selling drugs to, in reality, was an undercover officer. Secondly, his presence would be required when a jury that no doubt will have a number of black members, will view the filmed meetings where he expressed his bigoted remarks repeatedly. This will definitely come back to bite him in the rear!

Those that are fortunate enough to work in covert situations, get a very unique perspective of the underworld. We see it as a criminal, in their world, playing by their rules. The same person that says, "Yes sir officer, No sir, I swear I'm not lying officer," will address you totally different when he thinks you are just another low life attempting to get your daily fix of narcotics.

Undercover agents will be called punk, bitch, whitey, cracker and nigger, just to mention a few. You are only as good as your money or worth. It is not uncommon to be asked, "What the hell is stopping me from just killing your ass and taking your money?" Believe me, as a Narc you better damn well have a convincing answer on hand!

It is quite apparent that Racism is a prevalent factor when dealing with criminals, and race has an obvious effect on the price that one pays for narcotics as well as the manner in which the transaction will take place.

As a white UC, especially at the lower level, it is not uncommon to be referred to as white boy, white motherfucker, peckerwood or cracker during a purchase. This is a form of intimidation, making one less likely to argue the price or quality. The average black dealer knows quite well that the typical white person is frightened of blacks, having a perception that they are more likely to commit violent acts, such as assault, rape and even murder far sooner than a white dealer. However, I assure you this is not entirely true, evil has no skin color!

This knowledge gives them a definite advantage during transactions and makes the probability of a "Rip" (robbery) much more likely. A good UC will quickly learn how to present them self when confronted with this attitude. Not too cocky, yet not like a sheep willing to be led to the slaughter either, you must display enough confidence to prevent the rip, while not being perceived as superior or defiant. A tool not every UC possesses or is capable of learning, you either have it or you don't.

Now, at the higher level, the atmosphere takes on a much more business like setting. The likelihood of being challenged specifically because of your race is not as common. Although race will always remain a factor, it will most likely take a back seat to the good old American dollar. With this said, one must be very aware of the fact that the upper echelon in the narcotics world has far more at stake than the street dealer, which means you can be taken out (Killed) in a minute if you present a threat to their livelihood.

Our case soon mushroomed to a level that required more assets then the Detroit Police Department could provide.

Consequently, the Drug Enforcement Administration became involved. They brought a lot to the table, financing, experience and prosecution at the Federal level, which would almost assure truth in sentencing.

There were several members of the crew that expressed concern about the joint effort, implying the feds would steal the case. There was a long history of distrust between federal agencies and local police departments. The feds had a reputation of approaching the local police to work a joint endeavor and eventually take the case in a less then honorable fashion. They often enticed informants with large sums of money, which federal agencies certainly had access to, a luxury that local departments very seldom experienced due to budget constraints.

I'm sure there was merit to some of these accusations, most likely on both sides. If I had learned anything during my career, it was the fact that recognition can make some folks do strange things, even ignoring their ethical beliefs. Everyone yearns for the "Big Case" and this is not unique to the federal agencies, it exists at the local level as well. My thoughts were I would trust them until they proved they were not trustworthy.

Even though this was a joint effort, it was decided that Sergeant Mills would be the OIC (Officer In Charge), while Special Agent Tom Kent, of the Detroit DEA field office, would assure the case progressed in a direction that would allow for a successful federal prosecution.

Tom, who sported blonde curly hair and a goatee eerily brought to mind General George Custer of the renowned 7th Calvary Regiment. S/A Kent was a hard worker who certainly wasn't opposed to stopping for a drink or two after work. He didn't come off like the stereotypical Fed I had been warned of, to the contrary, he was soft spoken and immediately gave his honest opinion on how the case needed to progress to satisfy the U.S. Attorneys requirements. Everything appeared to be above the table with no hidden agenda, providing a needed calm between the agencies. He soon became a partner and mentor. The stories of deception by the DEA soon faded and Tom was accepted as a trusted member of our crew.

Working with the DEA certainly presented many opportunities, not only with financial aid that allowed us to purchase large amounts of narcotics from the big dogs; it also allowed me to meet numerous agents, many of whom would eventually become my future partners and lifelong friends.

What I discovered immediately is that the agents with prior law enforcement experience were generally far more aggressive than those who entered the agency right out of college. I attribute this to having a real understanding of the street and the criminal element. Academies are essential for learning the basics in law enforcement; however, there is no better teacher then the street.

The case proceeded flawlessly, thanks to our professional team; the defendant count grew with each passing day. I attempted to introduce other undercover officers for the purposes of lessening my case load. Unfortunately, the "Family" was very reluctant to meet any new faces, their theory was this would decrease the chance of cops infiltrating their organization, an excellent rule, just a little too late because I was already inside.

What began as an average conspiracy case had now grown into a multi-state criminal enterprise that had their hands into every illegal activity that could possibly generate money.

After several months into the investigation it was discovered that we had corrupt cops involved in our case, one was from the Highland Park Police Department, a small city surrounded by Detroit, and the other was within our own department. This case couldn't get any more complicated, corruption took the investigation to a new level, I was now restricted from frequenting any local or federal courts as well as any police or federal facilities. My identity and personnel file was removed and placed at a secure location off site. I was officially a ghost. Just for the record, the majority of my defendants and the corrupt cops were white.

Our crew was very diverse, both genders white, black, old and young, which certainly was a benefit for us. Due to many of the neighborhoods we traveled. I had criminal locations out in the lily white suburbs as well as the inner cities of Detroit and Pontiac.

It was imperative that we had the right makeup concerning our surveillance team. If you put whites in a black neighborhood the risk of robbery increases considerably. On the other hand, if you put blacks in some suburban neighborhood, you can be assured of the police being notified.

A couple incidents come to mind, the first was involving my old partner, Ed "Lucky" Denith who was part of the surveillance crew covering me during a narcotics transaction at one of the Detroit locations. Three black youths walked past his vehicle, which was stationary, only to return a short time later approaching from the rear with their hands in their pockets. Lucky, who had gun in hand prepared for the worst, realizing he had been targeted as an old white guy who was easy pickings. As the youths approached the vehicle Ed heard the big guy say, "Naw, man, this dude has to be the police, it's way too easy" as they turned and walked away. They knew the average white man would not be in this neighborhood unless he was crazy, a junkie or the police.

The second incident took place after a purchase on the westside of Detroit. I was on Eight Mile, stopped at a light and waiting to go down the ramp to the John Lodge Freeway. My crew was already headed down to police headquarters with the evidence. Suddenly, I noticed a dark vehicle in my rearview mirror attempting to maneuver, through traffic in what appeared to be an effort to position his vehicle alongside mine. As a precautionary measure, I pulled my weapon and placed it on my seat. Once the dark sedan pulled next to me, I observed it was occupied by a lone black male who was screaming for me to roll down my window, which I did, asking what the problem was. The irate driver stated, "You white motherfucker, you're in the wrong fucking neighborhood" at which time he pulled a gun and pointed at me saying, I'll kill your white, mother-fucking ass." I immediately raised my weapon, at which time a gun battle ensued.

The suspect's bullets were ineffective and the only thing I killed was his vehicle with six rounds in his driver's door, none of which penetrated. While attempting to flee the culprit wrecked his car and was subsequently arrested and charged with assault with a deadly weapon. The charges were eventually negotiated down to "discharging a firearm within the city limits." You got to love the Detroit Court System!

After approximately a year, the conspiracy investigation ended and all members of the "Family" now became defendants and were convicted and sentenced to substantial prison terms for various felony charges, including attempted murder of a law enforcement official, me!

Ironically, criminals feel betrayed when they discover their partner was the very person they trusted explicitly is, in reality, an undercover agent. In Mike's case he was so upset I betrayed the "Family" that he put a murder for hire contract out on me, a contract that was never redeemed, thanks to an alert informant, great police work and divine intervention. The explosives he intended to conceal in my vehicle were discovered prior to their emplacement.

I remained with my conspiracy crew for approximately one more year, during which time my partner Jimmy "Iron

Man" Stone was shot on a raid by the brother of a homicide supervisor.

Jimmy was a great cop, partner and friend. He was a tall slim, good looking man with a great sense of humor. Jimmy was married to a lovely lady who spoke with a distinct German accent. They met while he was serving with the U.S. Air Force in Germany. This guy loved to party and often stayed out for days. I once asked him how he did this without repercussions from his wife, his response was hilarious. "Dave, it's all about the training, when we got married I told her that here in the USA, we have a marriage review board that convenes annually and should the husband give an unfavorable report, she could be deported back to Germany." What a character!

The intriguing thing about Jimmy's shooting incident is that the suspect was found not guilty and consequently filed a law suit against the city of Detroit, which graciously awarded him a million dollars without even going to trial.

My partner, who was forced to retire because of the severity of his wound, was so enraged by the city's decision that he hired an attorney and counter sued the suspect who shot him. When the dust settled Jimmy was awarded the money the suspect received from the city. A victory, I guess, but he would live the remainder of his life with a bullet next to his spine, a bullet that if removed could leave him paralyzed, a chance he was not willing to take.

CHANGE IS GOOD, OR IS IT? 13

SEVERAL MONTHS AFTER JIMMY'S SHOOTING, I was approached by our inspector who suggested it might be conducive for me to make a change, perhaps to another crew or an inside desk position. I'm sure he was concerned I was beating myself up because I called in sick the night my partner got shot performing my job as the point shotgun man. I must admit I have asked myself a hundred times, if I hadn't called in sick and led my crew through the door, would the results have been different, a question that unfortunately will never be answered.

A change appeared to be logical as well as appropriate under the circumstances; however, a desk job was out of the question, I have never worked an inside job and had no intentions of ever doing so. I take great pride in being a street cop. I advised the inspector, if at all possible I would appreciate an assignment with a Street Enforcement crew, a request that was honored with a smile and a nod, coming from a man who was far more than a supervisor; he had become a trusted friend.

A week later I was fortunate enough to get assigned to my old narcotics street crew, commanded by none other than Donald "Cobra" Burton, the Godfather of Narcotics. Now, I say I was fortunate to be assigned to his crew, however, I truly believe Cobra requested me, not because I was anyone exceptional, to the contrary, he knew I was bothered by the shooting and Cobra was well known for taking in problem children, misfits and those that others wanted to broom. In essence, they were good cops who in some cases may have made poor decisions or were troubled by an incident they had experienced.

The icing on the cake was the fact that I inherited Cobra's outstanding crew. A team that was very diverse, we had my partner for years Bob "Bubba" Field, "Bush" a beautiful Asian lady who was very small in stature yet one no-nonsense Gal when confronted, and "Fridge," who was a very large black gentleman, hence the code name Fridge. Bob and I really took a liking to Fridge because of his sense of humor and un-relenting courage; we adopted him as our own. We also had "Rapper," a muscular black man reared in the South, who had more heart than muscle, then there was "Milkman," a young white narc that also gave up the demon in the bottle (alcohol) years ago and, finally, there was a young thin black officer who was striving to become an attorney. What a combination narc/attorney, if he becomes a defense attorney, dopers will be fighting for his representation because of his insight and knowledge of the police world. Whereas, if he goes with the prosecution he will have a unique edge because he has been in the belly of the beast.

It didn't take long to get back into the buy-and-bust mode: (street-level narcotics purchases that are followed by the immediate raid and incarceration of the suspect). While it may be lower level purchasing, it, without a doubt, is the most dangerous transaction a narcotics officer will encounter. I attribute this to the fact the bad guys at this level are usually desperate, quite often three-time losers and junkies themselves. They are willing to sell you dope or just put a gun to your head and rip you off; it doesn't matter either way because they are at the lowest pinnacle of life, there is nowhere for them to go but up.

I thought I would miss the upper echelon purchasing in the conspiracy world, but, to the contrary, it was a welcomed change with no pressure to get to the "Main Man." We were just required to make undercover purchases followed by raids and arrests. Then at evening's end there was the traditional cold beers at the local tavern, drinks that were shared by the entire crew, black and white alike. The only exception to this tradition was, when Cobra would join us, he would have his typical cup of coffee, because he too, had given up the demon in the bottle to save his marriage and career.

It was now the mid-eighties and the makeup of the department had gone through a major metamorphosis, with many blacks and minorities promoted to command positions, some deserving and others simply being rewarded for their support in past elections. Narcotics had had a black inspector for a while now, a gentleman I got along with quite well, at least as the DPOA union steward. I learned a long time ago that when there are changes at the top, there is always a trickle down factor and the Detroit Police Department was no exception.

It wasn't long until the changes began to affect the narcotic division. Rumors were spreading through the ranks that there were going to be an abundance of transfers, with the majority being reassigned to precincts in uniform.

As the DPOA Union steward, I set up a meeting with the inspector to address the rumor. To which it was confirmed, there were going to be numerous transfers and the majority of them would be white officers. The reason given was that the high command believed that narcotics division personnel should reflect the racial makeup of Detroit, which, in this case was a majority of blacks. An answer that would not sit well with the narcs it affected.

I would suggest that any decent Detroit citizen who is unfortunate enough to have a drug house next door, could care less what the racial makeup of the raiding crew is, their only concern was having the contagious fungus removed from the neighborhood.

Within a month the transfers began and most of them as the inspector indicated were white. Many of these officers had been in narcotics since its inception and were excellent cops with unquestionable integrity. This move certainly did not help the racial divide. Some would argue there should be time limits in sensitive assignments like narcotics or vice, due to concerns of corruption or complacency. The rebuttal to this argument would be that these senior narcotic officers possessed a wealth of knowledge that without question would save lives and keep the drug world in check.

Those of us that survived the cuts were now hearing remarks coming from both sides, some of those transferred were making snide remarks such as "We were kissing up to the black regime just to save are jobs," and a few of the blacks would now flaunt: "It's our world now, and this is just the beginning, it's your turn to take the back seat." These remarks were often said in jest, but there was obviously a hint of under-lying seriousness to the remarks. One thing was for certain, for those of us that remained, we were going to be extremely busy training the newly recruited narcs.

After the massive transfers, one would think the enforcement pace would have slowed down, but to the contrary, crews were now required to obtain and execute up to three search warrants a day. This equates to 15-20 raids a week per crew. This pace was very concerning to us senior officers, because when focusing on quantity instead of quality, the risk factor for officers being harmed sky-rockets.

Unfortunately, our fears would come to light sooner rather than later. It was one of our black officers that was killed during a dope transaction that turned out to be a rip (robbery). Now, I'm not insinuating this was directly related to the multi-raid and arrest campaign, but any cop worth a salt will tell you: if you are rushing or going off halfcocked, you're creating a recipe for disaster.

Before long, the quality of the raids by narcotic crews were plummeting. Many crews would walk away with seizures consisting of narcotics residue, paraphernalia with one or two packs of suspected drugs. Dry Holes (houses with nothing illegal found at all) were becoming more prevalent with each passing day.

The morale of the narcs was wearing thin; we were working in a haphazard fashion to please a command and regime that appeared, in my opinion, to leave one with the impression that they could care less about the potential for injury within our ranks, as long as they could deliver the right numbers to the mayor's office.

This dilemma was not unique to the Narcotics Division, each night we would interact with the precinct officers who would reflect the exact frustration we felt. They, too, were experiencing the effect of the so called departmental restructuring by the new black regime.

Every complaint reported by the lowest level criminal was now to be investigated without question, whereas in the past, the desk sergeant or supervisor on the street could determine if the complaint held merit or was just fabricated, at which point it could be disregarded. Many working officers were becoming discouraged and reluctant to engage in real police work out of the fear of being crucified for some contrived accusation.

Those die-hard cops that still wanted to do real police work found it very difficult, if not impossible, due to a huge backlog of police calls. It was not uncommon for scout car crews to receive 15-25 radio runs a night, a grueling pace even for real go-getters.

Our crew was staying strong as a team, Cobra made sure of that and we now had a new addition, which would eventually replace Cobra as the Officer In Charge (OIC) of the crew. He was a young black sergeant with the code name "Bomber," a name derived from the famous boxer Joe Lewis, known as the Brown Bomber. He may have been a new sergeant, but he was certainly no stranger to the Narcotics Division. No sir, he earned his bones as a UC (Undercover Officer) and a damn good one, I might add, buying more dope than most. He was also a military veteran and as a vet myself, that suited me just fine. So there was no problem with him as our new boss, not from the whites or blacks. We knew he had our backs and we damn sure had his.

Several months have passed and Bomber was now our immediate boss. Following a legend like Cobra was not an easy task, but Bomber was pulling it off, he was a good fit and a born leader, who was very supportive of the entire crew. He would often rely on Bubba and me for advice due to our many years of experience in the drug world.

Bob "Bubba" Field was the crew chief and respected by the entire team, almost looked on as a father figure. This respect was proven on a hot night when one of our crew members called in sick, which was very unusual for this individual;

he was a man who never missed a raid, so this was totally out of character. This crew member will remain nameless at this time for obvious reasons.

Our questions concerning his absence were soon answered, when we received a call from the upper command indicating that our officer was involved in a domestic dispute with his wife. The officer in charge at the scene was requesting Bubba's presence at our partners' home immediately.

Apparently our partner told the responding officers and supervisors to get the hell off his property and the only cop he would speak to was his crew chief, Bubba. The command feared a barricaded gunman situation, which can be quite common in domestic disputes due to the fact that emotions can escalate, especially when the person involved believes you are patronizing them.

Bubba, Bomber and I drove to our cohorts home located on the westside of the city. Upon arriving, Bubba was allowed in the home where he had a one-on-one with our partner. How ironic, our black partner told the responding black officers and brass to get the hell off his property, yet, his white crew chief that numerous black officers have accused of being a racist, is the one person this man trusted enough to summon and reason with. Thanks to Bubba the Grand Dragon of the KKK, as some small-minded people would have you believe, is the one man that defused a volatile situation which resulted in restoring peace to a domestic situation as well as avoiding a fine officer from facing departmental charges.

I must admit this wasn't the strongest crew I've had the pleasure to serve with, but it was certainly one of the most entertaining. My previous crews consisted of senior officers that had walked the walk for many years, knowing pretty much every aspect of narcotic enforcement. They were effective in the areas of undercover purchasing, surveillance, executing search warrants and evidence collecting, and each and every one of them could put on any one of these hats upon request; there are no limits to what can be achieved when you work with giants like this!

Most of our current crew may have been young and inexperienced but they were hungry for knowledge and, more than that, were willing to learn. Believe me, there was no shortage of courage, to the contrary, we, at times, had to pull the reins back when our young heroes would get a little too frisky.

Like the majority of the crews in narcotics, we were family and very protective of one another, on and off duty. There were occasions when we were in a precinct laughing and joking as we often did, levity that at times generated expressions of disapproval from black and white uniform officers. Looks that appeared to indicate, "You may be required to work together, but you don't have to enjoy it." We just ignored these idiots. Our thoughts were that until they grow testicles and accompany us on a raid placing their ass on the line, they can keep their condescending looks and opinions to themselves. You might be in blue, but you're damn sure not family.

A few weeks later after processing our arrest and closing out the shift, we found ourselves at Kim's lounge having a couple cold ones, rehashing the day's events and laying out our strategy for the next day. During the lies and laughs session, one of our black partners shared a conversation he recently had with his young nephew. This young man expressed his opinion on the black man's perspective of white men. His impression, although coming from a young teenager, was shared with a large portion of the black community. The nephew advised his uncle that white men are cowards and terrified of blacks. All we have to do is stare them down and they run like scared rabbits.

Well, our partner educated this young fellow immediately, advising him that all white men are not cut from that cloth, even though there are those that perceive black males as intimidating, there is a faction that is not buying it. In fact, there are some white men like the ones he works with daily would welcome a confrontation with such an arrogant bully. He further explained his attitude could get him a well-deserved beating or worse someday if he didn't wise up.

This young man's opinion should not surprise any of us; after all they inherit their parent's beliefs and fears. Historically, white children are warned from childhood to stay clear of all black areas because they are infested with drugs and crime. Whereas, blacks often caution their children not to trust the deceitful white man, because, he will never accept them as equals and will only interact when beneficial or necessary.

Despite these man made challenges, our crew stayed focused and functioned as one. We put all our biases on pause so we could complete the mission, of fighting those dealing in illicit drugs, all the time watching each other's back.

This is not to say we didn't discuss race, it was a topic that was discussed daily in one form or another. There were the serious discussions, many of them involving the city politics and the mayor. Most of the whites believed the mayor over the years had destroyed the city, causing many families to relocate to the suburbs. Whereas most of our black partners believed he had done a fine job, looking upon him as if he were the Messiah. It was so odd that the blacks on the crew would see something in one respect, while the whites viewed the issue in a totally different light. Both sides were amazed that the other couldn't understand their position.

Then there was the lighter side with traditional humor, jokes about barbecues, fried chicken and red pop, along with the whites talking like Richie from the "Happy Days" sitcom and dressing like a hick farmer.

Joking is fine and I would even suggest it's great therapy for cops. Even though we never took it personal, our humor could become pretty ruthless at times. Anyone on the outside looking in would think we were ready to get into a gun battle.

While we enjoyed our big boy humor, we knew when to turn it off and put our game face on. Nothing was more serious then raiding or covering your officers while they were undercover. All of us have witnessed how quick things can go south! There was a time to play and a time to be vigilant; losing another one of ours was not an option.

Months passed and the self-assurance within the crew was becoming evident to all. Our once inexperienced crew had become a well-oiled machine, and with their new found competence came a whole new level of confidence.

As comfortable as I had become with this team, I once again had another career altering decision to make. Recently, I was approached by a DEA supervisor who solicited me to join his taskforce team, the renowned "Group One" working out of the Detroit federal building. A group second to none, made up of local cops and federal agents, most of whom had prior law enforcement experience before joining DEA, as I have indicated this is a real plus! After much thought and running it by my best friend and partner Bob Field, I humbly accepted his offer. Unbeknownst to me, I just accepted my final assignment as a Detroit Police Officer.

THE BEGINNING OF MY END

DURING THE NEXT FEW YEARS AS a member of DEA Group One I would have the opportunity to work the most notorious drug gangs in Detroit. Infamous Young Boys Incorporated (YBI), Chambers Brother Gang, Pony Down Crew, Curry Brothers, Best Friends and White Boy Rick to mention a few.

Our crew consisted of Detroit Police Officers, DEA, ATF and INS agents who without question were the cream of the crop, a great bunch of guys and gals. Each member of the team brought unique skills to the table, expertise that would prove to be invaluable in our battle against the drug world.

Special Agent (S/A) Dick "Gator" Crooks, a former Cleveland narc, led the charge in attacking many of the major Detroit gangs, implementing conspiracy cases that for the most part were irreproachable. Then there was S/A chuck Moore a former Maryland state trooper who found great joy in attacking outlaw motorcycle clubs in the metropolitan area. Ron McIntosh, one tough cop and former Marine, was our crew chief, a very easy man to follow and S/A Greg Henderson who was a leader in his own right, taking undercover work to a whole new level, a real professional. These gentlemen were a reflection of the entire crew, a real dream team! Little did I realize, the relationships that I would build with many of my new federal partners would last for a life-time.

Then there were those that I could care less if I ever laid my eyes on again. One of these individuals I refer to was an officer, and I use the term lightly. By his own admission he was a self-proclaimed opponent of the white establishment. I will not dignify him by using his name, he's not worthy of the recognition. Let's just refer to him as Mr. X.

I was warned about this character upon my arrival, being told he was bad news and incapable of playing well with others, especially whites. I advised my group supervisor that I had worked with some far left black officers in my time, but never had found a partner I couldn't get along with or at least find a common ground. Consequently, I volunteered to work with this low-life, a decision I would learn to regret.

Mr. X was just another professional victim; everything he didn't have or achieve in his life was the fault of the white-controlled world. In many of his assignments, his bosses would be threatened with a grievance of race discrimination if he was counselled or required to do his job.

I attempted to befriend this loser, thinking maybe, just maybe, there was something salvageable in this man. I worked out with Mr. X at the gym, invited him to join the crew for drinks after the shift. We seemed to be getting along fairly well; maybe this guy wasn't given a chance, a thought that would soon be proven to be anything but correct.

Our Supervisor Alan Nederland was a former Gary, Indiana narcotic detective prior to joining DEA, a city with an over whelming black population. Alan had a reputation in the community as an honest, fair cop who worked in harmony with black partners his entire career. Nederland was well-liked and respected by all races within and outside the agency. He truly cared for anyone carrying a badge, a real cop's, cop.

Alan went out of his way to mentor this guy, with hopes of turning him into a halfway decent cop. A task that would not be easy due to the chip this "victim" had on his shoulder. Mr. X actually believed he had all the solutions for a better world and, needless to say, whites did not have a significant role in it. A man who looks through the glasses of hate has a very narrow view of life.

I recall on one occasion Alan requested Mr. X to submit a report that was days overdue, to which he threatened Alan with a grievance, accusing Nederland of badgering him be-cause he was black. Well, needless to say, the fabricated threat didn't sit well with this supervisor. The young officer was ordered into the supervisor's office, at which time the door slammed, this clown obviously threatened the wrong boss.

Approximately 15 minutes later, Mr. X emerged from Al's office sporting a huge frown, a bruised look that can only be found on a spoiled child that didn't get their way. We later found out that Alan advised Mr. X to grieve all he wanted because his complaint was meaningless. He was further warned that if his reports were not submitted by the day's end, he would be written up and possibly sent back to his department. If you play with the bull, you will get the horn!

Months passed and Mr. X was still an island and the odds of a change in character were highly unlikely. The general opinion was a leopard doesn't change its spots, especially when hatred is so imbedded. So we worked together tolerating one another at best. The entire crew felt uneasy with Mr. X being part of the raiding party, because we all knew if anything went down and force became necessary, this guy would make an issue out of it regardless of the facts. He was right and the world was wrong, what a lonely planet this guy lived on.

Mr. X also had built a close rapport with numerous DPD high-level black command officers, many of whom were considered very radical. He had attended unauthorized meetings at police headquarters as well as socializing with these supervisors off duty. Sure seemed like trouble was brewing!

The straw that finally broke the camel's back happened in the month of February while I was working an off-duty security job at the Michigan Auto Show in downtown Detroit. The show only lasted for two weeks, not a long gig; however it brought extra money into our household. By department policy, we were required to get an authorization letter from the chiefs office to work a part-time job off duty. I had received this signed letter of permission in previous years but for whatever reason, I neglected to apply for one this time.

As always, I invited my entire crew and their families to come down to the show as my guest, and if they arrived prior to the show opening, I would be able to give them a golf cart allowing them to tour the show as if they were VIP's, which in my eyes they were. It was just a small token of my appreciation for their loyalty. Well, as much as I didn't like Mr. X, he was still a member of our crew, so I extended the same invitation to him.

Two days later I received an odd call from Mr. X who said, "Brother Dave, I would like to take you up on your offer, all I need to know is what hours you're working and exactly where I can find you." I advised him it wasn't necessary to locate me because the guys on the doors will be aware that he and his guest are coming down and were to be admitted free of charge and given a golf cart to enjoy the show. My sixth sense began to kick in, a sense that had protected me on so many other occasions; something did not pass the smell test?

The next day everything would come to light, Judas would reveal himself. I took compensatory time to work this day so there would be no conflict with my DEA duties and hours. At approximately 10a.m., I received a call from Mr. X, "Brother Dave I'm on the way down to the show, where will you be? I thought, what the hell, why the infatuation with my location? "I'll be at the main door on the first floor, but as I said you can go to any of the doors because all of the security officers are aware you're coming to the show."

Something wasn't right, flags were going up left and right,

and I was getting that same feeling I would experience during a drug deal going south, Beware! Approximately 15 minutes later I was radioed by the guys at the main entrance advising me several black DPD High Command Officers were at the main entrance asking for me and inquiring if I was working the show?

Well, as you may have surmised, Mr. X never showed up and never intended to. It certainly appeared it was a set up. This racist SOB turned me into his brothers at police head-quarters for working a part-time job without authorization from the chief's office. This was hardly a felony, but was with-out question the closest thing to an arrest that Mr. X experienced since joining the group.

As you may or may not know, cops are not at the top of the food chain when it comes to salary. Detroit is one of the lowest paid major city police departments in the country. Cops are always willing to work a side job to supplement their income giving the families a little something extra. So if this is considered a crime, I'm busted!

Let me be perfectly clear, I have never been involved in any form of corruption and firmly believe that any law enforcement agent that crosses the line committing felonies should be prosecuted to the fullest extent. However, a cop working a side job off duty to supplement his marginal in-come, please!

The news spread like wild fire through the DEA and the entire federal building, Mr. X's trap had backfired. The blacks wasted no time expressing their dissatisfaction for his despicable ploy. His hatred for whites far superseded his loyalty for the men and women that would have laid their lives down for him, how sad! He was pretty much black balled and was never to be trusted again, at least by those in the Detroit office. His actions were shameful and unacceptable by both races.

One thing was now perfectly clear; there were several of DPD's Black High Command that had me in their sights. Why they wanted me was unclear at this time, but the ugly truth would reveal itself soon enough.

It was very interesting how I could work for a black chief, who in my opinion was one of the top chiefs of our time and understood his officers, uniform as well as undercover. I attribute his understanding of the undercover officer to the fact he himself had worked the vice squad in a covert capacity. Yet, I was considered a threat or problem child to some in the new regime.

For those that want to immediately bring up the fact that Chief Heart was charged and convicted of a felony, I concede this is a fact and do not condone his actions. While I'm unsure when he crossed the line, it doesn't matter, because once you go to the dark side, there is no return, you can't ride both horses. However, I will say he served his time and finds no respect for his actions from those of us who once admired him. With that said, unlike the command that relieved him, he truly treated all officers equally, no matter the race or gender, never considering an allegation a conviction.

The new chief and his command staff appeared to rule through intimidation not diplomacy, destroying anyone who disagrees with their policies. It appeared that any officer receiving a citizen complaint was considered guilty until proven innocent. The word of this new mindset within the department quickly spread to the streets, adding another weapon to the criminal's arsenal.

Those of us taskforce officers from DPD were so thankful we were assigned out to the DEA, an organization that was known for its integrity, treating its agents with respect, judging them by their merit not their race or beliefs. They truly played by the big boy rules.

Life couldn't be better. At work, our crew was doing great cases, investigations that yielded huge arrests and lucrative seizures, funds that would be divided under the forfeiture law between the local agencies participating in the taskforce. And, making it even better, my old partner Bubba just got transferred to our group. At home, my lovely wife Paula and I were blessed with a newborn, a beautiful little girl we nicknamed "Special," an angel who captured our hearts from the moment she took her first breath.

As good as things appeared, there were times headquarters and politics hindered our investigations. We were approached by one of the DPD upper echelon commanders who requested us to discreetly find out if the feds had anyone in the department or mayor's office under investigation, and if so, we were to supply them with the particulars ASAP. A request that would not be complied with, if there was involvement by city government in criminal activities, our thoughts were "Hang the bastards." I guess they were forgetting that little thing called an oath. This unethical request was reported to DEA command who frankly weren't very surprised.

There was no love between the Mayor of Detroit and federal agencies. It was common knowledge that he had been targeted by the feds for years. But as far as I know all investigations were either unfounded or evidence for an indictment was just not there.

The closest I ever came to witnessing wrong doing out of the mayor's office took place during the investigation of one of the major Detroit drug gangs. While executing a search warrant at a condo on the lower eastside of Detroit, the mayor's niece along with a kingpin drug dealer were found to be the only occupants. They were found to be in possession of an illegal hand gun and placed under arrest. The two were subsequently transported to police headquarters for processing.

Well, to our surprise, there was a high ranking officer awaiting our arrival, at which time he demanded we release the mayor's niece and surrender the confiscated pistol. Against our better judgment we reluctantly complied. The weapon disappeared, and charges were never filed. I guess there are some who are above the law after all!

My assignment with DEA had taken me all around the country working with various agencies. To my disappointment, I found that DPD was not unique as far as the dissension between races. What I did perceive is that racism in none of those agencies had escalated to or were as blatant as in Detroit. We had a cancer and the prognosis wasn't very bright. I didn't see it improving anytime in the near future at least not without some sort of assistance from higher powers.

The new upper echelon was making drastic changes throughout the department and the Narcotics Division was not exempt. Those of us assigned to the federal taskforce were given a heads-up by our command that there was going to be some restructuring in Narcotics and cut-backs in personnel assigned out. This was not good news, because if there were transfers, I'm sure I would be one of the chosen few.

As with most rumors, there was a shadow of truth. The report of transfers was confirmed by our group supervisor, who indicated I and Tim "Big Bird" Milosky were the two being transferred and were being reassigned to precincts working in uniform. I would like to suggest it was just a coincidence that both of us were white, but I think not, it was payback time!

After completing a drug transaction where I wore a concealed recording device commonly referred to as a wire, Tim and I decided to visit the Detroit Narcotics Division and meet with one of our supervisors to confirm the transfer and get an explanation for our reassignment. What we were told by this command officer was amazing, after apologizing for the way this entire incident evolved, he advised us that he had nothing to do with the transfers; the decision was made at the upper-level in headquarters.

The supervisor then advised Tim to keep a low profile for a year and then resubmit a transfer back to narcotics, at which time he would do his best to make it happen. He then addressed me, "Dave, you've always been one of our best and this has absolutely nothing to do with your performance. The deputy, (one of the same black command officers that came to the Auto show attempting to make the arrest of the century) said' You will get rid of that pretty white boy and he will never work narcotics again, I want his white ass gone.' So as sorry as I am to lose you, it's out of my hands."

I could not believe what I was hearing. "So you're telling me it's not my performance, he's actually having me transferred because he doesn't like the pretty white boy?" "That's right Dave that was his exact orders."

The supervisor was unaware that I activated the wire I was wearing prior to our meeting, taping the entire conversation, a tape that I have to this very day, a recording that that clearly identifies the command officer by name. Not that I intended to use it, I respected this boss too much, he was a good man and fair leader who was caught in the middle. But when you're dealing with a despicable racist such as this headquarters command officer, one needs insurance to protect his family. There was no doubt in my mind this man would not stop until I was fired. I can only imagine the hell that would be unleashed if the races were reversed in this situation!

My career in narcotics, which spanned 16 years, had come to an abrupt end, an assignment that was my life, all because of a self-centered egotistical man. He put professionalism aside for his personal prejudice against a working cop, just because, in his eyes, he was a pretty white boy. Ordinarily I would be flattered being called a pretty boy, but when you must prefix it with the word "white." it's not flattering, it's an outright insulting racist remark.

My passion for the narcotics division and officers that were courageous enough to work in the ugly world of illegal drugs inspired me to compose the following tribute to these exceptional men and women subsequent to my retirement.

They are Special

They accept the task of infiltrating the darkest side of society and living the life style of those they have incarcerated from the time they left the police academy.

They are asked to appear, speak and mimic that element which they are sworn to protect society from, while at all times staying within the guidelines of the law and maintaining the highest level of integrity.

They themselves become an oxymoron, while enforcing the law they must convince those around them they are breaking the law.

They enter locations daily that are infested with rats, roaches, lice and human scum, which frequently are infected with incurable diseases.

They bury their partners all too often and are expected

to understand that their death over a ten-dollar rock of crack cocaine is simply part of the job.

They shield their families from the disgusting world they work in, a world that can only be described as the closest thing to hell on earth and pray their loved ones stay ignorant, remaining silent when asked, "How was your day?"

They are expected to understand when their defendants who they have had under investigation for the last year, are released at trial on a technicality and receive a monetary settlement because their search warrant did not contain the proper verbiage.

They can only find comfort and understanding in the arms of those who have walked in their shoes. However, when doing so they are declared arrogant, superior or overbearing.

They must unquestionably understand when they are pulled off a case and reassigned, due to the fears of their supervisors they are becoming lost in the ugly world of illegal narcotics.

They are expected to go into Rome but not do as the Romans do, or to lie down with dogs without becoming flea infested.

They are truly a notch above the rest, filled with enthusiasm and ambition, while having an unachievable goal of stopping drug trafficking within our communities.

Yes, they are special, THEY ARE NARCS!

Dave Stealth

GUILTY IS IN THE EYES OF THE BEHOLDER

WELL SEVERAL YEARS PASSED AND THE country was now struggling to recover from the riots in LA following the Rodney King incident. As a law enforcement officer who has been there, I must tell you the video tape was quite compelling and excessive force certainly could be argued. Now, while the evidence appears to be overwhelming, one may think the jury missed the mark, which regrettably happens from time to time.

Many factors can effect jurors, including being human. While we would like to believe that all jurors can be totally impartial and evaluate with blind justice, I assure you this is not always the case. We are only fooling ourselves if we ignore the fact that race, gender, age and geography's can definitely play a role in the jury's decision. This is precisely why defense attorneys request a change of venue in high profile trials.

However, with that said, I will propose there is an appeal process in the judicial system when a verdict is less than desired by the prosecution or public and it's not killing, looting nor robbing! Exactly what took place in LA and many other cities, all in the name of justice or the lack there-of?

I would also suggest that if one could interview the looters or savages that killed an innocent truck driver whose only crime was being white and making a wrong turn, would find the rioters would not be able to explain why they were looting, at least not until they got home and viewed the news on the TV they had just stolen.

It wasn't about a cause or justice for most, it was about liquor, cases of cigarettes, TV's and clothes. It's called Opportunism, when a faction of society seizes the moment, knowing that arrests are highly unlikely, with anonymity being provided by a mob, which permits them to blend into the forest. Yet, when these same criminals are caught, they scream bloody racism, police brutality and declare they are protesting for civil rights, a real slap in the face to great men like Martin Luther King Jr.

With that said, I know from experience in such heated situations, there are things the camera doesn't reveal, such as the events leading up to the physical encounter. For example: resisting arrest, not complying with a lawful order, fleeing from the police, putting themselves and innocent citizens in danger, all of which takes the adrenaline to levels the average person cannot begin to comprehend. I'm not insinuating this is a justification, but I do believe these factors should be taken into consideration.

Back here in Detroit, we had our own problems as well. Two of Detroit's finest: Larry Nevers and Walter Budzyn, both white officers, were attempting to effect an arrest of a black suspect, an arrest that went terribly wrong. This event would soon become Detroit's police incident of the decade: the Malice Green episode.

The two officers, whom I was somewhat familiar with due to their stellar reputation, reportedly were attempting to apprehend a suspect for Violation of the Controlled Substance Act (VCSA) on the Southside of Detroit. The suspect began resisting and fighting with the officers, at which time he apparently was struck with a flash light while struggling, and subsequently died later that night.

The way the department and city handled the aftermath of this incident I found totally unethical and disgraceful. In my opinion the mayor in fear of a reoccurrence of the Rodney King riots in LA, ordered the chief to immediately suspend the officers and seek criminal warrants ASAP. All measures that were against department policy, but the chief of this period, who was considered a weak man by many, anxiously complied.

Officials of the city and police department immediately went on TV and radio announcing the officers involved would be brought to justice for the death of Malice Green. How great it is to work for a city that hangs you out to dry before you have even submitted a report. A hundred years ago I believe organizations like this were referred to as "Lynch Mobs."

Once again our city was divided, both seeing the accused from totally conflicting perspectives. Much of the black population declared both officers murderers, while demanding they go to prison or else! Then you had the white element that suggested that the suspect was dealing in narcotics and resisted arrest leaving the officers with no other alternative but to use what force was necessary to effect the arrest, a departmental rule that we were all taught in the police academy. Both conflicting opinions would soon be argued in front of a judge at the 36th District Court.

The family of Mr. Green filed a lawsuit against the officers and city as everyone expected. What wasn't anticipated is that the city settled with the family for millions before the investigation or trial was hardly underway. Typically these cases and settlements can linger on for years in the judicial system. You talk about giving the store away. Although it has been said the city would rather pay off lawsuits than endure a lengthy trial, not to mention the mayor's office and police department had already portrayed Nevers and Budzyn guilty as charged, which pleased the angry citizens and assisted the prosecution immensely.

Once the dust settled Nevers and Budzyn would be charged and convicted of second degree murder and eventually sentenced to twelve years in prison. After the guilty verdict, one of the white jurors came forward and advised the media that he only went along with the verdict because he was intimidated by the other jury members, a decision he now regretted. This was a short-lived story and never gained much traction, because in my view this city didn't want any other verdict, so much for blind justice!

It certainly appeared these officers never had a chance, there was no way in hell a not guilty judgment would have been delivered. Not when you have protesters marching outside the courthouse threating to burn the city down if a not guilty verdict came in. How jurors could be fair knowing that if they acquit the officers, their lives may be in danger, not to mention the promise of riots in the street. Between these mobs, the biased media and the pressure coming from the mayor's office, a fair trial was highly unlikely if not impossible; they were without question in my opinion found guilty through intimidation.

With Nevers and Budzyn away in prison, hopes were that the city could finally begin a healing process. Yet, there was a dark cloud now hanging over the Detroit Police Department. Many officers black and white were very reluctant to engage in solid police work because of the constant fear of repercussions. Most officers were pondering; if an offender resisted arrest and force became necessary, would they have the support of their supervisors and the city, or would they become another sacrificial lamb?

I personally knew a number of fine officers who were now turning a blind eye to non-violent crimes rather than facing the consequences of department discipline or prison. How pathetic, once excellent cops, now reduced to security guards to be politically correct. We certainly didn't want to offend the radical cop haters, a faction of society that found pleasure in the death of an officer. The same people that were so quick to pick up the phone and dial 911 at the slightest sign of danger!

I'm sure there will be those that feel I'm being very one-sided on this particular incident and I must admit, I am, for the following reasons. I know the kind of cops these two men were, they were out in the streets, hunting down the very element that you protect your home and loved ones from nightly with alarms, barred windows and doors. Over two decades of loyal service with thousands of felony arrests yielding only a few citizen complaints. Hardly a record of rogue white supremacist cops. Certainly not officers who suddenly snap and decide to execute an innocent black man, I think not.

I would suggest they were merely doing their job, attempting to arrest a man who reportedly was struggling while refusing to reveal the contents concealed in his hands, causing the arrest to go south quickly. As tragic and sad as the death of Mr. Green was, it could all have been avoided if he simply complied. This horrific incident left one man deceased and two dead men walking!

The next incident that would drive another wedge between the races would take place in southwest Detroit affecting many lives, including mine. My former partner who now had 34 years'-service with DPD was arresting a surly individual who was known for his involvement in narcotics and prostitution. The suspect began to resist arrest, refusing to comply causing a struggle to ensue, which led with the suspect receiving a small laceration on his head. This entire incident was captured on the scout car video cam, which undeniably reveals Officer Field tapping the suspect on the head with his handcuffs while advising him to stop resisting and comply. What the camera doesn't show because it was reportedly out of frame is the defendant struggling and refusing to be hand cuffed. Just for the record, this suspect was white.

Well, by the time Officer Field and his partner reached the precinct, the supervisors were already considering a plan of disciplinary actions against him for injuring this fine citizen. A citizen who will most likely file a complaint, placing his name in the Detroit City lottery, which appears to pay off more than not, in some cases offering better odds than Vegas for fallacious allegations.

As with any working cop, the more arrests you make the more visibility you have and with high visibility, the chances of citizen complaints increase considerably. What society in general fails to realize is that when you work in a predominately black precinct, a majority of your arrests will be black, with the exception of an occasional white coming down for sex or drugs. The same can be said about black officers working in a white precinct; their arrests will reflect the populace. Yet these stats are sometimes used and twisted to benefit hate filled radical groups or overzealous department supervisors. It's very elementary, when in Rome you arrest Romans!

It was anti-police outlooks like this that gave birth to an activist group in the lower end of the Fourth precinct, an organization that had little love for the police and especially Officer Field. They actually had a wanted poster made up with his photo displayed, declaring him a rogue racist cop! A title given to him because of his constant presence and direct effect he had in the crime-infested area, a region avoided by many cops because of the risk factor. Field's contention was basic: "We are policemen and because of the overwhelming crime stats in this area, it needs policing." What a profound concept!

The fact of the matter is, in the world of law enforcement it is very easy to be average, making an occasional arrest, avoiding the high crime areas and writing a ticket or two when necessary. This mindset will allow you to remain under the radar, preventing citizen complaints and keeping the management happy.

Whereas, being exceptional, takes far more effort and comes with a price, because you are constantly hunting the worst of the worst, the criminals who appear to be conscienceless and search out the innocent with the soul intent of doing evil. These exceptional lawmen risk death, lawsuits, and reprisals from management as well as radical activist groups for not being politically correct. Yet these courageous men and women hit the streets daily, largely because they honor an oath they took and much of society fails to appreciate.

Shortly after this incident, Officer Field was advised he was going to be charged with felony assault, which could lead to incarceration and or dismissal from the department. Even though the suspect in this incident was white, the black activists were demanding Officer Field be charged and arrested. I must admit I had never seen my partner so upset, not because of the charges, but because he realized the love of his life being a lawman, was now over.

The pathetic thing about this incident was that Bob was being charged with a felony and the suspect was released with all charges dropped. This same suspect would be shot during a drug transaction gone bad, some three weeks later. One must wonder, was this justice or karma?

Months later, the city with the prosecutor's approval contacted Officer Field's attorney and offered a deal. If Field would plead guilty to a simple assault and battery, a misdemeanor, they would drop the felony charge and all this would go away.

After much thought and weighing out all options, Field reluctantly decided there was no other alternative; he was not going to risk imprisonment for simply doing his job. As much as it was ripping his stomach out, he was going to accept the offer and plead to a simple assault and battery just to put this stressful situation behind him.

It was only fitting that on the morning of sentencing it would be dreary with a hint of a cold mist in the air. Bob would stand before a judge this day, a justice, who no doubt, he would be familiar with from his countless appearances in court. Unlike past court appearances, he would not be entering through the law enforcement entrance today, nor would he be seated in the officers' section once in the court-room. No, he would be entering the room as a defendant.

My instructions from my friend, was that there were to be

no support groups at court, no family, no comrades and no officers. This was degrading enough for a man that enforced the law for over 30 years; he didn't want anyone to witness his humiliation.

As I pulled in front of Bob's home I wondered how he would look, I'm certain he didn't get a wink of sleep all night; I don't believe any cop would have. As he exited his home with his new bride Jenny, I could see the anxiety written all over his face, he was clad in a dark suit and as always he had his American flag pin attached to his lapel, a sign of respect for all who had served. He was not only a great cop; he is one hell of a patriot.

"Good morning partner, you OK?" "Yea, I guess Dave; let's get this shit over with." To which I replied "This is the last day Bob, this department is not worthy of a hard working cop like you, it's their loss. I know you don't want to hear this, but better a misdemeanor then a felony, and with the powers to be placing a bull's eye on your back, it's time to get out of Dodge!" "Yea you're right, it's just that I put my heart and soul into this job and it ends this way, unbelievable!"

My biggest fear this day was that there would be protesters and camera crews outside waiting our arrival. Another concern was that the court room would be packed with officers and those that would take pleasure in observing his career demise. To my pleasant surprise there were no picketers or camera crews outside and the only officials inside the court room were a couple black Internal Affairs officers and the sheriff's deputies assigned to court security.

What only took moments for Bob to plead guilty seemed like hours. It was finally over with Officer Field receiving probation along with court costs. We could not wait to get out of there. Thank God there was no media outside waiting to ask ridiculous questions such as "How do you feel Officer Field? Do you regret what you did?"

"How about getting some lunch partner?" "I'm not hungry but, I sure could use a cold beer." We found ourselves in the Eastern Market District on the eastside of Detroit off of Gratiot Avenue, at one of the local pubs. Most of the pubs and restaurants in this area were set backs of the early 1900's, with wooden tables and chairs, long oak bars with brass foot rails and dim lighting. Typically the food was to die for. We were joined by Bob Jr. one of Bob's four precious children, which consisted of one daughter and three sons, two of whom are fine police officers.

The cold beers were appreciated by all, and it was apparent Bob was finally beginning to exhale; it was over, now he could move on and begin creating a new life, a life without law enforcement, which was very difficult for him to comprehend.

The jovial conversation we were engrossed in was suddenly interrupted by a cell phone ringing, it was mine and the caller ID indicated it was Bob's attorney. My first thought was we must have neglected to sign a form or two in the mountain of paper-work that is required when pleading guilty. What I heard from the attorney absolutely astonished me; to the point that I excused myself and stepped outside to complete the call.

Once outside, the attorney clarified the unfortunate news. After departing the court-room earlier, Bob's plea agreement and file was conveyed to the U.S. Attorney's office in the federal building by Detroit officials. The same representatives that offered the deal and said everything would go away if he accepted the lesser charge and pled guilty, were now attempting to have Bob indicted and tried for civil rights violations. These underhanded, lying low life's had planned this move all along. It was now obvious they didn't just want Bob off the job, they wanted to bury him. A legal move like this must be approved from the top; an Internal Affairs officer cannot arbitrarily submit a request like this to a U.S. Attorney without the blessing of the upper echelon. Here we go again!

When I returned inside, the expression on my face must have been quite obvious, because Bob immediately asked, "What the hell is wrong now?" Once I explained the situation, Bob turned pale white and just dropped his head, a gesture that pretty much said, "That's it, I give up!"

Once again that small faction of the Detroit Police regime went to levels lower than even I thought they would go, confirming that they would use whatever means necessary to appease city government and self-serving activist groups, even if it entailed destroying honest cops, simply because they refused to comply with or practice their one-sided policies.

It appeared this command based many of their new policies on race or revenge. There were those in the high command that ruled through fear and intimidation, eerily bringing to mind third world dictators. A hate driven command officer can be just as dangerous as a white or black supremacist. Both have the same agenda: eliminate those who do not look like you or think as you do!

Bob was advised by his attorney to just lay low and wait, because it could be months before the U.S. Attorney made a decision one way or the other. It was now a waiting game, a grueling period that can drive one insane; wondering is today the day? Each time the phone rings your stomach feels like someone is ripping it out with a pitchfork.

All the while his accusers go on with their daily lives having no regrets for destroying a good lawman, just aspirations of unlimited promotions and approval from the mayor's office. I suggest they will die lonely men and will eventually be accountable to our maker.

Six months later we were unofficially advised that the US Attorney concluded that there was no civil rights violation and federal prosecution would not be pursued. Officer Field, now retired Mr. Field, was elated to say the least. Finally the spiteful threat was no longer hanging over his head. A just man can now move on with what's left of his life. A job well done Detroit!

CHAPTER 16
A FORCE OR COUNTRY DIVIDED?

FOUR DECADES HAVE NOW PASSED AND the city of Detroit finds itself emerging from bankruptcy while being governed by a newly elected white mayor. This, after the death of Coleman Young and the election of three succeeding black mayors, one of whom was found guilty of corruption and is currently serving a lengthy prison sentence.

The citizens of Detroit were able to look beyond race and elect a person because of their qualifications not considering color a major factor, an unfortunate trend that appears to be taking place across our great nation. Detroiters elected an individual based on his merit and past performance, not because of ethnicity, race or promises; attractive promises that typically contain entitlements and are often forgotten after the election.

We also have a new police chief who by all accounts is a real professional that is making significant changes within the department and appears to be a breath of fresh air. He inherited a police department that for all intents and purposes had been run into the ground with morale levels at an all-time low.

This chief, a former LA police executive, was an external hire, which will be very healthy for the city, bringing experience, new ideas and no axes to grind. As a black man with a sterling reputation that precedes him, it would be highly unlikely that he would adopt the ill-advised policies of the previous commands, neglecting to use nepotism and revenge, motives that almost brought the department to the brink of collapse.

These two positive changes may be an indication that Detroit has made it through the worst of times and may now be ready for the revitalization of our great come-back city. I pray the Motor City will become an icon of hope for our entire nation.

We are beginning to see corporations and businesses returning to Detroit along with a new generation of enthusiastic citizens moving into our down town area. A renaissance appears to be underway, a welcoming change that I believe is totally possible as long as the politicians, race pimps and bigots cease interfering, which unfortunately is unlikely due to the enormous amount of money and power that is generated from dividing our country with their hateful, racist agenda.

The country, much like Detroit, has gone through major changes, we now have our first black president, Barack Hussein Obama. A man who ran on Hope and Change, a promise that was appealing to all but in time would prove to fall short. One prevalent change I have observed is that race relations between law enforcement agencies and the public have deteriorated considerably, which I attribute to the president, his attorney general and many within his administration who all too often interfere in local law enforcement matters merely to enhance their political agenda.

Each time there is a high profile incident involving race, this administration is quick to address the media and initiate an investigation searching for civil rights violations. Yet, when there is an incident like the massacre at Fort Hood by a self-proclaimed radical Islamic who targeted and shot soldiers of all races in the name of Allah, the president is quick to declare it a random act of work place violence. Really! You got to be kidding me, talk about selective recognition.

It appears this administration is governing in the same manner in which the city of Detroit had been ruled for the last 30 or so volatile years. Leading by intimidation, advising States if they do not comply with his executive actions, they will no longer receive government funding. This is a very dangerous example, governing in this fashion could not only set race relations back 40 years, it can quite possibly destroy our country!

With that said, I would suggest if there is a verified civil rights violation, the defendants should be prosecuted to the fullest extent. However, I do not agree in the manner in which this government arrives in a town following an incident involving race even before the investigation is complete and begin making inflammatory remarks to the media and public. They know quite well their abrasive remarks leave the accused with an appearance of guilt, not to mention it gives the black activist a platform to cause unrest, which could possibly lead to civil disturbance.

A few of the disheartening statements I have heard come from this president and his staff during volatile incidents around the country are; "As a black man I have experienced injustices." "I assure you we will have a thorough investigation bringing the guilty parties to justice." "For the first time in my life, I'm proud to be an American." Or, "The police obviously acted stupidly." Let us not forget, "If I had a son he would look like the victim." Statements that certainly are not impartial, not to mention they will leave an impression of guilt before an investigation has even been initiated, all the while appearing to give a subliminal authorization for radicals to take the law into their own hands if dissatisfied with the outcome.

Let me be perfectly clear, if there is a civil rights violation at the local level and that particular agency is not enforcing the law accordingly, then the feds should intervene, bringing justice to any person or party violating our laws. No one is above the law including the men and women wearing the badge of honor, a badge that has been paid for with the blood of far too many. Yet, I witness this commander in chief time and time again attacking law enforcement agencies across the country because of an allocation against one officer in one city.

On at least three occasions where the president and his administration have stepped in prematurely on high profile incidents which ignited civil unrest and dissention among the races, the accused were exonerated through overwhelming evidence. Yet, even when the facts indicated that the allegations were false, this haughty administration never apologizes, to the contrary, they choose to double down, remaining arrogantly silent, indicating they are not accountable and are, indeed, above the law!

While this White House appears to anxiously attempt to find evidence of wrong doing by law enforcement personnel, they choose not to pursue or prosecute witnesses that have beyond a question of a doubt, been proven to commit perjury against the accused officers.

It is very difficult to respect a president that has been less than truthful to the American people on numerous occasions. His organization often leaves one with the impression that we should do as they say, not as they do, simply because they know what's best for us. This same mindset has been displayed by socialist dictators throughout history. Here's a unique idea, attempt leading by example!

If this administration truly cared, they would be far more proactive, appearing in these troubled areas prior to the unfortunate incidents occurring, not afterwards! It certainly appears their involvement is for no other reason than political gain, grasping any unfortunate incident as a high visibility opportunity to appear compassionate. Yet, in reality, their presence is noticeably absent until they need votes or money. It often appears that the Obama administration believes that the blacks in these crime-ridden areas will vote for them merely because of race and entitlements, so why waste precious time in regions that are already locked in? How condescending!

There are several activists who now seem to be on this administration's speed dial, appearing to have an open door policy with the White House, allowing them to share their incendiary views on law enforcement and race issues whenever needed, certainly not an impartial environment. Yet, when you disagree with this administration or their advisers, you are immediately declared a racist who is merely attempting to make the White House appear incompetent because the president is black.

One must wonder what the president is thinking when he aligns himself with radicals who hold such one-sided extreme views. His associates include those that have allegedly been involved in bombings and illegal narcotics trafficking. Also radical rappers who advocate violence and racism in their lyrics and clergy who preach hate from the church pulpit, as well as self-proclaimed civil rights leaders that only appear when there is a volatile situation which in their minds equates to money.

Presidents are supposed to represent all of the people not just a select faction. Yet, this Commander in Chief appears to gravitate to groups that certainly display anti- American views. I would suggest that if these associates lived in any other country they could possibly be doing 5 to 20 in a federal penitentiary for the questionable self-serving tactics they use; thank God they live in the good old USA, because their hate filled antics would not be tolerated anywhere else.

In my opinion, this commander and chief is one of the most polarizing leaders I have witnessed during my life time. He has divided this country by race, religion and class with his socialist views, constantly playing one side against the other. The one man that could have made a significant difference in race relations and world affairs, earning a respectable place in history, has instead appeared to do everything in his power to derail the process, creating skepticism between blacks and whites, while leaving a shadow of distrust with the world leaders as well as our law enforcement agencies.

Bigotry and favoritism toward a race or ethnicity is not unique to this president. I will concede that there have been white presidents that practiced these same ugly policies in a similar deceiving fashion, although not nearly as blatant as this commander in chief. However, one would think we would have learned from our embarrassing past and attempt to move our country forward by forsaking these sinful policies. This is not a time to become arrogant with power and consider this an opportunity for pay back!

In my 40 plus years involved in the world of law enforcement, the only thing that appears to have changed is that many of the officials running our police agencies, cities and country are now black. One would think this would be a positive indication that our volatile country is finally evolving into the place our God and founding fathers intended it to be, one race under God indivisible with justice for all.

Unfortunately, the sad fact is there are a percentage of these black elected bureaucrats who have lost sight of their mission, becoming exactly like the radical white element they have fought against their entire life. Its business as usual for some, deals being cut, broken promises and carrying out hidden agendas, the only thing that has changed is the color of the skin. For some, it's no longer about race and doing the right thing it's all about power and politics. One step forward and two steps back.

This country, for the time being, remains majority white, which would indicate many of these officials of color were elected by the white voter as well as minorities. This obviously reveals a hunger for honest change within the system, looking beyond race, voting for a person who they believe will sincerely work for the community with no hidden schemas.

It's quite apparent the American people were looking for an adjustment, a change, which the primarily white politicians were not delivering.

In 2007, while serving in Iraq with the 101st Airborne Division, I was asked by a friend of mine, a young black captain, what I thought of the newly elected first black president? My reply was simple and to the point. I thought America and history were ready for a change, and all I would ask of this president is that he represents all of the people all the time and serve with honor. The captain agreed saying. "That's what we all want; only time will tell Dave."

Unfortunately, when some black politicians are caught with their hands in the cookie jar, their reaction is typically swift. They immediately play the race card and attempt to deflect the attention away from themselves, proclaiming it is the white system attacking them because of their color, a dishonorable defense to say the least.

These politicians were voted into office by various races, all of whom you have pledged you would represent, yet when you break the law it becomes the fault of the white society. Then you have the nerve to ask the black citizens to support you, the very people you have betrayed, amazing!

Nevertheless, there are those in the black community that will support these politicians blindly no matter what, declaring them as black figures that have beat the odds in a predominately white society. This faction truly believes these wolves in sheep's clothing will protect the little man on the street even when they're wrong.

This mindset has been proven with an incident involving one of our large city mayors, who after being convicted of a felony drug charge which subsequently led to his incarceration, was re-elected upon his release. Is there no accountability? Not to mention the pathetic message it sends to our children.

President Obama has promised his black supporters the world and given them a small village. He has offered the inner-city residents cell phones, extensions in unemployment benefits along with small monetary subsidies, yet generally their income remains below the poverty level, all the while he has become wealthy many times over and brushes elbows with the elite in fabulous settings.

He declares himself as a man of the people, yet has provided the less fortunate with these small subventions, which look great on paper yet in reality are mere crumbs. I would submit he is very generous with the taxpayer's money, while securing his wealth! If he cares so much about the lower and middle class why doesn't he reside in the neighborhoods he says he is fighting for? I wouldn't hold your breath. He won't be joining you for dinner any time soon, not unless it's a photo-op; you are merely a means for him to achieve his goal as the first black president, a president who fundamentally changed America. However, I will predict history will reflect many of his changes and achievements were self-serving and accomplished underhandedly through intimidation, apologies, and deceit.

It is my opinion this president misled the vast majority of his supporters with his divisive remarks and false promises, while sporting his sly grin or concerned look to convince the very people that believed in him, simply to promote his socialist ideas. Some would say it appears he attained his apparent dream of increasing division between the races all the while making us a far less superior world power!

I recognize that the majority of Americans, black and

white, are living their short time on this earth with one common goal, to raise their families in a dignified manner, teaching our children the basic core values of life ; i.e.: honorability, humility, respect for fellow man and being diligent throughout life will pay huge dividends. Elementary instructions that if practiced will allow them to achieve the American dream.

Then we have that element in society who believes the world owes them a living. Many activist and politicians feed off this percentage of the population by advising them that they are entitled to government handouts because of the injustices they and their ancestors have endured. Most citizens in this mindset will never recover, remaining professional victims dependent on the government and our tax dollars for the remainder of their lives; and unfortunately this cycle will most likely continue with the generations to follow.

Certainly, there are those that need government assistance, the elderly, young, homeless, sick and the legitimately unemployed. As God-fearing people we would be remiss if we as a society ignored their needs. However, I would propose that there is also a faction that prefers being professional victims, collecting food stamps, money, housing, cell phones and child care assistance indefinitely, all on the taxpayer's dollar. Many of the recipients of these crucial subsidies can be found at casinos around Michigan daily, gambling with taxpayer's hard-earned money. This is not a bigoted allegation it is an act I have personally witnessed.

Recently while gambling at one of the larger Detroit

casinos, I noticed a large young lady seated two stools away playing a slot machine. Each time the lady would win she became noticeably upset. Upon looking at her machine I noticed she was playing the maximum on each spin and had accumulated over $1700.00. I could not resist asking her why she was so upset over winning, to which she explained "I'm on government assistance and I'm trying to get my winnings below $1200.00 so I don't have to claim it as income, because the state will take away my food stamps and some of my money." This professional victim could have been any race, but in this case she happened to be black.

During my 65 years on Gods earth, I have found four areas in which there exists a gleam of hope for us as a society, situations where blacks and whites have existed in harmony, even if only for short periods.

The first area of compatibility is during the heat of battle. Whether in the sands of Iraq or the streets of Detroit I assure you there are no niggers, peckerwoods, beaners, or crackers when you're fighting for your life and country. You fight as a team, willing to give the ultimate sacrifice for your cohorts, never once taking into account their race or ethnicity. The only prevalent factor is you all are wearing the same uniform.

Isn't it incredible? A hundred years ago blacks could not drink out of the same water fountain, yet today we find ourselves on the urban streets of big cities as well as faraway lands fighting side by side for common goals, justice and freedom, it almost gives one hope!

Secondly, we have our children. Even the darkest hearts hold compassion for a child that is ill or in danger. On the streets of Detroit, I have witnessed white and black officers alike, with total disregard for their safety, run into a burning building without hesitation because a child is reportedly inside. Not a black child, not a white child just a child of God. If we could only take that moment and turn it into hours or days!

In Iraq, while on a mission, I personally observed my fellow soldiers hold their fire putting themselves and our team in harm's way because a child was in danger of being injured. They very well could have taken the shot as our enemy has done and been totally justified under the rules of engagement, yet the respect for innocents kept their safeties on. Humanity prevailed!

Faith is one of the most important factors, without God we have nothing! I have found that faith often prevents the lid from blowing off, allowing ignorance to escalate to a level of hate or violence. As powerful as faith maybe it can be challenged when dealing with evils such as racism, revenge and greed, all traits that many of us have sadly displayed at one time or another during our lives.

The final cohesive factor that both races find common ground is our elderly, proud citizens who have survived life's challenges requiring little other than peace and a small place on earth to live out their final days. Often, hardened racist and criminals pause and change their direction rather than confront, harm or disrespect our senior citizens. I'm not sure if this is out of respect or fear of the repercussions from citizens and law enforcement, both of whom feel somewhat responsible for their safety and well-being. They have raised, educated and protected us, now it's our turn!

If we could only take the innocence of a child, the wisdom of our elderly, the comradery found in battle and faithfully apply these emotions to all of society, then, maybe just maybe we could become one people!

While respecting history and acknowledging there have been immoral deeds inflicted upon blacks as well as all races, I truly believe unless we wake up and smell the roses putting our differences behind us, we will be the cause of our own demise.

Our enemies around the world are literally laughing at us, they need not plan future 911's, they can watch from afar as we destroy our society from within. If we continue to live in the past we will not have a future! I'm not insinuating we should forget the historic evils, I'm merely suggesting we learn from them and move on. This will not be an easy task due to the hate mongers and the radical activists whose lavish lifestyles are dependent upon spreading dissension and hate between the races, knowing quite well if they allow the candle of hate to go out, their status and income will evaporate!

This is no longer just a white and black issue. We now have various races and ethnicities some legal, many illegal in our country some of whom are claiming they believe they are being discriminated against because of race, demanding retributions they believe they are entitled too. The word obviously has gone worldwide, sending the message that if you come to America the borders are wide open and the entitlements are plentiful. We have opened the flood gates and closing them is not an option anytime soon.

While I and the majority of red-blooded Americans accept any and all legal immigrants into our great country, just as our forefathers were welcomed as they entered via Elis Island NY a hundred years ago. However, we must also recognize that our government has blatantly ignored our laws at the borders allowing thousands of illegal aliens to enter at will, some of whom are hardened criminals and suspected terrorists, a strategy that is totally inexcusable. Not to mention the dangers of not screening for diseases that could possibly be brought into our communities is a genuine concern.

If this immigration policy was properly regulated and done in the name of humanity, I believe we all could possibly come to an agreement on how to temporarily accommodate those that are sincere immigrants. But, once again it appears there is a hidden agenda within this administration, especially when they evade the law leaving our southern borders unprotected; one would almost think they are attempting to recruit an additional voting base.

During the 2008 presidential election, Barack Obama promised the entire country that if elected to office his administration would be the most transparent presidency in history, I would now suggest that they have unintentionally achieved their pledge!

Four decades have passed since I first realized we in Detroit had a force divided. While it appears we have made significant progress within the ranks of law enforcement concerning the racial divide, which I attribute to education, trust in our God and the realization that black or white it doesn't matter, if you are wearing blue you are expendable to administrations like our current one. In today's society, sacrificing a cop of any color generates votes.

Liberal politicians across the country have tapped into a faction of society that believes, or would like us all to believe, that our country is under siege by rogue law enforcement agencies. Hence, come's the cry for criminal justice reform. When in reality, we have the best criminal justice system in the world. Have there been injustices by a few bad apples? Absolutely, and the vast majority of law enforcement officers want them prosecuted in a fair trial and, if found guilty, the only thing that should beat them to prison should be the head-lights on the sheriff's bus.

However, I would suggest these rogue thugs wearing a cops badge are truly the 1%ers. Yet, many of today's politicians who portray themselves as civil rights activists that are simply looking out for the everyday citizen, grasp this hot issue and run with it. They are quick to declare that the entire criminal justice system needs reform, leaving the impression that the majority of cops want to hurt or kill minorities, an outrageous notion I assure you.

Many representatives embrace this cause, not out of commitment to sincere beliefs, but, rather, because it is the flavor of the day and out of the necessity to lock in votes at the next election. Have they no souls?

This president has inadvertently united many black and white police officers around the country by revealing the fact that all law enforcement personnel are expendable and will be thrown under the bus without hesitation if it furthers his agenda of dividing our country by classes to obtain the necessary votes.

It is clear this contagious disease of racism and hate is being spread across our great country, infecting our cities, states and even Washington DC. This disease, unlike others, targets our innocent and elderly, stripping them of love, compassion and trust, replacing it with hate, mistrust and envy. Unfortunately many who contract this illness will never recuperate.

Even though it appears we are in a tailspin, which will unavoidably crash in the near future, I sincerely believe it's not too late. I have faith we can fix this if we approach it as humanitarians, disregarding the toxic venom spread by our politicians, radical activists and supremacist of all races. We must approach this with no agenda other than repairing the years of injustice. It can only be reconciled from the bottom up; we have attempted to remedy this from the top down for years to no avail.

Equality is a God-given right and no human being should be denied this gift. With that said, we do have factions in our culture that will intentionally never achieve equality, because if they do so they will no longer have an excuse or platform from which to complain. This in essence, would mean that they would no longer have a defense and would now be required to become responsible citizens, determining their own destiny along with their fellow countrymen.

Racism can be very lucrative for those that want to continue stirring the pot; it's their livelihood, a business that pays in votes, donations and recognition to many who would otherwise just be another common thug.

Hence, comes my theory that the reconcile movement must be initiated at the home level, teaching by example one home at a time, educating our children that we need not be a country divided if we listen to our hearts instead of our politicians and hate mongers.

We have had politicians since the beginning of the civil rights movement that gravitates to the unfortunate in our country, those who are vulnerable and for the most part prove to be minorities. While there are some that sincerely care for the less fortunate, there is that faction who considers them simply a voting base, telling this group they feel their pain, assuring them the promise land, yet after the vote is cast, these trusting souls remain in the ghetto with little, if any change at all. Politicians of this character often attempt to portray themselves as John F. Kennedy-like, when in fact they view this percentage of society simply as a means to get free media time, votes and riches at the expense of taxpayers, all the while sporting a transparent smile, a smile that I envision a snake oil salesman exhibiting as he rips off a trusting customer.

These same soulless politicians melt and succumb when confronted by radical activist groups, surrendering to the loud mouth aggressive ruffians who disrupt events often charging the stage, choosing to use rude force instead of well-mannered dialog, all in an attempt to prevent one from practicing their 1st amendment right. This submissive behavior by todays politicians, brings to light a very transparent agenda, which is, it's not about "Black or All lives Matter," it's simply about, "Black Votes Matter!" Once again the puppet masters wins.

I would suggest, that many of today's activist groups would be better served, if they concentrate their efforts, not only on the minute number of cops who are involved in the questionable death of a valued black life. But, also focus and demonstrate in front of the abortion clinics, gang and dope houses, which are responsible for hundreds if not thousands, of young and unborn black lives monthly!

The radical hatemongers that spread detestation throughout our nation, fail to realize that the vast majority of law enforcement officials, leave their love ones daily, knowing quite well they may have to lay their life down protecting our citizens, which also includes the same despicable element that chants: "Pigs in a blanket fry-em like bacon" or "What do we want? Dead cops, when do we want-em? Now! " Rhetoric I would expect to hear from groups like ISIS or Al Qaeda, not Americans!

I suspect, if these rebel-rousers were asked to place their lives on the line protecting strangers of a different ideology or race, they would proclaim, "It's not my job, call a cop." Isn't amazing how we are hated, until we are needed.

We must all realize our maker doesn't make mistakes. He created a variety of races by design; a decision that I'm sure was intended to generate a pure and diverse civilization. Yet, the human race succumbed to the evils of greed, hate, power and an unfounded sense of superiority between the races.

One must wonder how historic leaders of the past such as Abraham Lincoln, Frederick Douglass, John F Kennedy, Martin Luther King or Ronald Regan would react if they could see the state of our great nation today? I truly believe their heads would be hung in disgust, asking the question, do sincere patriots no longer exist?

Until we as a people regain consciousness and realize there is a faction of society, black and white that is just pure evil and has a decisive plan, an agenda that for the most part is hidden, yet, with each passing day, it is becoming blatantly obvious. Their plot is to divide our country, our world, with ugly exaggerations of inequality, charging racism on both sides and calling for retribution or else. This small faction will cause unrest and even war, spilling blood just to achieve recognition, money or public office.

Scholars for centuries have attempted to find common ground for mankind to no avail. We all appear to fall short of a peaceful solution because of our one-sided views of race and beliefs. Yet, I often think if we as a world society would simply adopt or consider the teachings of a humble tablet that contained Ten Commandments, none of which penalized entire cultures if not adhered to, or banishes those that choose not to follow the mandates. These rules never suggested we scorn or kill those that have an opposing philosophy. To the contrary, these teachings suggest we respect, honor and love our fellow-man, praying for them rather than calling for their annihilation simply because they disagree with your belief, or they take on a different appearance.

Therefore, in my humble opinion; civilization must recognize this evil for what it is and begin to live by the premise that we are all one in the eyes of God, refusing to be held hostage by these shallow self-serving individuals with hidden agendas, adversaries who come in all races and religions. It now appears that Americans not only need to be sheltered from enemies abroad, we also must be cognizant of the deceiving enemy within our own borders. It is imperative that we never forget that united we stand and divided this great nation as we know it, will surely fall!

Made in the USA
Lexington, KY
12 January 2017